For Alice & Ted
with personal gratitude
& the best wishes
of the Archive Staff

The Longest Shadow

Geoffry Hartman

March 27, 1996

The Helen and Martin Schwartz Lectures
in Jewish Studies, 1994

Sponsored by the
Robert A. and Sandra S. Borns
Jewish Studies Program,
Indiana University

The Longest Shadow

In the Aftermath of the Holocaust

Geoffrey H. Hartman

Indiana University Press

Bloomington and Indianapolis

Library of Congress Cataloging-in-Publication Data

Hartman, Geoffrey H.
The longest shadow : in the aftermath of the Holocaust /
Geoffrey H. Hartman
p.   cm. — (The Helen and Martin Schwartz lectures in
Jewish studies)
Includes index.
ISBN 0-253-33033-5 (alk. paper)
1. Holocaust, Jewish (1939–1945)—Influence.   2. Holocaust,
Jewish (1939–1945)—Historiography.   3. Holocaust memorials.
I. Title.   II. Series.
D804.3.H359   1996
940.53′18—dc20   95-22267

1 2 3 4 5   01 00 99 98 97 96

For Renée and Hertha

Contents

Acknowledgments

I wish to thank Alvin Rosenfeld for encouraging me to give the Helen and Martin Schwartz Lectures and to publish this volume.

My specific debts are, I hope, adequately acknowledged in the text. But for support, intellectual or moral or both, I wish to single out Dori Laub, Larry Langer, Walter Reich, Saul Friedlander, Sidra Ezrahi, James Young, Richard Weisberg, Al Solnit, Miriam Hansen, Alaida and Jan Assmann, Margarete and Horst Meller, Yannis Thanasseikos, Annette Wieviorka, Larry Kritzman, and Joanne Rudof.

For permission to reprint I thank the following: Random House, for "The Longest Shadow," from David Rosenberg, ed., *Testimony: Contemporary Writers Make the Holocaust Personal;* Harvard University Press, for "The Book of the Destruction," from Saul Friedlander, ed., *Probing the Limits of Representation: Nazism and the "Final Solution";* Blackwell, for "Darkness Visible," from G. H. Hartman, ed., *Holocaust Remembrance: The Shapes of Memory;* the *New Republic* for "The Weight of What Happened"; Indiana University Press, for "Bitburg," from G. H. Hartman, ed., *Bitburg in Moral and Political Perspective;* Routledge, for "The Voice of Vichy," from Lawrence D. Kritzman, ed., *Auschwitz and After: Race, Culture, and "The Jewish Question" in France;* *Raritan Review,* for "Public Memory and Its Discontents"; Oxford University Press and *Holocaust and Genocide Studies,* for "Learning from Survivors: The Yale Testimony Project" and *Salmagundi* for "The Cinema Animal." A version of "Holocaust Testimony, Art and Trauma" was given as the 1994 Freud Lecture at Yale, sponsored by the Muriel Gardner Group for Psychoanalysis in the Humanities and the Western New England Psychoanalytic Association. A version of "Learning from Survivors" was delivered at a 1992 Auschwitz Foundation Conference at Brussels and published in French in its *Bulletin trimestriel.* I also thank HarperCollins Publishers Inc. and Yehuda Amichai for permission to reprint lines from "In the Mountains of Jerusalem," copyright © 1982 by Yehuda Amichai, from Yehuda Amichai's *After a Great Tranquillity: Questions and Answers,* translated from the Hebrew by Glenda Abramson and Tudor Parfitt, and the Jewish Publications Society for the lines from Dan Pagis's "Testimony," © 1981, from his *Points of Departure,* translated from the Hebrew by Stephen Mitchell.

The Longest Shadow

Introduction
On Closure

The French philosopher Jean-François Lyotard surmised that the shock of the Holocaust was so great that it destroyed the very instruments by which it could have been measured. But the after-shocks *are* measurable; we are deep into the process of creating new instruments to record and express what happened. The instruments themselves, the means of expression, are now, as it were, born of trauma.

There is, in any case, no lack of serious attention to the Shoah; after a slow start, after a stunned reaction, historians, philosophers, psychoanalysts, and artists have entered what has been characterized as a period of obsession. In fact, because fifty years have elapsed since the death camps were revealed, voices are heard that call for closure. The enormity of the event, we are told, blocks thought and leads to a black hole that swallows the haunted interpreter. Continue to note the historical facts, we are told, but please desist from a brooding that has gone beyond mourning to melancholia. With so many museums, monuments, and commemorations, you are in danger of fetishizing, or erecting a cult of the dead. Nietzsche's phrase that life is not possible without forgetfulness is often recalled; and Jews, in particular, are admonished to remember their entire history, their more than bimillennial culture, not only this darkest moment of victimage.

Yet closure is elusive for many reasons. The most obvious of these is that in fifty years little has changed. "Has the world learned anything?" is the despairing question we hear so often in the testimonies of survivors. In many places, antisemitism diminished or disguised itself; then it crept back, with rightist or leftist politics, and seems by now completely recovered— witness a virulent underground press or the open, prewar level of slander in Russia and Central Europe. Even in certain quarters of the U.S., roiled by ethnic turmoil and competition, a rhetoric of hate and contempt returns.

We continue to face, moreover, with greater sensitivity but also with an increased sense of impotence, genocidal episodes in Cambodia, Rwanda, and the Bosnian conflict. While there are clear differences between a "Final

Solution" that aimed at the extermination of every Jew and these "terrorist solutions" that have a distinct political end, media coverage of Bosnia has made us involuntary bystanders to a shameless "ethnic cleansing."

These developments raise questions about our species, our preconception that *we* are the human, the "family of man." Or, less dramatically, we wonder about the veneer of progress, culture, and educability. Through the focusing power of the Holocaust we look at both past and present, and what we see is insane. Yet how do we deal with that, how do we convert what lies plainly before our eyes into a potent and thoughtful rather than simply an emotional and burdening part of education?

This last question, which parallels Adorno's concern for "Education after Auschwitz," points to the confines of this book. My essays do not analyze in detail the events of 1933–1945, culminating in the Holocaust, or ask whether our inquiry should not start earlier, with the shock inflicted by World War I, a humiliating peace treaty, and deep-rooted socioeconomic factors. I am not a historian and have only a conscientious reader's competence in this area.

What I undertake is to write about the aftermath of the Holocaust. "The disaster always takes place after having taken place," Maurice Blanchot has said. I discuss artistic, scholarly, and pedagogical responses, their relation to the possibility of closure, how extreme experiences are represented and transmitted, links between representational techniques and ethical concerns, first- and second-generation witness. While there is no attempt to follow in the rigorous, subtle, sometimes tortuous steps of thinkers like Blanchot and Adorno, who have not let go of the question of what went wrong with civilization, I hope to engage them in another book, *A Fateful Question*, on the idea of culture after two world wars and the Shoah.

In these initial remarks I do want to suggest, however, why a focus on the Holocaust is not obsessive. The call for closure, though understandable as an expression of hope (that a deep wound is finally healing), remains premature. Wherever we look—at a potentially murderous racial politics, or at the work of mourning, or at public education (which now includes the media and multiplying networks of information)—wherever we look, the events of 1933–1945 cannot be relegated to the past. They are not over; anyone who comes in contact with them is gripped, and finds detachment difficult. They deliver a warning more decisive than that which gave Nineveh a second chance.

If this appears obvious to those who are likely to read these pages,

I should add that we are only at the beginning of an understanding of the Shoah. The last fifty years have been a period of testimonies and fact-gathering. No other event, it seems, has been so thoroughly documented and studied; therefore the implication that we are illegitimately fascinated by it. But understanding comes and goes; it has not been progressive. Perhaps it is too hard to take in Jean Améry's sober assertion concerning the discontinuity between Auschwitz and any other suffering the human mind has faced, and sometimes faced down. Améry writes: "The axes of [the intellect's] traditional frames of reference then shattered. Beauty: that was an illusion. Knowledge: that turned out to be a game with ideas."

Certain fundamental questions, moreover, though raised early on, are in need of being restated and developed. The passion with which Adorno delivered his strictures on poetry after Auschwitz is followed through, for example, by Berel Lang in a book which examines the "moral space of figurative discourse." And although Lang's argumentation—at once firm and finespun—restricts that space in the case of the Nazi genocide, it does not foreclose it but opens up once more the issue of literary representation as an act with an entailed responsibility. "[T]he enormity of the Nazi genocide in its historical or nonliterary character necessarily affects—enlarges—the risks incurred in its literary representation. . . . The most radical alternative to any particular representation of the Nazi genocide is not a different or contradictory one—but the possibility of not having written at all; that is, the writer's decision for silence." Here silence returns, not as theological dogma or the effect of intellectual impasse but as a value whose displacement must be justified.[1]

Yet does not that same responsibility affect *any* Holocaust representation? There is always a decision for or against silence. In that respect fictional elaboration is not different from history-writing or other non-fictional forms of description and commentary. Indeed, the shattering of traditional frames of reference also puts in question the resemblance of words, which can become false friends when their task is characterization of the death camp experience. "Martyrdom," "victim," "suffering," "choice," "resistance," are inadequate phrases even though we may have to use them to communicate and restore a semblance of normality. There is, here, the basis of an argument for fiction, or rather, for the defamiliarization of words and events in great poetry, like that of Celan and Pagis. "The universe of dying that was Auschwitz," Lawrence Langer has written, "yearns for a language purified of the taint of normality."[2]

Though the 1990s continue to be marked by a gathering of further evidential detail (the opening of the Soviet archives is a major development), the years have increasingly brought us to confront a dilemma. To integrate the Holocaust into our image of human nature is to despair of humanity, as well as of language. Yet to conclude that it cannot be integrated is also to despair—if it means abandoning the hope that a remedy may be available through collective action based on self-understanding and tradition. As new details or new perspectives emerge, can we draw any practical consequences from what we have learned?

Two generations have come into their own since the end of the Second World War. Yet there cannot be a statute of limitations either in research or interpretation. Perhaps this is true of any field of inquiry. Let me try to explain why it is *more true* of Holocaust studies.

The legitimacy of academic fields is based on a promise of their intelligibility. That promise is not so readily available in this case. Even though there has been a gradual shift away from doubt about the intelligibility of the Holocaust, from a pessimism that anything redemptive or corrective can be learned from this catastrophe, the scholars most deeply involved often admit an "excess" that remains dark and frightful, while they continue to generate explanatory hypotheses. We can, of course, suspend the search for meaning by adopting a purely descriptive approach, or point to the fact that fields are constituted by areas that have become intelligible, and the hope that other areas will follow suit. Yet something in the specific case of the Shoah remains dark at the heart of the event, not just in its peripheral regions; and it leads to reflections that seem "theological." Emil Fackenheim, as is well known, posits a caesura or rupture in historical time, the emergence of a *novum* that must be recognized as such, even when it cannot be understood.[3]

A comparison with the French Revolution is useful. The sequence *French Revolution: Enlightenment* cannot be matched by *Holocaust: Enlightenment.* What should be placed after the colon? "Eclipse of Enlightenment" or "Eclipse of God"?

We don't really expect closure in the intellectual sphere. Yet even in the political and moral sphere the scandal provoked by President Reagan's visit to the military cemetery at Bitburg showed the prematurity of closure, and the issues have not subsided. Today, the highly publicized fight over the Carmelite convent at Auschwitz seems finally resolved. But the commemorations in Poland on the fiftieth anniversary of the liberation of Auschwitz revealed once more embattled sensitivities concerning the symbolic and memorial status of the camp. There is increasing tension, moreover, between Jews and blacks in America, and one hears the charge that Jews, by exceptionalizing the Holocaust, are monopolizing suffering. What of the "sixty million" victims lost in the Middle Passage and still being lost in the urban carnage? (The figure of sixty million is Toni Morrison's, from the dedication to her novel, *Beloved*; Farrakhan is reported to have upped it to "six hundred million".)

The politics of memory continue to be troubling. In France political agitation centering on the Holocaust is a relatively recent thing: there was a successful campaign in 1993 to have President Mitterrand institute an official day for Jewish victims in France, in addition to the day commemorating all deportees. The full discovery of Vichy's policy toward the Jews is a story unto itself: but for Ophuls's film, *The Sorrow and the Pity*, and two non-French scholars, Paxton and Marrus, it might have been delayed even longer. Chronological distance from a catastrophic event may exacerbate and embroil rather than quieten public memory.

In fact, public memory itself now becomes an important subject of reflection. How is that memory formed, what is its relation to historical research on the one hand and fictional or media treatments on the other? The popular impact of Spielberg's *Schindler's List* has only heightened the debate as to whether a fictional treatment of the Shoah is appropriate, however accurate it tries to be.

The debates I have mentioned, and even the graphic details that continue to be revealed, may cause a natural impatience: "What more can be said about the Holocaust?" Lawrence Langer gives this question an answer: "Every future generation will have to be educated anew in how to face the historical period we call the Holocaust." Those who study it must "reverse history and progress and find a way of restoring to the imagination of coming generations the depth and scope of the catastrophe."[4] The specific debates may sometimes seem distracting. But if we keep Langer's principle in mind, we cannot go wrong. Time is not on the side of remembrance.

To resist closure (and its double, forgetfulness) means that we must think more closely about the action of time. As time passes into history, the "uniqueness" of what happened is contextualized, and many object to this as a "relativization." Yet a shift has occurred, as I have mentioned, away from claims about the Shoah's caesura-like or unexplainable character, its sinister sublimity as a *tremendum*, and toward a focus on what has been disclosed and made intelligible.[5] In her early interpretive essays, Hannah Arendt had already rejected the idea of demonic evil, which expressed our horror but made the event unintelligible.

Unfortunately, Arendt's follow-up thesis on the "banality of evil" (based on Eichmann, the super-typical Nazi bureaucrat), which intended to exorcise once more the idea of some demonic mystery, was misunderstood. It targeted Eichmann's "thoughtlessness" (i.e., not ideological conviction, extraordinary corruption, or "satanic greatness"), a negative quality that might be compared—at least in the writing-desk murderer—to that of the contemporary launderer of drug money who insists he is not a killer but merely "manipulates money" (*New York Times*, December 1, 1994: B1). Arendt's picture of the bureaucratic personality, banal through and through, and talking in "elated clichés," demystifies evil and shifts the focus to a dangerous element in modern society as a whole.

Steven Katz's *The Holocaust in Historical Context* examines genocidal actions in all of recorded history and compares the Shoah to them: it is an act of contextualization (not relativization) that does not diminish the scope or suffering of other democides. And Terrence des Pres's "a new shape of knowing invades the mind," refers to the way the Holocaust has sensitized us. It makes us aware of global political wretchedness; and he focuses on that rather than on the Holocaust's exceptionality or the fascination with evil it often induces.

The issue of closure, then, always there on the level of the affected individual, or of communal need, or as a question about the legitimacy of consolation, through art or myth, invades the political, sociological and historiographical realm. In history-writing, it gives a sharper edge to the problematic of narrative: whether narrative is more than a presentational device, whether its teleological or rhetorical thrust should be avoided, or cannot be (as Hayden White's "metahistory" seeks to demonstrate), and how, if it is unavoidable, historical differs from fictional emplotment. In sociology, the topic of closure provokes questions about the truth, falsity, or structure of what has come to be named, after Durkheim and Halbwachs, the collective memory. Lyotard, for example, does not deny that there is a collective memory marked by solacing fictions, political myths and the "grand récit," but he defines the postmodern condition in part as the demise of their legitimating power. In literary studies, the questioning of closure is often prompted by semiotic or deconstructionist theories whose concern is with false or falsified endings to the act of interpretation, the equivalent of forced reconciliation (Adorno's "erpresste Versöhnung") in the social or political sphere.

Finally, there is a philosophic dimension to closure—I call it philosophic for want of a better word. This aspect emerges as we become aware of two

Introduction

factors, whether they are characterized as modern or postmodern. The two factors are, quite simply, that there is an "after" Auschwitz, without any sign that we are "beyond" Auschwitz, and the continuing impact of technology on our sense of reality.

We recognize a technologic fatality, reflected by the Nazis' instrumentalization of murder, by their ability to carry out, in the name of national policy and racial metaphysics, so large and inhuman a project. We also become aware that, today, our sense of what is real is mediated by the media, by electronic phantoms that extend the confusion of reality and propaganda, or place events on the same level. We would like to think of the Nazi regime as an exceptional and aberrant development, but can it be entirely isolated this way, in German history or our own? How fatal has administrative or instrumentalized reason become in the modern era? Will the anxiety about reality-loss (that modernization and the media are destroying an "organic" relation between persons and of person to place), continue to scapegoat immigrants, and especially Jews, portrayed as a subversive threat to principles of blood and soil that supposedly guarantee both national and personal identity?

As to the "after" which gives little indication of becoming a "beyond": many are increasingly suspicious of the drive for fixed meanings. From this point of view an insistence on uniqueness may seem like closure. Derrida has pointed out that should we seek a moral imperative (an *il faut*) that takes the Holocaust into account, we will have to create links for what refuses linkage (*il faut enchaîner sur Auschwitz*). This is true even if Auschwitz, in terms of meaning or history, is a "negative" that cannot be integrated by any kind of dialectical move. How to "not talk" about it (*comment ne pas parler*) is the challenge. Yet it is hardly the first time that such an injunction has weighed on discourse.

There is also an intensified awareness of the retroactive effect on the significance of events by the future—by time's "reversal of alliances" and other unpredictable changes. (The Holocaust survivor, for instance, was not always a near-heroic figure: Edward L. Wallant's novel, on which the film *The Pawnbroker* was based, presents a tainted as well as haunted person, a larger-than-life but ambivalent depiction.) Such historical mutability both heightens and subverts the stakes in the area of representation. We notice, on the one hand, a reactive anxiety to settle and secure the meaning of an event, to win the generational battle over its place in history by deploying all our modern and augmented means of publicity. But there is also, on the other hand, an uncertainty about any such fixed meaning or about the constructed—mediated—nature of it, an uncertainty that may become a skeptical opportunism of the sort exploited by the negationists. Quite mistakenly, the vicious ideological turn that is taken by Holocaust deniers is sometimes associated with deconstruction's care in avoiding premature or forced closure, a care which has no ideological motive but is directed against an anxiety that produces shortcuts to meaning.

If art, then, is under heavy pressure when it comes to Holocaust representation, a pressure amounting almost to an interdiction, history too, as a discipline, feels a special burden. Even as we multiply historical treatments, in addition to novels, films, monuments, and museums, the split within memory-institutions, noted by Yosef Yerushalmi in *Zakhor*, becomes larger and less bridgeable. Yerushalmi describes it as a rupture between modern historiography, its tremendous fact-gathering and technical expertise, and the desire for closure through official interpretation and communal, ritualized forms of meaning-bestowal. "Remember" for the historian means something quite different from the "Remember" inspiring a collective memory shaped by folklore, prayer book, and Bible, and also, after the political emancipation of the Jews, by art.

One reason for the difference widening is generational: the children and now grandchildren of the survivors, as well as those who have become witnesses by adoption (who have adopted themselves into the family of victims), seek a new way to deal with a massively depressing event. They cannot testify with the same sense of historical participation, for it did not happen to *them*. This does not lessen, however, a moral and psychological burden. Despite missing memories, and though "suffering takes the place of inheritance" (Nadine Fresco), they look for a legacy, or a strong identification with what happened.

To illustrate that search, let me cite the Israeli film *Because of That War*, which tells the story of two children of survivors who join to write and compose songs about their own and their parents' struggles, and the first part of David Grossmann's novel *See Under: Love*, which has a touching account of what it feels like to grow up with adults who try to protect youngsters from a disastrous knowledge, but leak it anyway and compel them to imagine their own Holocaust scenarios. The literature of the survivor generation is well known; but what is equally impressive is the fiction, or sometimes mixed creative and documentary genres, produced by second-generation witness, both in the U.S. and abroad.

Indeed, one thing which counteracts despair is the surprising energy and creativity that has emerged from devastation. The search for "hope in the past" goes beyond macabre identity props.[6] In addition to classic works of literature by survivors like Primo Levi, Tadeusz Borowski, Arnost Lustig, Nelly Sachs, Paul Celan, Dan Pagis, Ida Fink, Aharon Appelfeld, Robert Antelme, Elie Wiesel, Jorge Semprun, Jean Améry, Charlotte Delbo, and outstanding films—I name only a few—Sidney Lumet's *The Pawnbroker*, Kadar and Klos's *The Shop on Main Street*, Louis Malle's *Au revoir, les enfants*, and Claude Lanzmann's *Shoah*,[7] the sons and daughters of the victims, and those who have made themselves witnesses by adoption, have contributed, in Israel, Europe, and America, significant projects.

If some of these are hard to classify, it is because they are often not conventional histories or fictions but *supplement* an oral tradition in danger of dying out. Moreover, as Vidal-Naquet has said, the historian has an "obligation to be both a scholar and an artist." Increasingly, the younger generations writing about the Holocaust incorporate a reflection on how to write it, a reflection on representation itself. Literary theory since 1960 has encouraged this self-reflective turn.[8]

Even in nonfiction and scholarship, then, there are creative gambits. Jonathan Boyarin plays the American in Paris in a moving and unusual way: his *Polish Jews in Paris: The Ethnography of Memory* argues that "Commemoration requires filiation," and tells the story of how the author became for a while the missing generational link for a Paris *landsmannschaft*, the sociological son who records its hypercommunalized (and dying) ways. James Young, who has devoted himself to the study of Holocaust monuments in *The Texture of Memory*, has found a similar filiation. "Because I was born in 1951, some six years after the end of World War II, I don't remember the Holocaust. All I remember, all I know of the Holocaust, is what the victims have passed down to me in their diaries, what the survivors have remembered to me in their memoirs. I remember not actual events, but the countless histories, novels and poems of the Holocaust I have read, the plays, movies and video testimonies I have watched over the years. I remember long days and nights in the company of survivors, listening to their harrowing tales, until their lives, loves and losses seemed grafted indelibly onto my own life's story." The result is an autobiography written as the story of his reception of the biography of two survivors: Aharon Appelfeld, the Israeli novelist, originally from Czernowicz, and Toman Brod, a Czech historian. This joining of lives, as well as of history and literature, strikes me as exemplary rather than sentimental. There is something similar in John Felstiner's way of translating Paul Celan's work: the act of translation itself is dramatized, not for self-aggrandizement but as a caring and careful act of both personal reception and cultural transmission.[9]

The new forms of ethnography and biography I have cited show that the split between history and (collective) memory is not as despairing as Yerushalmi suggests. Forms of representation are developing that mediate between them. At the same time, a more theoretical understanding of history and literature as memory-institutions is catching on. If memory, as the French sociological tradition claims, is always social memory, then history-writing too has a social context. Moreover, Saul Friedlander and Dominick LaCapra have recently emphasized that historians are not exempt from psychological defenses, including the temptation of closure, or "an obvious avoidance of what remains indeterminate, elusive and opaque." In the case of the Holocaust, Saul Friedlander adds that, notwithstanding a fifty years' accumulation of factual knowledge, "we have faced surplus meaning or blankness, with little interpretive or representational advance." Despite that admission by a major historian, I remain optimistic. Though, as Blanchot has said, we must be "guardians of an absent meaning," I do not find that this negative labor closes any avenue to memory or the creative intellect.

Since most Holocaust researchers are also educators, let me conclude by recalling the fact that we have entered a period of transition. The era of direct knowledge of the Holocaust as of the Second World War is rapidly coming to its end. Soon education will have to replace all eyewitness transmission of those experiences. This is as it must be, as it has always been. But there are distinctive features to this era of transition. The first is that denial of the Shoah does not always take the form of an egregious negationism. Denial, as Freud pointed out, is still a form of acknowledgment: with denial, the fact remains in the public eye, it does not disappear into oblivion or indifference. The episode of Bitburg, however, exhibited symptoms of a more insidious negation, one that does lead to amnesia. There is a simplification of memory, which both history-writing and significant art seek to prevent, the substitution of what might be called *anti-memory*— something that displays the colors of memory, like the commemoration at Bitburg cemetery, but drifts toward the closure of forgetful ritualization. Rampant analogies between the Holocaust and other catastrophes or disputed actions (such as claiming abortion leads to "a holocaust of babies") also weaken memory and the truth. As teachers we have to make sure that courses on the Shoah do not share in that drift: that they are not sentimental, or burdening in a purely emotional way (for that leads to defenses that again produce forgetfulness) but as tough, as intellectually and morally challenging, as any offering in history, sociology, or literature.

Introduction

The second difference I see in this period of transition is the immense energy of Holocaust Studies, even though they lack an establishment form. Except in Yehuda Bauer's Institute at the Hebrew University, very few teachers, so far as I know, are being formally trained (I mean, beyond a summer course, useful as that is); and very few slots are reserved for the Shoah in our curricula. A course here and a course there, by good and interested but basically untrained teachers, is the norm. History departments in America still regard the Holocaust as a Jewish affair, rather than as an event belonging to European history as clearly as the French Revolution. (The situation, Vidal-Naquet reminds us, is not different in France: "it is not inaccurate to say that the extermination of Jews, Gypsies, and the mentally ill by the Third Reich is a subject which has been neglected by French historiography. This negligence gave rise to the role which a legal expert such as Léon Poliakov, a biochemist like Georges Wellers or, at a very late date, a specialist in ancient Greek history such as myself were destined to play in this historiography.")[10]

Despite this inadequate academic situation, artistic and scholarly responses flourish: I have suggested a few of them. Memory in space, the interesting monuments and anti-monuments springing up everywhere, should also be mentioned at this point. The sophisticated ideological analysis brought by George Mosse to World War I (and prior) monuments, has in effect created a new field within cultural history. It is enlarged by Robert-Jan van Pelt on the architecture of Auschwitz. Pierre Nora's work on memory-places (*lieux de mémoire*), and a sociology (sometimes a psychology) that clarifies the relation between commemoration and national identity, have also extended our perspective.

I have not discussed what is closest to my thoughts: the emergence of a testimonial literature, in particular the videotestimony as a genre of representation. Those who have read Lawrence Langer's *Holocaust Testimonies: The Ruins of Memory*[11] can gauge the importance of this resource. While traditional paradigms, drawn from the treasury of Bible, midrash, and martyrology continue to exert a strong influence (the work, in that direction, of David Roskies and Alan Mintz is well known), there is less rigidity and more tolerance of detail and anecdote in the testimonies. This detail— vivid, human, direct, insubordinate—often escapes not only traditional paradigms but also a standard *histoire événementielle*. It strikes home so vividly precisely because it cannot be easily ordered or closed out. Vera Frenkel's *At the Transit Bar* suggests that the medium (helped by its mobility) will also be important in recording a postwar generation in Europe, its continuing wanderings and exilic temperament.

The video format, moreover, acknowledges the audiovisual receptivity of most of our students; I don't mean it exploits it but rather that it takes up the challenge of creating a counter-cinematic form that will set remembrance in this format against an amnesia which easily flows from this format. The videotestimony is a representation that lies "between" documentary history and oral tradition, as well as "between" history and artistic transformation. It keeps the original trauma before our eyes while modifying the breach diagnosed by Yerushalmi.

Many of the genres that are springing up (also in painting and photography) remain controversial mixtures, influenced by technology or by the conviction that fictional seduction must now carry its antidote within it, that commentary must accompany creation. This is one area where theory becomes passionate, where *how* or even *whether* to represent aspects of the "Final Solution" is hotly debated. Especially when these works, like Spiegelman's *Maus* or Spielberg's *Schindler's List* (very different from each other, of course), are powerful enough to gain a large audience and seep into popular culture.

This opening toward popular culture, at the same time, is as ominous as Pandora's Box. Popularization disseminates but also trivializes. Is there a way to prevent the cheapening of Holocaust memory? Should Elie Wiesel have appeared on the Oprah Winfrey Show? Will our Holocaust museums become a series of macabre theme parks? How can survivor testimony differentiate itself from testimonial video that promotes a cult of the victim? What if we can soon tap into thousands of such witness accounts through an access technology that allows video-on-demand? Is it possible to maintain the *quality* of knowledge in a media age, where public memory is under assault, pressured by information and disinformation, by sensational narratives, by the unceasing juxtaposition of trivia and extreme experiences? No wonder Lanzmann envisages a "ring of fire" encircling the Holocaust, to limit its exploitation, especially in fiction.

What makes the issue even more pressing from a historical point of view is that it was the preconditioning of popular culture, as George Mosse has reminded us, which allowed the spread of a bloody-minded antisemitism. It is astounding how many intellectuals, who were also journalists, supported antisemitic ideas of one kind or another in the 1930s. The slander and contempt of these intellectuals, and of "Hitler's Professors," as Max Weinreich called them, provided a rationale for persecution. This rationale was often an incitation: more inflammatory, that is, than the so-called "anger," popular or *völkisch*, which these same intellectuals attributed to the peasants and shopkeepers, to the "little man."

In an era of mass politics, in which the media play an essential role, a complete withdrawal from contemporary evils would be fatal. Yet public polemics alone are not a solution: however just one's cause, the noise level breeds confusion. Though we continue to write against silence, it remains "a compelling standard of judgment" (Berel Lang). Within our Pandora's Box there is supposed to be, at the very bottom, a winged hope: that art is fundamentally on the side of love rather than death, and that its kind of intelligence, the space it provides for deepened and independent thought through the variety of its forms of representation, will temper the demands of ideology and free the intellect rather than shut it down.

Notes

1. Lang, *Act and Idea in the Nazi Genocide* (Chicago: University of Chicago Press, 1990), 160–61. George Steiner's *Language and Silence* (New York: Atheneum, 1967), while more broad-ranging, and *In Bluebeard's Castle* (New Haven: Yale University Press, 1971), articulated the issue of silence (and of "corrupting fascination") in a way that has become more rather than less relevant.

2. *Admitting the Holocaust: Collected Essays* (New York: Oxford University Press, 1995), 93. See also his scrupulous remarks about "spiritual resistance" in the chapter on "Cultural Resistance to Genocide."

3. The issue of how to view the Holocaust in theological terms—"God after Auschwitz"—should be clearly distinguished, of course, from studies of the behavior of professional theologians during the Nazi era. This latter inquiry, cautionary and essential, and expanded to other professions, reveals not only widespread professional deformation but the impact of visionary and state-sponsored ideologies. Exemplary among such studies is Robert Lifton's *The Nazi Doctors* (New York: Free Press, 1986) on the "biomedical vision" that rationalized the genocidal practice of medicine. Other revealing studies are Ingo Muller, *Hitler's Justice: The Courts of the Third Reich*, trans. D. L. Schneider (Cambridge: Harvard University Press, 1991) and Richard H. Weisberg, *Vichy Lawyers and the French Holocaust* (New York: New York University Press, 1995).

4. Langer, *Admitting the Holocaust*, 179–84.

5. Raul Hilberg produced *The Destruction of the European Jews* (first edition, 1961), a pioneering work and a giant step forward in clarifying the policy that led toward the "Final Solution," while insisting that the "big question" of the "Why" of the Holocaust could not be answered, or displaced too many answerable questions.

6. The building up of Israel as a nation-state is part of this; yet the European past of the survivors who immigrated was for a long time (at least till the Eichmann trial) "redemptively negated" by the prevailing Zionist ideology.

7. An intelligent and comprehensive survey of major films is Ilan Avisar's *Screening*

The Longest Shadow

the Holocaust: Cinema's Images of the Unimaginable (Bloomington: Indiana University Press, 1988). See also Annette Insdorf, *Indelible Shadows: Film and the Holocaust* (New York: Random House, 1983).

8. For Pierre Vidal-Naquet's reflections on the historian, see "The Holocaust's Challenge to History," and for the obsession with the primacy of language and problems of representation, Elaine Marks, "*Cendres juives.*" Both essays can be found in *Auschwitz and After: Race, Culture, and "the Jewish Question" in France*, ed. Lawrence D. Kritzman (New York: Routledge, 1994). On the related issue of verisimilitude in Holocaust art, see the remarks on a necessary disfiguration in Lawrence Langer, *The Holocaust and the Literary Imagination* (New Haven: Yale University Press, 1975). Langer's challenging thesis is that "To establish an order of reality in which the unimaginable becomes imaginatively acceptable exceeds the capacities of an art devoted entirely to verisimilitude. . . . " (43).

9. Felstiner, *Paul Celan: Poet, Survivor, Jew* (New Haven: Yale University Press, 1995). It would be interesting to know if a gender issue is involved: are there similar filiations of American women with women survivors? Judith Friedlander's *Vilna on the Seine* (New Haven: Yale University Press, 1992) is an engaging but also quite impersonal work of scholarship. In the survivor generation, there are fewer female than male authors, and no "hypercommunalized" female communities. The support groups that exist bring together mainly the members of the second generation. I suspect that women scholars who are in the situation of Boyarin or Young gravitate to feminist writers, such as Duras and Cixous, who deal with questions of mourning and memory. Still, the number of women writers and artists is quite remarkable, even—especially—in Germany. See Sander L. Gilman, *Jews in Today's German Culture* (Bloomington: Indiana University Press, 1995).

10. Vidal-Naquet, 27.

11. New Haven: Yale University Press, 1991.

One

The Longest Shadow

In memory of Dorothy de Rothschild

I am sitting in a room with a dozen boys. We are glued to a small, crackling radio. On the wall is a map of Europe and Russia. As we hear the latest news we shift colored pins to indicate the progress of German armies that have invaded Russia. To us it does not matter whether the pins move forward or backward. It is just too exciting to follow one battle after another.

I remember receiving two postcards from my grandmother, left behind in Frankfurt, after my mother emigrates to America in December 1938 and I go to England in March 1939. She is sixty-five years old, perhaps more. The postcards come from a place called Theresienstadt, and the stamps (I am an avid collector) interest me. A message forwarded by the Red Cross says: I am in good health; everything is fine. The idea forms in me that Theresienstadt is a vacation spot, or where old people go to be cared for.

My passage to England was uneventful. But during the long train ride to the port in Holland, the boys with whom I traveled (all from Frankfurt, evacuated with the help of James de Rothschild on a Children's Transport) become restless; they fool about with the one family object I was able to take along, a violin. We all play on it, or rather with it; a string breaks. Later, in Waddesdon, we play some more with it; another string breaks. Eventually the case cracks, we can see a label inside. On it there is a signature. It identifies the unrepairable instrument as a Stradivarius.

I cannot say I was happy in England, my place of refuge. I lived there from the age of nine to nearly sixteen. But my unhappiness did not affect, and even stimulated, a thirst for knowledge that coursed through me and covered just about any subject. I devoured books about airplanes, learning each silhouette; books about trees, learning to identify them by shape and leaf; Latin grammars; botany texts; Penguin puzzle books; encyclopedias. I sat near the main road from Waddesdon to Aylesbury noting the make and registration number of cars. I collected stamps, poring over catalogue details characterizing the country of issue and memorizing prices, watermarks, valuable printing errors. Fantasies overcame me of how I would rescue Her Royal Highness, daughter of the King of England, and be awarded a thousand or . . . one hundred thousand pounds. I would then spend hours figuring out which stamps to buy.

My determination to know everything was part and parcel of a wish to communicate that knowledge. Learning was its own reward; nothing, I thought, could be more enjoyable than telling others what I had absorbed. This delight in passing on what had given me pleasure reminded me later of the child in William Blake's *Songs of Innocence*, who goes from church or schoolhouse straight into the fields to catechize the creatures:

> Little Lamb, who made thee?
> Dost thou know who made thee?

I did well in school; the absence of my mother (my father, divorced when I was an infant, had emigrated to South America), childish rebellion against the family in charge of the Waddesdon home, and ambivalent feelings about many of the Cedar Boys (named after two stately trees marking the large house in which we lived) merely spurred more delight in learning.

Only here and there did the consciousness that I was a Jewish refugee disturb me enough that I recall the very moments. At another level, of course, I was always conscious of it. The Germanic upbringing which continued at the Cedars stressed obligations and also therefore that our food, our clothes, our education were provided by charity. Not that James de Rothschild ever intervened that way. We saw him rarely. He sometimes appeared on Jewish holidays, accompanied by his young and beautiful wife. He would sit very straight, his gaunt face augmented by the aristocratic monocle covering an eye lost in a polo accident; Dorothy de Rothschild always stood beside him and tempered his severity with a smile as we passed in review. Whether my dislike of dependence and my intellectual passion to know the world through my own powers preexisted this experience of indebtedness, I can't tell. Brought up without father and mother, I would let no one else fill the vacuum.

Yet I was always aware of a greater debt: to creation itself. That sounds mystical, and perhaps it was. The joy in simply being alive was so strong that I noted with alarm when some of the delight faded—when a birthday or a vacation or waking early and feeling I was the only awake person in the whole world made the heart glad, but not as before. My social unhappiness had no bearing on a gratitude that "wasted" itself on the Bucks countryside with its ponds, open fields, and lovely old trees. English nature invited the trespasser: we went berrying or hunting or on long, aimless walks, leaping over hedge and stile. Wordsworth opened himself to my understanding as soon as I read him.

I distinctly recall brooding on continuity. What held matter together? Why didn't the table before me disintegrate? (I would later read with perfect understanding the famous question: Why does the world exist rather than not exist?) Who or what kept me alive, and so intensely aware, moment to moment? In school the only subject I failed was geometry. The idea of proving a theorem by extending a triangle did not make sense to me. I needed to know the principle behind the proof; mere extension was too much of a mystery in my own life.

Yet there were incidents which made me conscious of being Jewish and a refugee. One of them also revealed the pressure to assimilate, a pressure that did not come from admonition but from homelessness. The recreation hall in Waddesdon, the only place large enough for socializing in a village of two thousand, was packed full one day with a motley, unwashed crew. We were told that they too were refugees, but from the East, *Ostjuden*. The inhabitants of Waddesdon, who could scarcely distinguish German refugees from German spies, were faced with people whose habits were utterly unlike theirs or ours. These colorful D.P.s were given to talking and gesturing unintelligibly, and . . . to haggling in the shops! I remember disavowing them: *We* (the German refugees) have nothing to do with *them*.

The portion I read on my bar mitzvah happened to describe the attack of the Amalekites on the Israelites as the latter wander through the desert toward the Promised Land. The biblical writer is vengeful and does not mince his words. Amalek is to be destroyed, completely. "Remember the Amalekite. Thou shalt not forget." The good rabbi who traveled from London every week to give us an hour of Hebrew mingled with moral instruction or a schmooze on the virtues of the patriarchs, and who presided over the bar mitzvah of each Cedar Boy, did not fail to draw the lesson that the Nazis were the new Amalek. I was personally charged to remember and offered a Bible inscribed with that dire slogan.

In retrospect, it seems as if some God had wrapped me about and kept me immune from the worst. Though a quasi orphan, I felt at home in the gentle countryside of Buckinghamshire, my life somehow part of its life, and sheltered by an active sense of belonging. This curious trust in life rather than people may have been there much earlier. A separation from home that could have been traumatic at age nine was not. In Germany I was occasionally beaten up by Nazi youngsters, but that was merely part of life: I would have been beaten up anyway, by some group of kids. Only once did I return home crying, not only roughed up but pushed deliberately into dogshit. Where was God, I bitterly asked.

Nazi parades were thrilling; physical hunger was moderate. Because I didn't look Jewish, and was adorned with likable flappy ears, my mother would send me out to see whether a warmhearted grocer might be induced to sell me an egg. Every Saturday I came back with something. Perhaps the tendency then to protect children from adult knowledge made me understand very little of what was happening to relatives: Kristallnacht exists in my mind as a vague rumor of uncles who left home for a while. A month later my mother was in America. Unable to get a visa for me, she left anyway, but made sure I would be on a Children's Transport to England. When we said good-bye neither of us knew that it would be for seven years: by the time I rejoined her, I was an adolescent, and she a stranger.

My thoughts about the Holocaust did not gather momentum till after army service, in 1955. I had been drafted two years before and spent a funny and painful sixteen weeks of basic training at Fort Dix. During that period of methodical humiliation and physical exhaustion, I recovered "basic" feelings of a different kind—about the earth on which this strange training took place, about my dependence on sunrise and sunset. Solid, beautiful, encompassing, a sudden closeness to nature taught me more about companionship than the forced esprit de corps in the simulated hell the army provided. After the usual military mix-ups I ended in Heidelberg at Headquarters PID (Public Information). As an antidote to both army life and a country which had exiled or killed my relatives, I began to study Hebrew with another draftee—he was later to enter the Jewish Theological Seminary, a *hozer betshuvah* inspired by a vision of uniting, through Judaism, the wisdom of East and West.

We found a Holocaust survivor in Heidelberg with whom we read the Book of Job twice a week. As we knocked on the door of a dingy apartment, Herr Sprecher peered out, always with an anxious expression, as if expecting to be arrested again. His smile when he saw us was a relief. A Polish Jew, he had been through the camps and rarely talked about it. At that time (1954) the German goverment was not yet paying reparations or had not gotten around to him. Though in abject poverty, he was happy to be alive: a very small man with a ruddy, rotund face, who seemed supernaturally gentle and old. After my army service, during the first year of teaching at Yale, I wrote a play that included some of the stories he revealed. Basically, though, like many who had gone through far worse, I was building a life and not focusing on the past.

My grand scholarly project at Yale was a History of Interpretation which would do justice to the Jewish commentary-tradition in the context of patristics, allegoresis, and so on. I did not know at that time that David Hartman, my grandfather, a teacher of religion in Frankfurt, had published a doctoral thesis on Midrash and the Book of Ruth. None of this had a direct bearing on my duties at Yale: courses on English poetry took most of my energy, although I smuggled in biblical texts. I suppose that, as in the army, I was working against the environment. T. S. Eliot was everywhere as the spiritual heir of Donne; I too was impressed by his ironic, liturgical rhythms, but disturbed by the uses to which his poetry was put. It reinforced a gentlemanly sort of Christianity that allied itself with the unmistakable Anglophile bearing of my senior colleagues in the seventeenth and eighteenth centuries. Those centuries were the prestige fields at Yale, attracting great donors as well as scholars, and overshadowing the adolescent and faintly disreputable Romantics. I tried applying to law school—in revolt, I suppose, and in hope that it would help my interpretation project: law school would not accept me as a part-time student. I gave up my History of Interpretation, a task that needed total commitment, though twenty-five years later I was able to help in setting up Judaic Studies at the university. Today Jewish and Hebrew texts can be learned either in the context of other literatures or in the context of Midrash: its exegetical inventiveness and colloquial force are still not fully appreciated in secular circles.

Throughout the fifties and sixties I remained future-oriented. Yet I often thought of the German-Jewish community that had been destroyed and wondered what kind of intellectual I would have become if I had grown up in the shadow of Franz Rosenzweig, Martin Buber, Gershom Scholem, Ernst Simon, Abraham Heschel—not to speak of the Frankfurt School proper: Theodor Adorno, Walter Benjamin, Erich Fromm, and others. It was also, I suspect, a deep sense of separation that made Israel important for me. I have never been a conscious Zionist and went through none of the schools or youth movements fostering *ahavat Zion*. But already on my first visit, in 1952, Israel appeared to my feelings as an embodied dream. The sense of belonging to it, as if the land and not human parents had begotten me, especially an uncrowded, rural Jerusalem so close to the sky, intensified sensations that had bound me to the English countryside. This was starker, stonier, more primitive. I walked about with a barefoot mind, a spiritual vagabond having no sort of special Jewish identity, taking pleasure in every motion of sight and sound: goats and olive trees in Jerusalem; Mea Shearim with its market and numberless *stuebele;* the mystery of the Old City, walled off, inaccessible; Safad, more Oriental still, its beggars, Hasids, and hole-in-the-wall shops; Tel Aviv, the city built from the ground up within the memory of many then living, where a young cousin of mine could date every new building and even tree in the neighborhood.

An organic relation to place is what I lacked and would never recover. I rarely experience strong feelings of attachment, whether to people or to soil. Israel was different. The soil I walked on felt both very old and very new: ancient beyond belief yet still to be planted, by the imagination too. Even the people moved me, from the Jekes (German Jews) to the black-suited Orthodox, and the aggressively secular, open-shirted kibbutzniks. I was glad of the mingling and saw no need to take sides in an incredibly hardworking society where every group seemed to have its own rhythm. Enthusiastically I joined in, harvesting huge melons on my first day on a kibbutz, and was out with a sunstroke by noon.

We underestimate how important the feeling for place is as a physical memory. It is important for love, which often fuses person and place. But as *mystique* becomes *politique*, it can also grow into a fanatical passion: a self-sanctifying, place-bound nationalism that casts a murderous suspicion on the outsider. The Jew has been its major victim in the Diaspora. He is seen as an alien, however ancient and settled his claim. Those who cleave to Zion are not exempt from the dark side of that sacred passion. They must now confront it in themselves, in their own homeland and refuge.

It was toward the end of the 1970s that the survivors of the camps, now fully settled in America, with children grown up and grandchildren not far off, allowed the past a more conscious, public existence. Those who had entered the camps (or other extreme conditions) when their physical and mental resilience was at its prime (say, between fourteen and forty) had a better chance of survival. This age group was now close to sixty and some were over seventy. Most had rebuilt their families almost immediately without stopping to complete their formal education. The task of rebuilding had thrown them at once into making a living. Others became distinguished professionals, often returning to school at a later point. Now their children, the Second Generation, were beginning to seek a legacy.

To honor their parents meant also to honor the experience of their parents, however grim and burdensome it was. As children they had heard too much or too little. Both parents and children, moreover, were shocked by the growth of "revisionism," a phenomenon that became more aggressive in the 1970s. It denied that a systematic genocide had taken place. The deaths suffered in the Holocaust were attributed by revisionists to wartime conditions or exaggerated Jewish propaganda. Such malicious denial had to be met by an intensified act of witness. The movement encouraging ethnic affirmation also helped witnesses to speak out.

I too became directly involved at that time. What had haunted me all along, in addition to the genocide itself, was that it was not significantly opposed by local populations, who often even exploited it. I still felt German enough not to condemn the German character as such; other nationals had shown themselves indifferent or had actively promoted the crime. The exceptions—mostly compassionate individuals from all ranks of society, and even an entire village like Chambon or a nation like Denmark—only proved the rule. There was, then, the mystery of the bystanders as well as of the perpetrators, and among the bystanders were many well-educated persons (Max Weinreich called them "Hitler's professors"), who condoned or even disseminated a racial theory that justified the exclusion of the Jews from public life.

The behavior of these intellectuals was especially incomprehensible. But then it all was; and I could not find an access-point for either study or activism. Yet had I really tried to find it? Or had I sheltered myself from too heavy a commitment by overestimating the mystery and pretending that thinking could not grasp the facts? It did not help that I saw around me many who depended on the *Shoah* to reinforce their religious or political identity.

My wife, Renée, now played a crucial role. Her story was one of the first to be recorded by the Holocaust Survivors Film Project, founded in 1979 with the encouragement of New Haven survivors who wished to give public testimony. Born in Czechoslovakia, Renée and her deaf sister (a year younger) had been hidden on a farm near the Moravian border until their parents were deported to Auschwitz early in 1944. Payments for the children stopped and they were forced to return to Bratislava. The sisters (ages nine and ten) arrived and found no one to shelter them—no Jews officially remained. After a few weeks they went to the police and asked to join their parents. They were sent to Bergen-Belsen.

One year in the camp was almost fatal. Liberated in April 1945, Renée was seriously ill with typhus: to this day she regrets not remembering the actual day of liberation. In 1948 she came to America from Sweden, where the sisters had been evacuated by UNRRA and the Red Cross.

Renée's participation in the Survivors Film Project roused my own interest. I discovered that the immediate cause for organizing it was the television series *Holocaust.* This film, so effective in West Germany, struck the survivors as a sanitized and distorted version of what they had suffered. The vow they had made not to forget—not to let the world forget—came back to them. The *Farband,* a Labor Zionist group composed mainly of East European immigrants, cooperated with a psychiatrist in New Haven (himself a survivor) and a television interviewer active in Jewish affairs. Dori Laub and Laurel Vlock, with the support of William Rosenberg, head of the *Farband*, and many in the New Haven community, began to assemble the means to videotape witnesses to the genocide.

What is a professor of English good for, if not to write a grant proposal? That is how I was drawn in; but the real reason for my increasing participation in this grass-roots effort was that I saw how important it could be for education. It gave me my point of access. I thought: Even the survivors are mortal. In ten or twenty years, how many will be left? For the time being we can ask them to tell their story in person, to talk to a classroom or to a community audience; but who will represent them when they are no longer among us? Historians establish the larger picture, while verifying every fact; they are rarely interested in transmitting stories, however impressive the latter may be as a revelation of personality and often in psychological and textured detail.

What I wanted was a restitution: the survivors not only recalling what happened then, but their thoughts, *now* as well as *then*. The whole person, or as much as could be recorded in the space of two hours. Claude Lanzmann's great film, *Shoah*, has set a standard for sophisticated and relentless inquiry, but the kind of open-ended, unprogrammatic interviewing practiced by the New Haven group is quite different. The interviewer, as Dori Laub has said, is a listener and a companion; he or she asks a minimum of questions in the hope that memories will emerge from a deeper, more spontaneous level.

It was also a way of compensating for the fact that most visual documentation of that period comes from Nazi sources. Our Holocaust museums are full of photos drawn from the picturebook of the murderers. The mind is exposed to images magnifying the Nazis and degrading their victims. The witness accounts are a view from the other side: they restore the sympathy and humanity systematically denied by Nazi footage. And even if, being recorded so many years after the event, they cannot be reliable in all aspects, the passage of time also matures memory. The video project does not impinge on the province of historians, who sift and compare sources, but seeks to open the hearts and minds of both high school students and adult audiences. They see the testimony of a thinking and feeling person, rather than of a victim.

It was during the Eichmann trial in 1960–61 that I first understood the power of personal witnessing. At that time I wrote "Ahasuerus," a poem that assimilated the witness account of a *Sonderkommando* member to the archetype of this legendary Wanderer, doomed to survive and conscious of everything. He would have preferred to die; but (in my version) his fear that he might be the last and only witness precluded death as a way out. While I glimpsed in many testimonies a mythic dimension learned from Jewish storytelling, or a poetry of realism that was a natural reaction to unbearable and meaningless suffering, I also saw that they were as authentic a representation as was possible in an audiovisual era—where exploitation is inevitable. An Archive of Conscience was needed both for educational purposes and for the sake of the media.

In 1982 Yale became the curator of the testimonies. The Revson Foundation enabled the university to establish a video archive in its central library. We had become a witness to the witness. What started as a grass-roots project could now develop into an oral history of national scope. (There are also important audiotape collections, "Voices from the Holocaust," that should likewise be indexed, coordinated, and so made accessible to education and research.) As I write this, close to the fiftieth anniversary of Kristallnacht, Yale's video-testimony project is being extended to Europe, and our archive has grown to over twelve hundred accounts.

Yet who can render the workings of memory? A Proust, perhaps, had he been born in a more tragic period and passed through the destruction. Everything we do seems, at times, inadequate and external. The interviews can be uneven; there are bad days; both witnesses and interviewers have resistances to overcome. In moments of doubt I take comfort from such writers as Primo Levi, Jean Améry, and Aharon Appelfeld. They tell us about weakness as well as courage, about the repression that occurred within the survivor, about a vital need to forget and the struggle against what has bitten into the soul. It is true but not all the truth that the survivors were neglected or that people could not bear to hear them. Silence shelters; even the most confessional writing communicates quietly, in its own space. There came a point when the survivors did not wish to talk. That time is past, although it is never entirely past. It required the "bribe" of life, that is, their children, and also the fear that the Holocaust would not be forgotten so much as denied or distorted, to bring the survivors back to the injunction: Thou shalt tell.

Ezekiel was forbidden to mourn the loss of the Temple in public. For many years after the Holocaust it seemed impossible to find an adequate form of public memory. Now it is possible, but still precarious. There are memorials to the memorials in Poland, funeral monuments made by piecing together vandalized tombstones. In Czechoslovakia the dome of a burned synagogue is set like a gravestone into a cemetery. At Worms, West

Germany, you can admire the reconstructed medieval synagogue and the room where Rashi had his yeshiva. But these are cenotaphs. In the absence of a vital community the restored buildings and orphaned monuments recall painfully Hitler's Museum of a Vanished Race.

The most sensitive issue, both where there are Jews and where there are not, is how to communicate to the young what happened. The insemination of horror, or of horror and guilt, may produce terrible fantasies or else feelings of impotence. How does one teach a traumatic history without increasing inappropriate psychological defenses? The pedagogical question must be faced, especially when so many museums and educational programs are springing up.

Many times have I heard the nursery rhyme

Ring around the rosies,
A pocket full of posies,
Ashes, ashes,
All fall down!

without being aware of its sinister side, its possible origin in the Great Plague of the seventeenth century. The Opies, who mention that hypothesis in their *Oxford Dictionary of Nursery Rhymes*, have no proof. The catchy words absorb, so the hypothesis goes, that forgotten catastrophe: a red rash marking the disease, posies of flowers to ward off the smell of death and perhaps death itself, the burning of contaminated materials and corpses (though the version quoted by the Opies has "A-tishoo" not "Ashes"), and the sudden, macabre career of the plague. We don't trust such speculations, but they express our hope that deadly knowledge can be transformed from a traumatic into a bearable truth.

Our culture must look beyond the Holocaust, yet it can do so only by using ritual as well as realism. In the distant future we may stand before the most successful transformations as before certain traditional enactments: ceremonies, prayers, popular songs, even verses without an obvious reference to the tragedy. We need representations that do not founder under their weight of reality, that transmit more than images of victimage. In the search for authentic representations I believe testimonies can play a part. They are basic and archetypal, stories that are acts of facing in their very telling. A collective portrait is drawn and ordinary speech survives the burden of recollection.

In those testimonies there comes a moment when the loneliness is brought home: even into the home rebuilt with so much fervor and dedication. At family celebrations, such as a son's bar mitzvah, the survivor may realize that, among so many guests, the family from which he comes—all those aunts, uncles, cousins—is represented by no one except himself. That pang of loneliness remains; and it can swell to more than a pang, to a struggle with the Angel of Death, who threatens to vacate the entire achievement of a generation in which fathers and mothers started almost from scratch, like the patriarchs. It is as if they, the survivors, belonged to the dead after all.

At the end of the Israeli film, *Because of That War*, Halina revisits the death camp Treblinka, suffers a hallucinatory episode in which she acts out the struggle with the Angel, and returns home emptied rather than exalted, or exalted beyond the family. She realizes how much of her living strength has disappeared into a story she is able to retell or hysterically reenact, but not integrate into ordinary life. So we find that what is established on the flood is never established enough for the survivor.

I have not had to overcome so deadly a past. But sometimes in the midst of a bar mitzvah, when I realize once more how much communal experience is embodied in those prayers, I become enraged and argue with myself: How can you be so sad, so vengefully angry, just at this happy moment? I think of the sudden, pitiless removal of a family, or a community like the one in which I am praying, from their rooted and peaceful existence, to suffer a nakedness more terrible than Job's, and which resembles—if it can resemble anything—landscapes of hell in Christian painting. They are transported into that man-made hell, made naked, trampled on, massacred. It is not the image of death itself which gets hold of me, breaking past the safeguards, compelling imagination to look at that final transition. This Holocaust suddenness is worse than death, a denial of life so stark that it is hard to summon an affirmation to counter it, to decide that life, when such a shame and desecration come to mind, remains worthwhile.

My bitter feelings, in the midst of a community's joy, focus on the killers who tried to extirpate an entire people, classifying them as unworthy to live. A people who are among the ancients of this world, not in age only but in continuity, not in continuity only but in wealth of learning, not in learning only but in a moral wisdom centered on the preservation of life, *pikuah nefesh*. Their morality, despite messianic-volcanic outbreaks, has tied them to life on this earth, a practical life, leavened by two thousand years of Bible reading and interpretation.

What happened cannot be explained by an intolerance of difference, or disgust for the pariah, or the need to blame and eliminate the victim. It really was violent evil rising up against a punctilious moral knowledge and an Ahasuerus-like conscience.

The Longest Shadow

I am far from saying that Jews, who can be as stiff-necked, quarrelsome, and exclusive as any other group, have cornered the market on wisdom. They have their crazies, bigots, extremists, exploiters. And the Holocaust has hardened them: there are signs, especially in Israel, that the Bible can be a weapon turned against a world that is felt to be even more hostile now than *beyamim hahem*, "in those days."

Yet it is not a matter of the victims taking on features of the perpetrators, according to the pop psychology of unbenevolent observers. Israel is a state like any other and must defend itself. In the wake of the Holocaust, the 1967 and 1973 wars made its citizens intensely aware of the possibility of *hurban habayit hashlishi*, the destruction of the Third Temple. Where else, within a context of such danger, do you find maintained a culture of argument and a system of values that prize study so much and do not see faith demanding a sacrifice of intellect?

I think of a Yiddish song like "Yankele," or of the service on the Sabbath, when the Torah scroll, handled like royalty, is opened and read to all, then carried into the congregation to show that it is a shared possession. It was the Jews' textual, not their territorial, ambition which united them, their refusal to kill the letter and to cancel the contract of their fathers and mothers with God. Yet this very people was taken out of its place and transferred—*raus, raus*—to that ultimate *Umschlagplatz*, the death camp, in a matter of days or hours. We were like a great tree that had weathered the centuries and in a day is uprooted, dismembered, and thrown to the flames. Each community in the Diaspora was a tree like that. There can be no replacement for those communities, though new centers have appeared in Israel, and with them a transplanting of new learning, new life, new problems. But the shadow of the destruction is not something that the joy of the newborn or the joy of what has survived can lessen.

Two

The Weight of What Happened

There is a speculation by the well-known mythographer Mircea Eliade that major religious holidays are not only commemorative (celebrating a past event), but also soothers of a burdened memory. They cancel a debt by a sort of solemn orgy; they undo, especially in the Judeo-Christian tradition, a past that weighs on those who take history seriously, who cannot see it as merely contingent, as a meaningless and catastrophic accumulation. As Nietzsche said in *The Use and Abuse of History:* "Life is absolutely impossible without forgetfulness." The modern historical sense, he added, may prevent that forgetfulness and may injure our ability to live by enforcing a state of perpetual wakefulness.

The Jewish Day of Atonement could be taken to corroborate this insight. We remember all our debts toward God, all sins of commission and omission, but only in order to be purged of them, in order for a New Year to begin also within the individual. This paradoxical disburdenment of memory through ritual rememoration was also cryptically expressed in the Baal Shem Tov's famous "Memory is Redemption," now inscribed on Yad Vashem, a house that testifies to the most ruinous episode in the history of the Jews. Yad Vashem, the museum in Jerusalem, documents the Holocaust in the light of a phrase that is basic to every attempt to make sense of a catastrophe which threatens to turn us all into Nietzsche's insomniac philosopher.

To "understand" the Holocaust, we are using for the first time all the resources of modern historiography. What in previous eras of pogroms, massacres, expulsions, was remembered mainly by being absorbed into a repetition or extension of existing prayers—into that kind of collective mourning—is now much harder to treat ritually: first, because of the enormity of the event, many find no true analogy; then, because by a reversal of traditional procedures, the call to remember (*zakhor*) is no longer

This chapter was occasioned by the publication of two books: Yosef Hayim Yerushalmi's *Zakhor: Jewish History and Jewish Memory* (Seattle: University of Washington Press, 1982); and *From a Ruined Garden: The Memorial Books of Polish Jewry*, edited and translated by Jack Kugelmass and Jonathan Boyarin (New York: Schocken, 1982).

satisfied by Days of Remembrance alone, but aspires to a writing so fearfully detailed that it may never be erased from the conscience of the nations.

This modern turn to historiography may have significant consequences. Yosef Hayim Yerushalmi has argued that it is causing the first real rupture between Jewish memory and Jewish history. For to document something faithfully and endlessly cannot give the relief that comes from ritual observance, which stresses "not the historicity of the past, but its eternal contemporaneity." The collective memory, working through ritual and recital within the confines of Bible, Talmud, and similar texts, remains redemptive or integrative. Yet many today cannot choose "myth" over "history"—a possibility still open even after the expulsion of the Jews from Spain, which saw some history writing in the modern sense, but mainly a spreading mysticism. Nor does Zionism help settle the balance between ritual memory and historiography: it weakens Jewish memory by its revolt against Diaspora continuities, and also weakens historiography by vacating historical time between Masada and the founding of the state of Israel.

Yerushalmi fears that the historical sense, which modern Jewish writers themselves cultivate with luminous persistence, will hasten the decline of Jewish memory. The historian's task, therefore, "can no longer be limited to finding continuities in Jewish history, not even 'dialectical' ones. Perhaps the time has come to look more closely at ruptures, breaches, breaks, to identify them more precisely, to see how Jews endured them. . . . " Yet he does not guarantee this venture success: he refuses to substitute for myths of history a myth of the historian. To be a "physician of memory" is indeed the right vocation. But since among the Jews memory did not depend on historians in the first place (the "collective memories of the Jewish people," he writes, "were a function of the shared faith, cohesiveness, and will of the group itself, transmitting and re-creating its past through an entire complex of interlocking social and religious institutions that functioned organically to achieve this"), the historian, as he puts it sadly, seems at best a pathologist rather than a physician.

The collective memory is not easy to define. In principle, it should be possible to understand what is Jewish (or any other persistent group identity) from an embodied knowledge, a set of practices and symbols which have attracted a variety of explanations, some in the form of stories. To such questions as "What mean these stones?" or "What mean ye by these ceremonies?" there are various kinds of answers, not all convergent, not all official. Jewish tradition for a long time did not codify them. It preserved and kept probing; it expected scholars to memorize everything and find their own way among the authorities. Every scholar was immersed in this labor of reading, transmitting, and sorting the past; it was not left to someone called a historian.

This is clearly less true today, and in that sense it is correct to talk of a decline of the collective memory. Story and history separate. Yet this also liberates story, makes it stand in its own light, reveal its own character. We have learned that stories cannot be abbreviated by an intellectual method, or foreclosed by spiritual hindsight. Christian typology, which turns the Hebrew Bible into an "Old" Testament prefiguring a "New" Truth that completes it, suffers imaginatively from such a foreclosure, though Christian story generates, of course, parables of its own, episodes that are enigmatic enough to haunt as well as guide the reader. From Judah Halevi's twelfth-century theological work, *Kuzari*, advocating storytelling over philosophical argument, to Walter Benjamin's essay in our time on how storytelling is becoming a lost art because we insert too much explanatory material, there is an awareness, however easily trivialized ("Pepperidge Farm remembers," spoken in a great-grandpa voice), that something like a collective memory exists. Unlike Halevi, of course, Benjamin knew that the collective memory, as an uninterrupted or self-reparative process of handing down wisdom from generation to generation, seemed now in jeopardy, and that contemporary ideologies like Nazism were leaping into the breach by professing a politics of repristination, a violent return to an aboriginal state of purity that, in effect, elided both story and history.

It is not oral transmission as such which is crucial, rather the fact that ritual and recital combine effectively to make memorable stories which survive when other channels of communication fail. Whether or not we fully understand how this collective memory works, we know that in Jewish tradition learning and legend have reinforced rather than subverted each other. We also know that historicism in its earliest phase recovered the oral traditions of other peoples and that the major effort of nineteenth-century philology was to analyze ballad, Bible, and epic as the expression of a communal spirit. Even as individualism asserted itself, communal forms were retrieved. Often, however, a virulent nationalism took hold of that research and politicized it, so that the concept of a "people" or "folk," and of collective rather than individual expression, was used to censor and suppress nonconformist tendencies.

Any talk about the "collective memory" must be approached, then, with circumspection. The imputed character of such a memory may itself be the outcome of historical anxieties. It is premature to assume that a collective memory once existed that is now endangered by modern developments. The only certain thing is that the contemporary historian has a self-image of his discipline which sets up an opposition: "a Jewish historiography divorced from Jewish collective memory and, in crucial respects, thoroughly at odds with it."

Must we accept Yerushalmi's stark contrast between these two sources of knowledge and identity? It is certainly important to insist on a difference not sufficiently studied; yet there is a tendency, which one finds equally in literary studies (Yerushalmi admits that his distinction reflects an "ever-growing modern dichotomy"), to exaggerate the organic, or ideal and unitary character of a previous kind of memory, as if unconscious adhesion to a way of life were more genuine than a broken or born-again pattern. The breaches and breaks Yerushalmi wishes to identify more precisely, and the endurance that helped the Jews to overcome them, may have always existed. But now there are fears, more prophetic than realistic, that the rise of the historical sense will doom altogether a collective memory associated too easily with continuity and authoritative transmission.

This is a time, then, when we should ask what middle terms or significant links can be found between Jewish historiography and Jewish memory—links that might be strengthened once more. That such intermediate forms exist is suggested by Yerushalmi himself in certain of his comments on the Holocaust. He remarks that though it has engendered more historical research than any single event in Jewish history, "I have no doubt whatsoever that its image is being shaped, not at the historian's anvil, but in the novelist's crucible." The novel, he suggests, shows that Jews, while not rejecting the burden of history out of hand, expect to be relieved from it by a new metahistorical myth, like those Sephardi Jews who chose mysticism over history to explain the cataclysm of the Spanish expulsion.

I am less sure that fiction can play the role attributed to it by this distinguished historian, who speaks urbanely yet in bitterness of heart. He feels the need to acknowledge the rise of something (fiction) that is inherently profane and perhaps profaning, yet which in previous eras was kept within the boundaries of ritual and recital. Fiction is, no doubt, an image maker today, and open to popular misuse, especially in the form of televised simplification. But that is why, first of all, we have such an increasingly complex literary criticism, a hygiene of reading with iconoclastic overtones. Like the historian, the literary critic looks "more closely at ruptures, breaches, breaks," not to defeat tradition even more, but to show the heteronomic rather than hegemonic structure of every significant mode of discourse, sacred or secular. But equally important are "memorial" genres that perpetuate, even today, the collective memory in a nonfictional yet highly imaginative form.

Among these genres are the video memoirs incorporated, for example, in YIVO's film about Jewish life in Poland before the war, *Image Before My Eyes*, or the tapes being made by Yale's Video Archive for Holocaust Testimonies. This new oral history has not yet found its place: it looks suspicious to the positivist historian, yet it should not be left by default to the literary critic's tendency to turn everything into narratology. A second link to the collective memory is represented by another YIVO-inspired work, *From a Ruined Garden*, a selection from the "memorial books" of Polish Jewry indispensable to historians interested in the survivors of the Holocaust as well as the Holocaust itself.

As the editors tell us in their fine introduction, most memorial books, or *yizker-bikher*, are written in Yiddish, and they describe salient aspects of the life of both small and very large Jewish communities in Poland. At least six hundred such books exist for Eastern European Jewry alone. Some are in Hebrew or English or whatever language the survivors speak. Compiled on shoestring budgets, they are an unusual example of collective authorship, commonplace books that bring together whatever documents the survivors could save. They contain the records, known in each community as its *pinkes*, historical narratives based on all kinds of sources, from encyclopedia articles to eyewitness accounts. But they are interspersed with personal sketches and reflections, vivid characterizations of both eccentric and leading personalities, and learned summaries of folklore and linguistic habits. Some contain maps and photographs. The first modern books of this kind emerge after World War I and the Ukrainian pogroms. Most *yizker* books, however, were compiled in response to the Holocaust. They are the equivalent in words to communal tombstones erected by *landsmannschaften* (fraternal societies of emigrés and survivors) in their home cemeteries. "No graves have been left of all those who were slain," we read in such a book. "Beloved and precious martyrs of Koriv, we bring you to burial today! In a *yizker-bukh*, a memorial volume! Today we have set up a tombstone in memory of you!" The recently announced Yad Vashem project to build a "Valley of the Destroyed Communities" extends this work of mourning. It has to embrace not individuals alone, but entire communities in which the Jews were among the oldest settlers. Of three million in Poland, only ten percent survived.

Let me say at once how difficult and disconcerting it is, how moving and necessary, to encounter this collection. Every story or testimony in it is and is not like every other. I wonder whether such a treasury of sorrows has been published before. Who has not seen, in certain Catholic churches of Europe, a wall crowded with notes to the Virgin Mary, hopeful plaques and inscriptions in all sizes and shapes? To me it seemed as if I had come across an endless wall of such tablets, stretched across time, pregnant words snatched from an underworld of private and communal tragedy. The dead cannot speak; here the survivors speak for the dead as well as for themselves; or like Esther-Khaye, the *Zogerin* ("Speaker"), for the illiterate and the grief-stricken unable to talk:

> Just at daybreak before the High Holy Days, this picture is to be seen: a large crowd of women, led by Esther-Khaye bearing her book of supplications, set off for the cemetery. The way to the graveyard is not far from town, and as Esther-Khaye enters, she feels at home, among people she knows. "Good morning, God," she begins in a tragic melody, "Your servant Esther-Khaye has come. . . . " And approaching the grave, she looks over at the woman on whose behalf she is supplicating, and words begin to pour from her mouth, as if from a spring.
>
> First she calls out the name of the deceased and strikes the gravestone three times with her hand, speaking as if to a living person: "Good morning to you, Rive-Mindl the daughter of Hankev-Tsvi, your daughter Sore-Rivke has come, for she wants to see you and pour out her bitter heart before you. Look, Rive-Mindl, at what has become of your daughter, if you were to arise now and see what has become of your daughter, you would return to the grave. Request, Rive-Mindl, a good year for your daughter, a kosher year, that she may know no ill, exert yourself for her sake, why are you silent? Why do you not supplicate the Lord of the Universe?"

Taken from the Zabludow *yizker* book, published in Buenos Aires in 1961, this story, like many others, has no direct relation to the Holocaust. Yet it is recalled, together with grim and graphic accounts of the destruction, because these volumes memorialize a vanished life in its vigor. One finds depictions of the market, of special festivals, of a girl's schoolroom, of anarchist and other political demonstrations and deaths, of local quarrels, of Jewish fighters in the Spanish Civil War. There are reminiscences from the real Chelm (known in legend for its naive townsfolk), sayings attributed to the Dubner Magid, and a grotesque *fait divers* from the camps: "How I read Yiddish Literature to an S.S. Captain." The sections dealing specifically with the Holocaust and its aftermath take up only a third of the volume. Emphasis falls on the variegated, often joyful, culture of the Polish Jews, on what existed before the garden was ruined.

The task of anthologizing must have been trying. The editors, anthropologists by profession, chose what they found most compelling: humorous or tragic stories illustrating everyday life and its underlying tensions. Even if what they left out is important, at least the quarry of these sources has begun. A scholarly "Bibliography of Eastern European Memorial Books" is appended. There are also German-Jewish memorial books to be explored, though they tend more to the learned monograph. They can be found in the Leo Baeck Institute.

Can we reflect on the art revealed by this collection? The vignette presenting Esther-Khaye has the intimacy of Yiddish, and we cannot call such provincial stories "great" or "heroic," accustomed as we are to Western literature. Yet the intimate detail builds up typical characters or scenes, and evokes an acute sense of the difference made by speech—from lighthearted joking to bearing witness—in a universe of death. Esther-Khaye, seen in retrospect, stands for the difficulty of mourning, and for the increased strain of that effort after the Holocaust, when there is not enough voice to go around. Even the familiar prayers barely save themselves. Yet if the effect here is anything but heroic, there is a category of the memorable which is "above heroic," and which lies at the heart of all imaginative writing as it reanimates the colors and figures of a culture that should not be allowed to die a second time by becoming a nostalgic and frozen memory. What is delightful about Esther-Khaye is precisely her spontaneous, creative use of a traditional ceremony and its formulas. Everything is familiar, yet nothing is rigid.

From a Ruined Garden is an indispensable sourcebook that shows Jewish memory interacting with history. It renews a genre going back at least to the fourteenth century. Yerushalmi points to the famous *Memorbuch* of Nuremburg which summarizes persecutions in Germany and France from the First Crusade of 1096 to the Black Death of 1349. Without these books in modern form we would have only the records of the perpetrators: orders of the day, intake lists, lives reduced to itemized effects, names and numbers in endless series. By the poetic justice of the *yizker-bikher*, there is a *gilgul*, or a transmigration, of names—belonging to places, persons, and customs—extended as in a Mourner's Kaddish, though here by means of story and testimony.

Is it the literary scholar in me that responds so strongly to these names saved from obliteration, as if they were revenants who are offered the life from which they were cut off, if only in the body of these memoirs? Despite Yerushalmi's caution that "although *Memorbücher* may contain important historical information, they cannot be regarded as historiography," I regard them as a type of history with its own form and reason, a popular and restitutive genre. That genre is historical rather than historiographical: penetrated by contingency, by the fact that these survived and these did not, but also by an insurgent memorial tradition that gathered in and recorded, in a spontaneous and composite, rather than ritual and integrated form, the fullness of these names. On the one hand, the unutterably sacred name of God, called *haShem*, "The Name"; on the other, motley syllables often more like nicknames, sometimes short (Yosl, Schloyme Healer), sometimes evocative of rabbinic grandeur (Rabbi Reb Yoshuah Yankev).

As the *Sefer Kalushin*, the memorial book of the town of Kalushin, writes of a tragedy in the last century, when a synagogue was burnt: "The place stood empty; only the terror and the legends remained." That remains true here too. The names return; fragments of ordinary life are recovered; the *landsmannshaftn* piece together emblems and synecdoches of their former existence. Yet nothing fills up. Some of the terror is given shape and purged. But one cannot say that these memories bring relief, even if they take the place of tears. Nor do they drift toward a new myth. Relief comes only, perhaps, in glimpsing a life that is still familiar to us, that has not been estranged. It is not fantasy we view, but reality—a reality which knows how to make use of fantasy "year in, year out, every time with the same familiar pattern" as is written of Esther-Khaye's performance.

But there is not yet such "tranquility" as Yehuda Amichai's poem on Jerusalem offers, moving rhythmically from the task of remembering to a natural forgetting:

> Everything here is busy with the task of remembering:
> the ruin remembers, the garden remembers
> the cistern remembers its water and the memorial grove
> remembers on a marble plaque a distant holocaust. . . .

> But names are not important in these hills,
> like at the cinema, when the credits on screen
> before the film are not yet interesting and at the end of the film
> are no longer so. The lights come up, the letters fade,
> the rippling curtain comes down, doors are open and outside is
>   the night.

Three

Darkness Visible

No light, but rather darkness visible

—Milton, *Paradise Lost*

Not energy, not messages, not particles, not light.
Light itself falls back down, broken by its own weight.

—Primo Levi, "The Black Stars"

We think of memory as a residue left in the mind by the ruins of time, and capable of retrieving and even restoring the past. For modernity the great metaphor of such retrieval is furnished by Schliemann's excavations at the end of the last century. Searching for Homer's Troy Schliemann discovered in one of his digs a magnificent gold mask of a face. He boasted: "Today I kissed the lips of Agamemnon."

Freud's comparison of psychoanalysis to an archeological excavation like Schliemann's brought the metaphor directly into contact with memory retrieval as fieldwork both highly emotional and scrupulously scientific. Psychoanalysis cleared away each layer of mental sedimentation in order to find a buried object of desire. There is a beyond to memory in this scenario: myth becomes flesh, becomes history, when Schliemann kisses the mask of Agamemnon. The imagination leaps from fiction to life. That legendary Grecian commander really existed; that magnificent mask must be his persona. The tyranny of Greece over the German mind could not find a better illustration. The tyranny of an imagination that requires emblems of a heroic past could not expose itself more clearly.

The work of recovering shapes of memory from the destruction named the Holocaust has so little in common with Schliemann's successful quest that it stands rather as a terrible coda. Can we find a guiding image for that very different, mostly grim, always burdened retrieval? The Jews in Europe were decimated by the Nazi genocide and lost their communal identity. In Germany and Eastern Europe that loss of community has been decisive,

35

irreversible; in other parts of Europe, such as France and Italy, or in Israel and America, new communities have developed, though conscious of a perhaps fatal amputation, and caught between a morbid and a necessary remembrance. The ash that literally covered Jewish lives, and from which we rescue vivid and pathetic snapshots, or cultural and religious artifacts expressive of a civilization at least as old as the Greek, that ash is more contaminating than what may have buried a millennial Troy, or a Pompey calcified by natural disaster.

Acting to understand this recent and most disastrous episode in Jewish and German history, the imagination has little occasion to leap. The photographs shown, one after the other, at the end of Haim Gouri's film *Pnei Mered* (literally *Faces of the Revolt*, but publicized as *Fire in the Ashes*), or the different shapes, spiritual and psychological, that I will describe, are not heroic, or inevitably heroic; nor are they enlarged, gilded, totemic. They tell of "nothing more than what we are"—rather, of what *they* were who had to face humiliation, persecution, and systematic slaughter.

Because the genocide did not occur in the distant past, and because it was unprecedented in its virulent and obsessive focus, there are dangers for the historian greater than those attending other archival quests. The "black sun" of the destruction can produce a melancholy as disabling as any we have known. Dürer's famous picture of a figure sitting dejected, like a fallen angel, in the midst of accumulated instruments of knowledge, the very tools of Enlightenment, points in the present context not only to the role of technology in the genocide but also to the dark (I previously said "contaminating") light shed by the Holocaust on human history.

Even so, some creative impulse is felt, perhaps akin to what made Jewish chroniclers and diarists continue to record the destruction to the last moment. David Roskies has shown that many contemporary accounts of pogroms dated from the First World War, and how this kind of narrative began to assume (emotionally, but also for preservation purposes) quasi-sacred status. Dubnov's famous words—even should they be apocryphal—as the *Einsatzgruppen* are eliminating the Jews of Riga, take on symbolic character and darken Schliemann's ecstasy: *Schreib un farschreib!* Keep writing it down!

The same impulse has led to remarkable works of art after the Holocaust, despite the dangers of trivialization and sensationalism. Among artists who were survivors one thinks of such poets as Celan, Nelly Sachs, Pagis, Cayrol, Kovner, and Sutzkever, of Samuel Bak's paintings, of Primo Levi's and Jean Améry's essays, of Charlotte Delbo's fragments and David Rousset's *The Other Kingdom*, of the fiction writers Wiesel, Appelfeld, Semprun, and Fink. It was not uncomplicated for them to release that creative energy. The hope

Darkness Visible

for collective survival, still inspiring the ghetto writers, was revealed to have been an illusion: after liberation, the total, overriding Nazi commitment to genocide became all too clear. In the dawn of new life, moreover, the liberated were again shunned or disregarded, like the proverbial messenger of bad news. Aharon Appelfeld, the Israeli novelist, often depicts the survivors as lapsing into a Big Sleep, not unlike the charmed amnesia of national assimilation from which they were so traumatically torn; and Gouri, a member of the so-called "Palmach" generation, with its ethos of *gevurah* or heroism, has documented the eye-opening impact of the Eichmann trial on an Israeli memory-politics that had encouraged the dormancy of which Appelfeld writes.

"A consuming fever" is how Nietzsche described our era's passion for historical detail. He questioned what use history-writing had for the living. Every day it becomes clearer that facts that must be retrieved are pervaded by error, partiality, myth, and may sink under the weight of our very attempt to correct for distortion. Such terms as stratified, mediated, perspectival, polyphonic, and multidimensional enter the critical vocabulary describing both fictional and historical reconstruction. In addition, a post-history (*posthistoire*) trend emerges in contemporary thought, of which Syberberg's *Hitler* film is a chief exhibit. This trend takes a cosmic view of history, distancing it by a montaged and synchronic perspective, mingling German cabaret with a *theatrum mundi* effect, and inducing a frustrated feeling of equivalence as if everything were as spectacularly banal as the Fuehrer's valet. The trend "relativizes," as the expression goes, even the Hitler era, even the Holocaust. It does not deny the experience we have passed through but plays with it in a way that is at once mocking and challenging. This is a further troubling development within historicism, a feverish reaction to the "consuming fever" registered by Nietzsche; and I will return to it later.

For those who do not see the Holocaust as "just another calamity," or who think that even were it comparable to other great massacres we should not allow it to fade from consciousness—because of its magnitude, its blatant criminality, its coordinated exploitation of all modern resources, cultural and technological, and the signal it sends how quickly racist feelings can be mobilized—for those, and I am of their number, posthistorical is as unacceptable as historical relativization.

That weak though diplomatic word, "unacceptable," points to a moral dilemma. The issue of history in relation to memory—the issue of what is needful to remember—refuses to disappear. Even considering the exceptional nature of the Holocaust, why reiterate what happened in memoir after memoir, or in fascinated historical tracts outdoing each other in precision? One understands the scribal passion of contemporary witnesses like Dubnov. As family, as friends are killed, each becomes the last Jew, the only survivor: "And I alone have survived to tell thee." One understands, likewise, the need to acquaint relatives and a too-silent world immediately after the war. The French historian, Annette Wieviorka, has analyzed one such attempt, the *récits* of French survivors, who considered themselves French deportees rather than Jewish victims. But what of the next generation, and now of those growing up fifty years and more after the Final Solution was launched? What meaning can be extracted from an increasing mass of materials: multiplying films, novels, historical reconstructions, witness accounts, and even monuments?

One meaning is to expose and defeat what Primo Levi called the "War on Memory." This war takes many forms. In daily life, and especially in politics, the "blatant beast" of slander and defamation is among the most deadly of these. Extended into the writing of history it relies on ignorant or deliberate and expedient falsification, abetted by prejudicial stereotypes and ethnic or national myths. As Walter Benjamin observed, the dead are not safe from politics. It is well known, for example, that the Jewish identity of the victims was suppressed on monuments and memorial sites built in the Eastern Bloc countries. At the same time, the conflict over the convent at Auschwitz might have been avoided had both parties known the history and layout of this cluster of camps. It is never adequate to allow a memorial to elide its own history, so that it becomes nothing more than sacred and collectivized space. "The very term 'monument' has a treacherous sound," Giovanni Leoni, an Italian architect, has written. There is a danger that "once we assign monumental form to memory, we have to some degree divested ourselves of the obligation to remember."[1]

The rise of pedagogical museums helps to overcome this danger. But as the case of the museum at Auschwitz shows, even honorable intentions can lead to a distortive image—to actual physical (topographical) changes. If these cannot be avoided they should not be overlooked: the very process of building and rebuilding such memorial sites must become part of the record. The deeper issue, however, has to do with transmitting "Auschwitz" to the young, to succeeding generations. Recreating a visit to the camp, Eleonora Lev evokes the difficulty of taking one's child there, of accepting and not accepting the sanitized museum atmosphere. "The place we are visiting is only the bottle of formaldehyde where the corpse of memory is kept. . . . [Auschwitz] exists not here but is dispersed throughout the world, in fragments, in the survivors' memories . . . day and night, continuing to struggle and gnaw and consume, without refuge."[2]

Some distortion is inherent in every attempt to achieve stability or closure, as history changes into memory and its institutionalization. Otherwise all man-created disasters, as well as some natural ones (the Lisbon earthquake of the eighteenth century comes to mind), would draw us into an endless, emotional vortex. "Curse God and die" may respond to our bitterness of heart, but what we generally do is seek a redemptive perspective to save the good name of humanity or of life itself. Yet the Final Solution's man-made calamity is exceptionally resistant to such a perspective. It threatens to remain an open grave, an open wound in consciousness. In fact, the passage of time has eroded redemptive as well as merely rationalizing meanings faster than they can be replaced. We become, in Maurice Blanchot's words, "guardians of an absent meaning." And in a gesture that is meant to be theoretical rather than religious, we then reflect on the limits of representation, questioning under the impact of this corrosive event our cultural achievements in criticism, literature, and historiography.

Lawrence Langer suggests, in *Holocaust Testimonies: The Ruins of Memory*, that an older language of moral concern, that of civic humanism, cannot encompass the dilemmas faced by the victims in the camps. What is called for is not a redemptive or heroic vocabulary but, to quote Blanchot again, a "disaster notation" (*écriture du désastre*). Saul Friedlander, a leading Israeli historian, focuses on the related issue of representational adequacy in historical writing. For while no recent event has elicited more documentation and analysis, knowledge has failed to become understanding. Moreover, though historians generally do not let feelings color their research, in this case the topic is approached with a transferential complexity that makes the task of description shakier: there is a mixture of numbness (leading to over-objectification) and emotionalism.[3]

Friedlander offers two hypotheses concerning the deferred or absent meaning of the Holocaust. Each can only be tested by time. The first is that even as bystanders—as nonparticipant observers, either during the events or in the fifty years since—we suffer something like a trauma, a breach in normal thinking about human and civilized nature; and this breach needs more time to heal. Understanding may have to be deferred to a later generation. The second hypothesis, which parallels Langer's point, is that a new method of representation is necessary, and this too has not come about.

But he suggests that historians should heed the individual voice of the victims and introduce it "in a field dominated by political decisions and administrative decrees which neutralize the concreteness of despair and death." Recent attempts to recreate the everyday history of Nazi Germany have neglected, if not totally displaced, the everyday history of the victims—which their testimony, as well as Langer's attention to it, so powerfully brings back.

Holocaust testimony as a genre is not one thing, of course, but a complex act whose function may have changed both with the passage of time and the growing use of the tape recorder and video camera. In the years immediately after the war, testimony had the status of an archival document whose primary aim was an increase of knowledge; today it is rather a means of transmission that keeps the events before our eyes. The volume of testimonies is remarkable; it not only contradicts the notion of the Holocaust as an inexpressible experience (though that retains an emotional truth) but creates an internally complex field of study. There is a mass of chronicles and memory books, dating back to earlier in the century, a library or canon with traditional and specifically Jewish features.[4] Annette Wieviorka has enlarged the description of this canon by analyzing differences of structure, literary texture, and personal stance in French and Yiddish testimonies that came like a flood between 1945 and 1948.[5]

We live in an era of testimony, and this phenomenon in its very heterogeneity—memory having many shapes, which should not be prematurely unified—deserves to be looked at. Yet testimony does not become, because of its variety, a vague or insubordinate concept. Wieviorka's careful differentiation of testimonial narratives is supplemented by, for example, Shoshana Felman's analysis of the extraordinary layering of historical truth in Lanzmann's *Shoah*,[6] as well as Mary Felstiner's respect for the documentary strengths of Charlotte Salomon's powerful cartoon-diary, *Life or Theater?*[7] What is required is a deeper conceptualization of the act of witnessing (Felman) or an undoing of such simplistic dichotomies as artistic "inner quest" and "historical backdrop" (Felstiner).

Since few events have been documented more thoroughly than the Holocaust (though much remains to be sifted and clarified) our focus shifts, at this point in time, to memory in its vicissitudes, to the sequelae of a catastrophic experience. The struggle between memory and identity, for

Darkness Visible

example, including national identity, does not let up with time. Polish national memory and Jewish memory haunt many of the same places. And the testimonies already mentioned, recorded years after the event, are often less essential for their historical data than for the way survivors regard themselves now, in their "afterlife." Primo Levi's "The Survivor," a poem written in 1984, depicts a camp prisoner still haunted by his dead companions. "Stand back, leave me alone submerged people. . . . It's not my fault if I live and breathe. . . . "

From the beginning, moreover, historical research has been accompanied by a "collective memory" transmitted through popular as well as educated circles. This kind of recollection encourages a comforting, and sometimes politically inspired, form of closure. The very events that have jeopardized the community must now reinforce it. As the eyewitnesses pass from the scene and even the most faithful memories fade, the question of what sustains Jewish identity is raised with a new urgency. In this transitional phase the children of the victims play a particular role as transmitters of a difficult, defining legacy. Their situation is special, but it suggests a more than temporary dilemma in that the burden on their emotions, on their capacity to identify, is something we all share to a degree. "I had lived on the edges of a catastrophe; a distance—impassable, perhaps—separated me from those who had been directly caught up in the tide of events, and despite all my efforts, I remained, in my own eyes, not so much a victim as—a spectator. I was destined, therefore, to wander among several worlds, knowing them, understanding them—better, perhaps, than many others—but nonetheless incapable of feeling an identification without any reticence, incapable of seeing, understanding, and belonging in a single, immediate, total movement."[8]

It could be said that we are all part of that second generation dilemma: so Alain Finkielkraut defines a new character type, the "imaginary Jew," who lives after these events yet tries to identify with a vital, now ruined culture.[9] In the diaspora especially, Judaism is marked by this existential and nostalgic quest. *We remain*, facing the attempted murder of an entire people and brutal eradication of its lifeworld. But *we remain* also in a different sense, one that imposes a critical perspective and duty.

It is the "generation after" that struggles against as well as for Holocaust remembrance. In Israel (not only in Germany) the idea of overcoming the past has proved to be an illusion. On both the personal level and that of public policy there is enormous tension. For a long time Israel rejected the ethos of the refugees who flooded in, while legitimating itself (as it still does, and increasingly) through Holocaust memory. The generation after, because of its closeness to the survivors, yet sensitive to how the dead are exploited by the living, has the essential and ungrateful task of criticizing specific aspects of a Holocaust remembrance that turns into a politics of memory.[10]

"Those who are still alive," Czeslaw Milosz declared in his Nobel lecture, "receive a mandate from those who are silent forever. They can fulfill their duties only by trying to reconstruct precisely things as they were by wresting the past from fictions and legends." That mandate holds for many writers and artists of the generation after. Vera Schwarcz, for example, daughter of a survivor, shows how her father's memory tried to break through to itself using her as amanuensis, and how her very choice of a professional field, that of China historian, was influenced by the theme of memory.[11] Others identify stages in a return of the past after its repression or marginalization. Michael Geyer and Miriam Hansen, now American academics, but who came of age in postwar Germany, expand Habermas's concern over the public use of history. In particular, they analyze the "explosion into memory" of the genocide, an outpouring from the late-seventies on of memoirs and historical research, further stimulated by the TV serial *Holocaust*. In a country where the crime was planned, the Holocaust suddenly became "popular," thirty years after the liberation of the camps and more than a decade after the 1964 Auschwitz trial in Frankfurt. How should we interpret this shift from scarcity to excess, from the inauthentic silence that officially shielded both Germans and displaced persons to a national obsession?[12]

Even the survivors had fallen silent, especially in West Germany. It took the Auschwitz trial, the first serious accounting demanded by the German state of its citizens, to inspire in Jean Améry the role of what Alvin Rosenfeld has called his moral witness. The rest of Améry's short life was spent driving home the message that the evil that had occurred was "singular and irreducible in its total inner logic and its accursed rationality." It often seemed to Améry as if Hitler had gained a posthumous triumph: so many further crimes against humanity—invasions, tortures, genocidal expulsions, murder squads, and gulags—postdated 1945 and threatened to relativize the Holocaust, to make it no more than a large blip on the screen of history. Yet only a year before his suicide, in the preface to a re-edition (1977) of *At the Mind's Limits*, he continued to insist that "whatever abominations we may have experienced still do not offset the fact that between 1933 and 1945 those things of which I speak in my writings took place

among the German people, a people of high intelligence, industrial capacities and unequaled cultural wealth."

Nadine Fresco, also of the generation after, fulfills the mandate of which
Milosz speaks, with anger but also with historical and psychological precision. She writes intuitive essays on "Remembering the Unknown," that is,
on how those born during or after the war deal with missing memories,
with an imagination compelled to reconstruct the absent parents' culture
and experience. But she also lays bare the political and sectarian motives
of French "negationists" (a more exact term than "revisionists") who deny
that the systematic murder of five to six million Jews ever took place.

The Jews, according to the negationists, were victims only as a side effect
of a terrible war that also killed millions of others and did not single them
out by a genocidal act. In the U.S., the negationists call for an "open discussion" of the Holocaust, appropriating the language of rights, as if the
Book of the Destruction were not open, as if the massive facts and testimonies were not totally available. This notion that information has been with-
held or distorted is so absurd that it must immediately be reinforced by a
charge that goes to the heart of the slander. Motivated not by facts but by
an all-determining ideology, the negationists resort to defamation and assert the presence of a conspiracy: by capitalist society, the unacknowledged
cause of fascism and particularly its industrialization of death (a first "revision," by the extreme left), or by the Jews themselves, who still control the
media and impose this hoax on the entire world (a second "revision," by
the extreme right).[13]

To Nadine Fresco's decisive and bitter understanding of negationism I
want to add a coda. As Geyer and Hansen point out, the revival of *public*
memory in Germany and elsewhere took place only after many years (which
is understandable), but, more relevantly, it took place in a changed social
and cultural milieu—call it postmodern rather than modern. The exact
label does not matter; the significant thing is that now the pressure on memory comes from more than an evaded historical burden, or a post-Holocaust
conscience that opens our eyes to worldwide misery. In democratic countries, where the possibilities of recall have vastly increased since 1945, our
communication networks no longer allow the plea (if it was ever sincere)
that "We could not know" or "We had no idea." Hence the prospect of
human guilt becomes limitless again; and new defenses are erected against
an intolerable awareness.

These defenses, amounting to outright denial in the case of the negationists, point to the construction of an anti-memory—a representation that takes the colors of memory yet blocks its retrieval. So "Bitburg" was meant to close the book on Germany's guilt, and to foster an unburdened national present. So monuments multiply, not only to redeem but often to profit from a shameful past. The signs of such a disburdening of memory are everywhere. Even as public recognition of the Holocaust increases, so do charges about exploiting, profaning, or trivializing the suffering. Many of the more sensitive prefer a respectful silence.[14] Though critical of talkativeness, Elie Wiesel, whose *Night* was called in its earlier, Yiddish version *And the World was Silent*, deserves a special tribute for his insistence that keeping silent only strengthens those who wish to deny or evade knowledge.

The Holocaust should not have happened but it did happen; and so it is a momentous event that draws architects, artists, scholars, and intellectuals. Full of action as well as suffering, with episodes of heroism as well as banal failure, presenting evil in its starkest aspect yet also goodness and sacrifice, it remains a mystery that cannot be shrouded in a repressive quiet. Now that the public silence has been broken, it will remain broken; and no shame attaches to those who evoke that darkest time to give it meaning, or to dispute the meanings given. No shame, that is, except the one of which Primo Levi spoke, and which tends to corrode our image of the human. . . .

It will require both scholarship and art to defeat an encroaching anti-memory. And the drift toward it can be something commonplace rather than dramatic, something "in the air." Indeed, theorists of the postmodern such as Jean Baudrillard, and, as I mentioned previously, movie makers such as Syberberg, contribute to anti-memory in a peculiar way. They seem powerless to overcome, by their own spectacular idiom, the negative implication of a culture industry that can simulate anything and everything. In the light of media overexposure, the evil of the Holocaust becomes strangely weightless. Both Améry's stubborn refusal to relent as a witness, to allow Germany's present to free itself from its past, and Lanzmann's *Shoah* with its visual and verbal density, its exhausting quest to record every detail of the Nazi killing machine, do more than save the naked truth from forgetfulness or ideological distortion. They seek to force the return of an older and endangered sense of real presence.[15]

In *The Transparence of Evil*, Jean Baudrillard evokes a reality-loss, a phantomization of both personal and collective identity, and ultimately of the past—of history itself. This reality-loss Baudrillard links to our very capacity, now hugely expanded, for retrieving and disseminating knowledge: we gain a global information technology but it transmits images that could be simulacra. His vision of a mediatized world is so extreme that it runs parallel at certain points to that of the American high-tech fantasist, Philip K. Dick.

There is a new amnesia, according to Baudrillard, produced by an endless process of image-substitution, of representation after representation, of one theory after another. Our "necrospective" too is a symptom. "It is because we have disappeared *today . . .* that we want to prove we died between 1940 and 1945, at Auschwitz or Hiroshima—that, at least, was real history [*une histoire forte*]." The negationist paradox concerning the supposed impossibility of proving that the Holocaust occurred is only another expression of this sense of the unreality of the present; we have reached "the impasse of a hallucinatory *fin de siècle*, fascinated by the horror of its origins, for which oblivion is impossible. The only way out is by denial or negation."[16]

Baudrillard combines irony with hyperbole to drive his point home. "One of these days we will ask ourselves if even Heidegger existed." Yet something of this mad, posthistory perspective was anticipated by Walter Benjamin. His famous essay of 1936, on the changing status of art in the era of mechanical reproduction, suggests that when techniques like photography transport objects from their original site, from their specific historical locus, they lose the aura of uniqueness. The reproducibility of art—and, by extension, of the newsworthy event—brings us closer to it yet also creates a further distance: a world in which presence is increasingly displaced by representation. A new space for manipulation opens through photomontage, and since the means of reproducing "real" or "authentic" events are generally not in our control but depend on propagandists or the media, hermeneutic suspicion becomes even more necessary than before.

Benjamin's experiment with historical materialism may have been a way to compensate this loss of substance, of historical emplacement. He writes as if the potentially explosive impact of past on present were still possible. He refuses to let memory become remembrance or a mere "inventory" of the past. When I read *A Berlin Childhood* (written circa 1932–33, though not published till 1950), the book's magical realism, a pervasive blend of personal memory and *Kunstmärchen*, strikes me as dated yet also attractively solid: a fetish or talisman. I want to rub it like Alladin's lamp, or taste it like Proust's madeleine.

Benjamin is a transitional figure who sees the future rather than the past in a ghostly light. The future is dangerously abstract as a motive for progress; the past alone, its very ruins, can be an object of love, of motivating hope. This hope in the past inspires a backward glance like that of the angel of history Benjamin will depict shortly before his death. What the angel sees or remembers turns, however, into something fierce, driving and desperate: a Messianism that is not the goal but the end—the abrupt termination—of history. Yet Benjamin appeals, as I have said, as a transitional figure: it is impossible to think of his incursions into the "dark backward and abysm" of time as post-genocidal. Today the interior landscape is marked by ruined or vanished sites or else by a fantastic and facile "virtual reality": the relation between representation and reality, between mimesis and the object of mimesis seems to have undergone a quasi-geological rift.[17]

I agree with Baudrillard that our sense of reality has been affected; that a media-induced anxiety is promoting a greater or more subtle doubt about simulated evidence than Descartes' famous *malin génie*, his trickster or illusionist demiurge. Yet Baudrillard fails to acknowledge an ordinary and perfectly reasonable suspicion of the world of appearances, or of the way the immediacy of the lived event fades into the past before having been grasped or understood. The pastness of life seems to be a condition for understanding it; as Péguy already remarked, there is an "unbridgeable gulf between the actual and the historical event." Baudrillard also fails to note how the sadness that comes from this feeling of lost time or the unlived life is exploited by groups with a *revanchist* political agenda. This bears directly on denials of the Holocaust: a *civilized* fear of reality-loss is contaminated by a *savage* antisemitism that preceded the Holocaust and still continues in negationist attacks on the media as "Jewish."

The charge that Jews control the media, and through the media our very image of reality, has a paranoid structure. But already in the nineteenth century a feeling of reality-loss, linked to the weakening of place-bound identity, and redressed by nostalgic evocations of rural homestead, *Heimat* or *vieux pays*, could breed a new and virulent antisemitism. Jews began to be scapegoats for an imperfect transition of society from a rural economy to industrialization and urbanization. The move from the land to urban centers, the deracination it produced, and the growing role of financial middlemen during this time, led to a politically exploited antisemitism beyond the anti-Jewish feelings fostered by the Church. Identified with capitalism and its "abstract" money, the Jews were soon held responsible for the disintegration of the so-called organic community. Their supposed "semitic" status—however indigenous or settled, they were accused of being without loyalty to the land or the host-nation—imposed on them the image of perpetual aliens. T. S. Eliot's notorious lines from "Gerontion" (1919),

> My house is a decayed house,
> And the jew squats on the window sill, the owner,
> Spawned in some estaminet of Antwerp

express this stereotype: the Jew is a foreign trader, a parasite-usurper of other people's houses, and ultimately of the declining, ancient House of Europe itself, undermined by his arts.

The danger came, supposedly, not only from the traditional Jew of alien or "oriental" aspect. What alarmed even more, from Richard Wagner to Nazi racial science, was the assimilated Jew, Wagner's "plastic [i.e., shape-shifting] demon of decadence," who *seemed* to adapt and fit in. Philip Dick can dream of a machine to distinguish between humans and replicants, but no machine short of extermination could outwit this coldhearted, dissimulating stranger, using all the cunning at his disposal, all his free-floating, worldwide intelligence and capital, to undermine the national community. It was this anxiety that the Nazi regime cultivated, until extirpation of the "poisonous mushroom," of the entire antirace of simulacra or subversive look-alikes, became thinkable.[18] At the present time, when non-Jewish waves of immigration are a major concern of European countries, both from an economic and cultural point of view, and when nationalism and xenophobia are reaching another high, we see the old violence returning.

Despite the Holocaust, myths of national, ethnic, or religious purity continue to persist. While the issue of how to deal with the immigrant or resident stranger is never an easy one, the matter cannot be left to explosive popular feelings. Rituals that offer hospitality and laws that protect the foreigner are essential to both Homeric and biblical times, but episodes like those of the Cyclops and of Sodom and Gomorrah are vivid reminders of a chronic and murderous lawlessness.

In Coleridge's "Ancient Mariner," one of the best known of modern poems, the Mariner transgresses a code of hospitality by killing an albatross that had welcomed the sailors. The albatross turns out to have been the guardian spirit of the polar region into which their ship had strayed. The Mariner's punishment for this crime is perpetual exile, a homeless wandering from place to place. Through his powerful tale Coleridge evokes a cosmic and avenging memory that can be triggered even by casual infringements. The lesson seems to be that mankind is itself a trespasser in the universe, dependent on earth's hospitality; to respect other creatures, therefore, both man and beast, is not only a Noachite law prior to special religious revelations but also a symbiotic necessity.

By projecting a cosmic memory as retentive and resentful as our own, Coleridge leads us to understand the consequences. The entanglement of memory and revenge does not cease; persecution does not cease. What his poem presents as fantasy is our daily condition. The question remains what role laws play in this tragedy. Can they, should they, limit revenge by instituting a legalized forgetting (amnesty) or a forgiveness that is its religious counterpart? The issues are quite clear and they center on a perhaps unresolvable conflict. On the one hand, for victims of the Holocaust (and this includes their families, or victims by adoption, or all who have been radically affected) it is not justice alone but also reality—the very sense of reality jeopardized by postmodern amnesia, by anti-memory—that must be recovered through the Eichmann, Barbie, and similar trials. The crimes against humanity disclosed by such legal proceedings are wrested from an increasingly inert historical record and endowed with "judicial presence."[19] On the other hand, to burden later generations with the guilt of parents and grandparents will produce feelings of victimization and damaged identity that increase compensatory assertions such as nationalism and xenophobia. Geyer and Hansen suggest that all of us, and Germans in particular, should fight these assertions by relinquishing the illusory appeal of the unified personality (of a psyche in harmony both with itself, in the classical, Goethean sense, and with the state, in the Fichtean romantic sense); but their prescription may again be utopian. The politics of memory, the acute link of resentful memory with *revanchist* programs, is not likely to disappear.

Amnesty is lawful amnesia; and what takes place at this highly formalized level may also take place in the domain of the social or collective memory. This type of memory has recently intrigued scholars concerned with the impact of catastrophic events on nation or group. Can memory, individual or collective, when besieged by an insomniac stream of both trivial and fearful news—and by the *revenants* Levi depicts—tolerate all this pressure without a sanctioned principle of forgetting? If such a principle is essential, where does it come from and how can we choose critically between alternative modes of amnesia?

Perhaps cultures could be differentiated by describing the degree of their memory-tolerance. But it seems as if the socially constructed memory, no sooner discovered, is already in jeopardy. Following Nietzsche, some contemporary historians fear that it is being eroded by an overload of historical information and the assault of current events.[20] Even epoch-making incidents like the Shoah, swept into that current, are integrated not by distinctive communal forms but by politically motivated analogies. Such false integration is again a form of anti-memory. Rights activists proclaim an "animal Auschwitz" and the antiabortion movement a "holocaust of babies." What prompts these analogies is less inadequate knowledge than an overburdened conscience.

Indeed, some thinkers have made a distinction between ancient and modern memory. Mircea Eliade speculates that the ancient world used orgiastic festivals for the purpose of licensed oblivion. He claims that Christianity was less of a cargo-cult kind of religion; that it tolerated more history, more historical consciousness.[21] Given the ecstatic if not orgiastic excesses of fascism, including the antisemitic phobia of the Romanian Legion of Saint Michael to which Eliade belonged as a young man, one may be allowed to question his assertion of progress.

Moreover, and this is the paradox of a *non-orgiastic* solution, forgetting on a collective scale can itself assume the guise of memory, that is, of a religious or collective type of remembrance ("If I forget thee, O Jerusalem . . . "). It constructs, that is, a highly selective story, focused on what is basic for the community and turning away from everything else.[22] The collective memory, in the process of making sense of history, shapes a gradually formalized agreement to transmit the meaning of intensely shared events in a way that does not have to be individually struggled for. Canonical interpretation takes over, ceremonies develop, monuments are built. An event is given a memory-place (*lieu de mémoire*)[23] in the form of monument, museum, or concentration camp site, and an annually repeated day. The repetition involves public rituals that merge individual sorrow or joy with communally prescribed forms of observance.

How are we to distinguish, then, between this collectivized and integrative form of memory and what I have designated "anti-memory"? The natural scepticism which notes that history is not possible without memory can easily motivate the construction of memorial narratives in the service of an alternative history. The rise of *Pamyat* ("Memory") in Russia, with its blatant antisemitic nationalism, illustrates the problem. We have no choice, I think, but to accept both the collective memory and the factual burden it reacts to. They cannot substitute for each other. The collective memory uses and produces fictions, yet it must learn from art not to confuse fiction and history, and from history not to succumb to sentimental or mystical ideas about a community's "world-historical" destiny. In this learning process both historian and literary critic play a role.[24]

Today we are certainly more aware of the pathological potential in collective types of thought that claim to unify or heal a community. Yet the appeal of such thought has not seriously diminished, and it can penetrate even historiography. The effort to find an intelligible, comprehensive, and objective overview often produces nontrivial but still dubious historical analogies that function just like integrative simplifications in the collective memory. In the historians' debate, as Friedlander has shown,[25] a deep concern for national identity motivates an apologetic rather than objective discourse. Germany historians who are German historians and face "a past that will not go away" (Ernst Nolte), are forced into a very particular angle of reflection or subject position. They become actors in a national drama of conscience. For even if Nolte does not *identify* with Hitler's presumed state of mind—Nolte speculates that Auschwitz was Hitler's "Asiatic deed," analogous to and as if compelled by Stalin's Eastern (gulag) terror—he backs this empathic insight with enough meretricious detail to make us doubt the claim that he is unbiased. Another historian, Andreas Hillgruber, comes close to identifying explicitly with the point of view of the German soldier fighting on the Eastern Front in the final, apocalyptic months of the war. His retrospective (and autobiographical) self-stationing would be more credible in fiction, in a novelistic or dramatic form that could allow a shameful sentiment to emerge as powerful *ressentiment.*

Wound and cure, in this sensitive area, are hard to tell apart. Anthropologists and students of myth, moreover, have shown that death incites superstitious explanations. There exist older societies which do not accept even *natural* death as a possibility but see in it the work of demons. Every death is an act of witchcraft and requires the community to find and convict the guilty party. Once this is done, order is restored. The effort of Nazi propaganda to blame the Jews for Germany's defeat in World War I and to suggest a Jewish conspiracy to launch a second such war against the Reich created a witch-hunt atmosphere. An event like the Shoah, a political mass murder targeting for extinction an entire "race" of defenseless noncombatants, could not have occurred without a terrible superstition motivating it, and cannot now, after the event, be taken into mind without a severe disturbance.

It is not surprising that after the Holocaust so much guilt surfaces in the form of religious types of incrimination as well as reactive and exculpatory schemes of denial. With respect to guilt, there are many that question not only the treatment of immigrants but our entire history of behavior toward the other—the stranger at our gates or the conquered and colonized. Our confidence in the West, in its claim to be civilized, is shaken.[26] Yet, reactively, there are many that blame the victims or count themselves among their number or, seeing victims everywhere, equalize them all, undermining moral distinctions. So the Waffen SS, buried in Bitburg cemetery, are also deemed "victims" of the Third Reich—even though many of them may have committed war crimes and crimes against humanity, especially against the Jews!

The latest threat, however, diagnosed by Baudrillard as postmodern, affects history as well as memory. The influence of the media, the penetration of their simulacra into daily life, prompts a deep anxiety about forgery, or counterfeit evidence. Should historiography be viewed as a self-consuming artifact, and should our basic trust in the reported fact diminish, then conspiracy theories get the upper hand and put everything in doubt except disbelief itself. The world of appearances, the *mediated* world, is felt to have so strong a hold that nothing can disenchant it except a "gnostic" assault that makes of historical research an infinite and so impossible task. That so many regimes and their gods have fallen also contributes to a demystification without bounds, a fanatic incredulity. The result is not only a supercilious and treacherous lucidity but often the return of myth.[27] Because of the conviction that what passes for history is not reality but reconstruction, nostalgia revives for a world elsewhere, for an original sublimity. In his quest for the truth about his birth, Oedipus the King thinks at one point that he may be descended from a god. Those who seek an identity, personal, national or racial, with an intensity that is equivalent to religious passion, seem to have returned to that delusive moment.

Yet there are signs that art has not lost its aura or history its critical and evidential impact. We should not underestimate the counterforce of literature as it combines with testimony. I don't mean forms of fiction like docudrama or historical novel. These are, and always have been, problematic if influential constructs. There has emerged, however, a body of works "between history and literature," including witness accounts and remarkable essays that seem to defy the Freudian formula that where trauma is, consciousness is not. So Améry's clarity is not linked to mastering the past. He has not overcome his terror and pain. "No remembering," he writes, "has become a mere memory. . . . Where is it decreed that enlightenment must be free of emotion?" Primo Levi's *Survival in Auschwitz*, especially its last, Dantesque chapter, is as substantial a work of both testimony and art as we are likely to get. His subject is at the antipodes of Thoreau's *Walden*, yet shares with that tranquil book the sense of being a sequence of reflections. He has written essays from hell. And Lanzmann goes so far as to call the searing witness accounts in *Shoah* "resurrections."

The role of art remains mysterious, however, for art is testimony, as well as combining with testimony. Levi again is exemplary: his attempt to recall Dante's Canto of Ulysses in the Inferno of Auschwitz, and to communicate faith in his culture by that solitary and ludicrous act, moves the remembered text closer to scripture. If I limit my comments to an art of memory with explicit reference to the Shoah, it is because the historical referent of a more transformative method is difficult to retrieve.

Yet writers who were young children during the war, or for whom the Holocaust is an "absent memory"—Georges Perec, Alain Finkielkraut of *Le Juif imaginaire*, Henri Raczymow of *Contes d'exil et d'oubli*, and *Un Cri sans voix* (translated as *Writing the Book of Esther*), Sara Kofman of *Paroles suffoquées*, David Grossman of *See Under: Love*, reconstitute the past from anecdotes rather than direct knowledge. This generation creates its own, often exotic world coiled round that absence, and offers a glimpse of a transformative art. The eyewitness generation expressed a return of memory despite trauma; this "second" generation expresses the trauma of memory turning in the void, and is all the more sensitive, therefore, to whatever tries to fill the gap.[28]

The general claim I make is not that the historical memory should be held superior to other cultural virtues, for that could again lead to a simplified or exclusive identity claim. Memory, as the Polish poet and essayist Adam Zagajewski has said, "is an indispensable part of creating culture, agreed; but isn't it true that it records and preserves the creative act rather than expresses itself in it? The elements of creativity have little in common with memory. Innovation, for example, and rebellion: both are rather hostile to memory."

This too, however, simplifies memory's link with creativity. That the relation between them can be unpredictable is shown by Dan Pagis. The poetry of this child survivor from Bukovina moves historical reality off-stage, replacing it with an "absent memory" of a deliberate kind, one characterized by a disembodied voice, a discontinuous narrative and ghostly cosmic symbols. But in the last decade of the poet's life his rebellion against memory gives way to a project of retrieval that redeems a portion of the past and provides a historical key. Changing from a surreal and elliptical poetry to prose-poems, and then to short narratives with a documentary valence, Pagis returns from the "exile" of a fictive self-dispersal. On the brink of his own death he dies into life rather than fiction; more precisely, his imagination no longer conspires with the survivor's sense of unreality, of living posthumously. His last writings are a conversation with his dead father—spooky enough, but still a coming to terms with the past. The effort to recall the father who had seemed to abandon him, or the town that "forgot" him (Radautz), to reintegrate a deeply effaced reality—including his own first name, changed in Israel to the common "Dan"—produces a minimalism that makes us feel the charge and gravity of every autobiographical allusion.[29]

Art often moves away from topical or historical reference by a characteristic distancing. Moreover, even so estranging an event as the Shoah may have to be estranged again, through art, insofar as its symbols become trite and ritualistic rather than realizing. Such triteness (or overfamiliarization) overtook Celan's "Deathfugue" and can also turn the most telling photo into a cliché. No hostility to memory is implied by attempting to reverse this process; and Anselm Kiefer's paintings, by formally alluding to Celan, create a secondary evocation that acts like the collective memory, yet remains individual. The issue of how memory and history become art is always a complicated one; in the case of the Shoah the question is also whether they *should* become art.

Adorno's dictum, "To write poetry after Auschwitz is barbaric" was intended to be, as the context shows, a caution against the media and any aesthetic exploitation. Yet like other prohibitions against representation it heightens the stakes and inscribes itself in the work of those who confront it. For Günther Grass of the Hitler Youth generation, who inherited the evil fame of Nazi Germany, Adorno's caution was translated into "abandoning absolutes, the black and white of ideology; it meant showing belief the door and placing all one's bets on doubt, which turned everything, even the rainbow, to gray. But this imperative yielded wealth of another sort: the heartrending beauty of all the shades of gray was to be celebrated in damaged language."[30] Life is green, Goethe said, while all knowledge is gray; that, however, was another absolute, just like the abandoned white and black. Perhaps art must now give up its own absolutist pretension and accept some gray matter. It becomes suspicious of itself, of its aestheticizing drive. The reflective and the creative, therefore, often mingle conspicuously.

All these issues (estranging a too-familiar though traumatic history, the "barbaric" effort to wrest beauty or lyricism from it, or the anti-aesthetic mingling of creative and explicitly reflective styles) are seen in the surprising work of Art Spiegelman. His *Maus* and *Maus II* blend the folkloric beast-fable with American popular cartoons in order to retell the story of his survivor parents, together with its effect on him. Spiegelman's comic-book style is not a simple alienation effect; it mirrors the vision of an adult who becomes a child again as he attempts to absorb extreme knowledge. The cartoons serve as a transitional object helping us toward a difficult truth—though not as innocent an object as it used to be. For they recall the Nazi representation of Jews as rodents as well as our own uneasy conscience about "lower" orders of the creation we both slaughter *and* promote to comic strip immortality, such as Mickey Mouse, Bugs Bunny, Miss Piggy, Elsie, etc.

By his extraordinary adaptation of a popular medium, Spiegelman questions whether a fully human knowledge of the Holocaust is possible, or whether as adults, and especially adults in America, we must remain child-like, trapped in a Disneyland sort of truth, a "Mauschwitz." The unreality of this domestication, a consequence also of having to bring the traumatic past into a family context, afflicts the survivors themselves as well as their children. Spiegelman's tag-like inscriptions, not only his pictures, capture the absurdity of attempting to live a normal life after its rupture by Auschwitz. "My parents survived Hell and moved to the suburbs."

Art constructs, in brief, a cultural memory of its own, in which the struggle of the individual with (and often for) experience—including the collective memory itself—never ceases. In a media-mediated age, this struggle may center on the issue of communicability. *Maus* stays on the side of popular culture, which seeks a high degree of direct communication;[31] the transformative method here, the estrangement, is based on a formula that is transgressive yet easily reproduced. Though a shock is given to imaginative habits that assign extreme phenomena to high culture, *Maus* is neither a grotesque nor a gothic exploitation of the horrors of genocide. Its metamorphosis of the human figure recognizes that the Shoah has affected how we think about ourselves as a *species* (the human? race).

Most of the time, however, transmissibility and truth move into opposition. So Paul Celan's untransparent work seeks in the absent community—even among the murdered—a "you" to address. "Speaks true who speaks shadow." The space of conversation, precarious at best, seems fatally injured and a descent to the dead is necessary to restore it. Celan's archaeology is more exemplary for us than Schliemann's.

Darkness Visible

Even a less opaque artist, like Dan Pagis, can use dense literary allusions to create something strong and inimitable. A poem entitled "Testimony" compares Nazi guards to their victims. They, the uniformed, booted guards, "were created / in the image," but the writer-victim is said to be merely "a shade. / A different creator made me." The Hebrew word Pagis uses for "image" is *zelem*. The Hebrew word for "shade" is *zel*. The juxtaposition tells all and deepens the darkness of those root letters and the horror of the fact that Genesis, the act of divine creation, could have led to this. The poet's manichean acknowledgement of evil concludes with an ironic echo of Maimonides' creed, enshrined as a hymn in the prayer book, and thus in Jewish memory:

And he in his mercy left nothing of me that could die.
And I fled to him, floated up weightless, blue,
forgiving—I would even say: apologizing—
smoke to omnipotent smoke
that has no face or image.[32]

It is mid-October. In New England the leaves have turned. One or two begin to float in the crisp air. Further north many maples have already shed half their gold, a hectic treasure for the children. I see them in the large front yard of an old house, running and shouting, five of them, all sizes. A woman is raking the leaves, or trying to. The children, romping around, undo her work; she cuffs them with the rake, as tolerantly as a kitten a perplexing ball or comatose object. The pile of raked leaves grows, and the children invent a new game. They collapse into the pile, spreading out deliciously, while the woman—mother, housekeeper—abets their game, and covers them with the still fragrant, light leaves. At first giggles and squeaks, then, as the tumulus rises to a respectable height, total silence. But only for a minute. For, as if on signal, all emerge simultaneously from the leafy tomb, jumping out, laughing, resurrected, to the mock surprise of the one who is raking and who patiently begins again.

I am on my way to give a lecture on the Holocaust, when I come across the pastoral scene. What am I doing, I ask myself. How can I talk about such matters, here? I cannot reconcile scenes like this with others I know about.

In a fleeting montage, I see or dream I see the green, cursed fields of Auschwitz. A cold calm has settled on them. The blood does not cry from the ground. Yet no place, no wood, meadow, sylvan scene will now be the same. Something more fearful than any gothic horror has entered the landscape. Even in quiet Concord or Unadilla. This moment of contagion does not last, yet it returns unpredictably. I cannot forget any more than I can truly remember. And every morning, punctual as the news, a daily corruptness, page after page, associates with that pang, that pain, and shames the hope I have left.

Notes

1. Giovanni Leoni, " 'The First Blow': Projects for the Camp at Fossoli," in *Holocaust Remembrance: The Shapes of Memory*, ed. Geoffrey H. Hartman (Oxford: Blackwell, 1994); James E. Young, "The Counter-Monument: Memory against Itself in Germany Today," *Critical Inquiry*, 18 (1992): 273. Deborah Dwork and Robert Jan Van Pelt, in their essay on Auschwitz in *Holocaust Remembrance*, describe an architectural project of 1954 that aimed to defeat the inert and aggrandized space of monumental sites by turning Auschwitz into a monument to oblivion—one that would have, in effect, cursed those grounds and left them to become more of a ruin. Another paradoxical solution is proposed in Leoni's essay. "[O]ne seeks to restore to the victims not so much a voice as an image, to 'embody' them in the midst of an architecture that expresses the oppressor's will." Young, in his essay on the counter-monument cited above, describes actual attempts to build a self-destructing memorial. George Mosse's *Fallen Soldiers: Reshaping the Memory of the World War* (New York: Oxford University Press, 1990) includes a superb account of the relation of monuments to memory as the cult of the war dead—shared by all European nations—reaches its apogee in Nazi Germany and then fades after World War II. The issue of monumentalism converges on that of architecture in general: for a non-Holocaust related discussion, see Denis Hollier, *Against Architecture: The Writings of Georges Bataille* (Cambridge: MIT Press, 1989).

2. Eleonora Lev, "Don't Take Your Daughter to the Extermination Camp", *Tikkun* 2 (1987): 54–60.

3. For Friedlander's earlier analysis of the inadequacy (perhaps intrinsic) of historical language in the face of extreme events, and above all of "Auschwitz," as well as the different though related inadequacy of literature and film, see *Reflections of Nazism: An Essay on Kitsch and Death* (French publication 1982; English translation, New York: Harper & Row, 1984). Also Friedlander, ed. *Probing the Limits of Representation: Nazism and the "Final Solution"* (Cambridge: Harvard University Press, 1992). The historian's "transferential relation" to his subject and the way it is worked through are a major concern of Dominick LaCapra's: see, inter alia, his essay on the Historians' Debate in the Friedlander volume on *Limits of Representation*.

4. See David Roskies, "The Library of Jewish Catastrophe," in *Holocaust Remembrance*.

5. Wieviorka, "On Testimony," in *Holocaust Remembrance*.

6. Shoshana Felman and Dori Laub, *Testimony: Crises of Witnessing in Literature, Psychoanalysis, and History* (New York: Routledge, 1991).

7. Mary Felstiner, *To Paint Her Life: Charlotte Salomon in the Nazi Era* (New York: Harper Collins, 1994).

8. Saul Friedlander, *When Memory Comes* (New York: Farrar Strauss & Giroux, 1979), 155–56.

9. *Le juif imaginaire* (Paris: Seuil, 1980). I have mentioned in the introduction Jonathan Boyarin's *Polish Jews in Paris: The Ethnography of Memory* (Bloomington: Indiana University Press, 1991). Basing himself on the elderly rather than, as Finkielkraut does,

the maturing generation (on the Paris *landsmannshaftn*), Boyarin not only records their way of life but provisionally substitutes for the missing generational link who has to "assume"—take upon himself or herself—the status of participant-observer. A tension remains, of course, between his role as ethno-persona and as American Jew. For why is this American in Paris if not because he needs the *landsmannshaftn*: in his own country these elders are not as cohesive or "hyper-communalized." For a sensitive, inside view and portrait of the children of survivors, see Helen Epstein, *Children of the Holocaust: Conversations with Sons and Daughters of Survivors* (New York: Putnam, 1979).

10. See Saul Friedlander, "Shoah: Between Memory and History," *The Jerusalem Quarterly*, 53 (1990): 115–26. For memorial politics, see also my article on Bitburg in the 1985 *Yearbook* of the *Jewish Encyclopedia* and the chapter on Bitburg in this book.

11. See Schwarz, "Chinese History and Jewish Memory," in *Holocaust Remembrance*.

12. "German-Jewish Memory and National Consciousness," in *Holocaust Remembrance*.

13. See *International Review of Psychoanalysis* 11 (1984): 417–27, and "Negating the Dead," in *Holocaust Remembrance*. The most thorough account of negationism, Pierre Vidal-Naquet's *Les assassins de la mémoire* (Paris: La Découverte, 1987), has now been translated (with an excellent foreword) by J. Mehlman as *Assassins of Memory: Essays on the Denial of the Holocaust* (New York: Columbia University Press, 1992).

14. A balanced review of the issue is given by Michael R. Marrus, "The Use and Misuse of the Holocaust," in *Lessons and Legacies: The Meaning of the Holocaust in a Changing World*, ed. Peter Hayes (Evanston: Northwestern University Press, 1991).

15. David Tracy's call for Christian theology to continue its "return to history" after the Shoah goes in the same direction, and he describes this as a "postmodern" development. I see it rather as a strong reaction to the postmodern and its "ether of discourse" (Charles Maier). The meaning of the term postmodern may differ according to different disciplines; it has not fully crystallized. See David Tracy, "Christian Witness and the Shoah," in *Holocaust Remembrance*.

16. Baudrillard, *La transparence du mal: essai sur les phénomènes extrêmes* (Paris: Gallimard, 1990). The basic argument is found in his earlier *Simulacres et simulation* (Paris: Galilée, 1981). The section on "Holocaust" begins: "Forgetting the extermination is part of the extermination, for that also bears on memory, history, the social, etc."

17. Erich Auerbach's *Mimesis*, a distinctly European book written in exile and published in 1946, may also derive some of its appeal from still being on the far side of that rift: it foresees something that has already happened.

18. I develop this point in Chapter 8, "The Book of the Destruction."

19. See Alain Finkielkraut, *La mémoire vaine: du crime contre l'humanité* (Paris: Gallimard, 1989), now available as *Remembering in Vain: The Klaus Barbie Trial and Crimes against Humanity*, trans. Roxanne Lapidus with Sima Godfrey (New York: Columbia University Press, 1992).

20. Yosef Hayim Yerushalmi, *Zakhor: Jewish History and Jewish Memory* (Seattle: University of Washington Press, 1982), chap. 4. For a more sanguine view of the rupture between history and "collective" memory, see Michael Kammen's massive and magisterial *Mystic Chords of Memory: The Transformation of Tradition in American Culture* (New York: Knopf, 1991). A thoughtful overview of "Can there be too much memory?" is offered by Charles Maier's Epilogue to *The Unmasterable Past: History, Holocaust, and German National Identity* (Cambridge: Harvard University Press, 1988). Further scholarly considerations of the issue can be found in *Kultur und Gedächtnis*, ed. J. Assmann and T. Hölscher (Frankfurt a/M: Suhrkamp, 1988); *Mnemosyne: Formen und Funktionen der kulturellen Erinnerung*, ed. A. Assmann and D. Harth (Frankfurt a/M: Fischer, 1991), esp. 342–49; *Usages*

de l'oubli (Paris: Seuil, 1988), with contributions by Yerushalmi and others; also Amos Funkenstein, "Collective Memory and Historical Consciousness," *History and Memory*, 1 (1989): 5–27. The notion of a collective memory is indebted, of course, to Maurice Halbwachs's *La mémoire collective*, published posthumously in 1950. Halbwachs anticipates the history/memory split: "General history starts only when tradition ends and the social memory is fading or breaking up."

21. Eliade, *Cosmos and History: The Myth of the Eternal Return* (1949), trans. Willard R. Trask (New York: Pantheon, 1954). What Saturnalia remain can be described as feasts of memorization, and embrace one's entire life, as in Talmudic scholarship. The contemporary quiz show, with its built-in recognition of contingency, or "Wheel of Fortune," is a trivia feast and a conspicuous consumption of memory compared to such scholarship.

22. Cf. *Usages de l'oubli*, cited previously. Recent sociology has done significant work on institutional or systematic forgetting and generally on "the rhetorical organization of remembering and forgetting." See *Collective Remembering*, ed. David Middleton and Derek Edwards (London: Sage, 1990). British and American sociology often combines Halbwachs with F. C. Bartlett's *Remembering* (1932), because, though the latter continues to emphasize the individual, he studies "remembering as a form of constructive activity, emphasizing that memory is not the retrieval of stored information, but the putting together of a claim about past states of affairs by means of a framework of shared cultural understanding." See Alan Radley's essay in *Collective Remembering*.

23. See Pierre Nora, "Between Memory and History: *Les lieux de mémoire*," *Representations* 26 (Spring 1989).

24. For the literary critic, see, e.g., James Young, *The Texture of Memory: Holocaust Memorials and Meaning in Europe, Israel and America* (New Haven: Yale University Press, 1993). Young seeks to break down any monolithic notion of collective memory in favor of a "collected memory," that is, a socially constructed process that enables us, through shared forms and spaces, to attribute collective meaning to memories that remain, nevertheless, personal and disparate; for the historian, cf. Hayden White, *The Content of the Form: Narrative Discourse and Historical Representation* (Baltimore: Johns Hopkins University Press, 1987), chap. 3.

25. See Martin Broszat and Saul Friedlander, "A Controversy about the Historicization of National Socialism," *New German Critique*, 44 (Spring–Summer 1988).

26. An attempt has begun to analyze cultural discourse itself, in its over two-century-old vacillation between forms of nationalism and universalism. But this attempt, revealing that no group which aspired to autonomy and a place (homeland) of its own was free of a discriminatory and if not Nazi-like then violent and self-exalting rhetoric, seems to compromise our quest for an absolute post-Holocaust fixing of blame. In the difficult closing pages of his article on "The Force of Law," Jacques Derrida suggests (in the name of Benjamin, but perhaps also in the name of deconstruction), that our judgmental, historiographical, and interpretive terms are still "homogenous with the space in which Nazism developed up to and including the final solution." Is there a "complicity" between the discourses we honor, or tolerate, and the worst of these, the murderous discourse of Nazism? See *Deconstruction and the Possibility of Justice, Cardozo Law Review* 11 (1990): 1042–45.

27. Alain Finkielkraut speaks of a "scenario of the lost illusion," which is the myth into which the demystifiers lapse, or the object of their automatic respect as they vow never to be deceived again. See his "La mémoire et l'histoire" in *L'avenir d'une négation: réflexion sur la question du génocide* (Paris: Seuil, 1982), 97. Oliver Stone could be said to create just such a scenario in his movie *JFK*. He calls it an "outlaw history" or "counter-

myth." Historical films like *JFK* are complex symptoms expressing the fact, as Anton Kaes has observed, that certain photographic images are everywhere, "impossible to topple and destroy." These images take on a life of their own in the collective memory until the originating historical event is displaced into a movie myth, or what Baudrillard (in his earlier book on simulacra) defines as "models of a real without origin or reality: a hyperreal." See Kaes, "History and Film: Public Memory in the Age of Electronic Dissemination," *History and Memory*, 2 (1990), and his epilogue "History, Memory and Film" in *From Hitler to Heimat: The Return of History as Film* (Cambridge: Harvard University Press, 1989).

28. Cf. Ellen S. Fine, "The Absent Memory" in *Writing and the Holocaust*, ed. Berel Lang (New York: Holmes & Meier, 1988) and cf. 95–96 in this volume. Raymond Federman writes in his novel *To Whom It May Concern* (Norman, IL: Fiction Collective Two, 1990), which explores that absence in two children who survived the war but lost their families in the Holocaust: " . . . the void of their lives can only find its fulfilment in the circumstances of that void. . . . [Their] remembrance is of an absence, and they have made a lifetime occasion of it." Federman, at the same time, generalizes the "circumstances of that void" to challenge, in the name of (postmodernist) fiction, what he calls "the paralyzing holiness of realism." Norma Rosen's novel *Touching Evil* extends what she names "witnesses-through-the-imagination" to non-Jews. See also her "The Second Life of Holocaust Imagery," in *Accidents of Influence: Writing as a Woman and a Jew in America* (Albany: State University of New York Press, 1992).

29. See Sidra Koven Ezrahi, "Conversations in the Cemetery: Dan Pagis and the Prosaics of Memory," in *Holocaust Remembrance*. A comparison between Pagis and Amir Gilboa suggests that there is no absolute divide between the representational modes of the first and second generation. One of the finest second generation poems, dating from the early 1950s, is Gilboa's "Isaac." Its ellipses also express an "absent memory": that of the son who went to Israel before the Holocaust and, many years later, recalls the father(s) who stayed and perished. Rarely has a short poem succeeded more in conveying, through a powerful modification of the Akedah story, but without any explicit historical reference to the Shoah, a youngster's terror in having to face that event, and the accompanying fear that it may have amputated his generation.

30. "Writing after Auschwitz," in *Two States—One Nation?* (New York: Harcourt Brace Jovanovich, 1990). Moshe Kupferman's painterly minimalism also seems to explore those "shades of gray": here the art of a survivor has chosen a non-figurative mode, works on paper that create a different kind of "newspaper," that evoke the fragility of paper as it bears its always "new" constructions without the full palette of painting. Where Adorno can talk of "damaged life" and Grass of "damaged language," it is harder to conceive of "damaged color," which is one reason Grass celebrates gray. Kitaj's painting "Varschreibt!" confronts in addition the absence of a strong imaging tradition in Judaism.

31. Charlotte Salomon's operetta in pictures, although bravely concentrating on the *normal* joys and pains that link her exile to her previous life—"a little bit of love / a few rules / a young girl / a large bed / after so much dying / is this a life . . . " also recovers something "barbaric" from a popular genre and transfers it quite starkly to painting.

32. Dan Pagis, *Points of Departure* (Philadelphia: Jewish Publication Society of America, 1981), trans. Stephen Mitchell. Quoted by permission. The allusion to Maimonides's *Yigdal* is noted by Robert Alter in his introduction to the volume.

Four

Bitburg

The theme of memory haunts us increasingly. As events "pass into history," and they seem to do so more quickly than ever, are they forgotten by all except specialists? "Passing into history" would then be a euphemism for oblivion, though not obliteration. That something is retrievable in the archives of a library may even help us to tolerate the speedy displacement of one news item by another. The storage capacity of the personal memory is, after all, very limited. But what of the collective memory, with its days of celebration and lamentation, and the duty to keep alive a community's heritage?

The actual memories are likely to be what they have always been: joyful, painful, or both together. Yet recently the tonality of the word "memory" has darkened and moved toward lamentation. We complain, for instance, about the shortened memory-span of the young, and their refusal to extend personal experience by the study of history. One scholar has talked of the death of the past. Another has characterized the historian as a physician of memory. Paradoxically, or so it seems, we plan more and more rites of memorialization, unveiling monuments and instituting days of remembrance that dot the calendar with new holidays. Is there a concern that the burden of the past on the individual consciousness will prove too heavy? Perhaps, then, the mechanics of commemoration are being used to achieve a disburdening of memory, to "construct" forgetfulness, and so—unfortunately—to forestall real, continuous thought about catastrophic events that mark our recent past.

Nineteen eighty-five was the fortieth anniversary of both the end of the Second World War and the liberation of the Nazi death camps. Public speakers remarked on the symbolism of the "forty years" that the Israelites were compelled to spend in the Wilderness. Only after the older generation had died out were they permitted into the Promised Land. But that parable for our time was applied in two very different ways. There were those, including the president of the United States, who felt that Germany, now a bulwark of democracy and NATO, had passed through its exile years and should be rehabilitated spiritually. (Its economic and political standing had been restored long before.) But there were also those who saw that the survivors of the Nazi camps were approaching the term of their life. Soon very few would remain. This occasion was a chance to become more aware of how *they* felt about past and present, including events the president wished to distance. The historians had documented in necessary and fearful detail the Nazi killing machine; the politicians had agreed to establish a Holocaust Memorial Council and annual Days of Remembrance; but the survivors' experience as experienced, their personal story and individual memories—everything too easily characterized as "Oral History"—was only beginning to be heard.

The "forty years," then, meant different things for these two groups that came into collision when the president agreed to honor a German military cemetery at Bitburg, having previously declined to visit a concentration camp memorial site. The full rehabilitation of a perpetrator nation by Mr. Reagan clashed with the survivors' sense (shared by the Jewish community) that they were passing from the scene with their message still unheard, though repeated many times.

Nineteen eighty-five may also have brought to consciousness a related, and more universal, conflict. Life is characterized by a contradictory effort: to remember and to forget, to respect the past and to acknowledge that the present is open to the future. Associated with this common tension are issues that reach into the most sensitive area of morality as it intersects with a nation's political agenda. However hostile the relation between states, a realignment of alliances can occur. It is always possible that a Sadat will fly to Jerusalem and begin a peace process that was unimaginable just months before. The ties between America and Germany, moreover, had grown and intensified over the space of thirty years, aided by a shared anxiety about the East.

Yet the moral question remained, because the guilt incurred by Germany during the war was exceptional. The war brought to light the crime of genocide. The Nazi regime had deprived its own Jewish citizens of profession and property, then of life itself. An entire people was hunted down in the Occupied Territories and slated for extermination. The War against the Jews was prosecuted with as much zeal as the military campaign against the Allies, and even interfered with it. An incredible obsession, it still has not found its explanation and may never find it. But the death camps altered forever the landscape of memory.

There could be no forgetting, then. By 1985, memorials to the victims of the Holocaust were going up everywhere in America. Yet by 1985, too, the memory of that era belonged primarily to the historian rather than to the general public, for the majority of citizens in America and Europe were born after the beginning of the war. For them knowledge about the war and the Holocaust comes primarily from history books and the media rather than from personal recall or contact with individual survivors. This is a turning point, then, and a crucial one. Education and ritual must supplement personal experience; and these, *in less than one more generation*, may have to carry the entire burden of sustaining the collective memory.

The prophets of an older time knew that ceremonies were not enough. Ceremonies would substitute for, rather than inscribe, what should be known and acted upon. Few will quarrel with the fact that to deal with the moral issues raised by the Holocaust, or to transmit a knowledge of it without causing new trauma, is basic. Yet many think they already know about the Holocaust, and that it has received too much attention. But their attitude is a sign that they have no direct memory of the events and learn about them mainly from ceremonies and the media.

This "I know, I know" is only one of many defenses. The fact is that each new generation, German as well as American, has known *something*. The events of April–May 1985 are not unique. There are recurrent crises of consciousness involving the Holocaust.[1] But each crisis—triggered by the Eichmann trial revelations, for instance, or the full disclosure of how much American leaders (Jewish as well as gentile) knew and how little they did— simply brings about new mechanisms of defense. If this pattern of disclosure and defense is allowed to continue, it will achieve nothing except an occasional catharsis. Each decade will have its "punctual agony," after which things return to normal. So Theodor Adorno (a German philosopher who survived the Nazis by spending the war years in America) anticipated in his 1959 essay "What Does Coming to Terms with the Past Mean?" what has become only too clear in 1985. It was also Adorno who raised the question of what education meant "After Auschwitz." The Holocaust should not be assigned to the history of the victims, as if it were not of the utmost consequence to every thoughtful person. This is where education enters as a responsibility that cannot be delayed.

It is an education, quite specifically, that will have to pose questions for which the answers are lacking, while not abandoning its obligation to find answers. Such questions as: how do we transmit so dark and debilitating a knowledge? There are righteous and kindly acts to be reported, but they stand out in their rarity. Can any culture, including that of pre-Holocaust

Jewry, help us to absorb or integrate the damaging picture? Our concern for the human image, moreover, could extend itself to the divine image. For the Holocaust acts as an eclipse of the *imago Dei* (of the God in whose image man is said to be created), even if the faith of many survivors was unshaken. As we consider such large questions, we realize that they connect, as in the case of Bitburg, with something daily and immediate. What does "forgiveness" or "reconciliation" mean? Especially in circumstances where the offense may not be forgotten?

This issue of *response* cannot be separated, in short, from that of *responsibility*. How do we handle the imputation of collective guilt? Can the offended and injured evolve a statute of limitations, not of course toward individual criminals but toward the perpetrator nation, or bystanders (the church and others, not just the average German) who did so little to help? We surely cannot invoke a collective guilt of the kind that bloodied the record of history long before the Nazis translated it into their atrocious practices against the Jews.

Education must raise these issues formally. But there remains an ultimate question and the most subversive of all. Can a method be found to prevent the recurrence of genocidal regimes by instituting a more effective system of law and education? The question is subversive because we know all too well that Germany was a law-abiding and civilized country. The fact that the Holocaust occurred among an educated people, and where the Jews had achieved a remarkable symbiosis, requires us to rebuild our faith in education itself. It is not just a matter of gaining more space for the Holocaust (more textbook pages) in the curriculum. To have predicted the crimes against the Jews and other "racially inferior" groups by that cultured nation, Germany, was as impossible, one commentator wrote during the Bitburg turmoil, as imagining that Goethe ate human flesh.

President Reagan's decision to visit Bitburg during ceremonies marking the fortieth anniversary of Germany's "liberation" from the Nazi yoke may simply have been a blunder, caused by bad advance planning. Blunder or not, the story of that visit as it unfolded occupied the media for two months, from the end of March to the end of May. It was a remarkably intense period. The anguish, especially though not exclusively within Jewish circles, and particularly among those who survived the Holocaust, has still not passed away.

Americans may have been ready for what Mr. Reagan called "reconciliation," but not in *that* form. All at once we realized again the crucial importance of symbols, as well as the difficulty of finding any symbol or ceremony that could have served Mr. Reagan's aim. The time had not come for so global an act of political absolution. Any place chosen for its symbolic value might therefore seem flawed—though some less than others, as Raul Hilberg points out. Even so moving a gesture as Willy Brandt's, when he fell to his knees before the Warsaw Ghetto memorial during a 1970 visit, was questioned by the press.

Every monument or ceremony seeking to honor the collective memory can be "forgetful" in the sense that its design is influenced by policy. But the choice of Bitburg not only raised a question as to whether the ceremony was necessary, or what ceremonies really achieve—it gave the impression of wishing to recall *nothing* of the past except common sacrifices and a shared code of military honor. Yet was it not that very code which was breached by Nazi "crimes against humanity"?

Mr. Reagan treated the matter as if it were an internal American affair. There had been some fuss when Gerald Ford, after assuming the presidency, pardoned Nixon and asked the nation to heal its wounds. This time, on a divisive issue involving the international community, we were asked to accept a formal act of reconciliation that would take place not only on German soil but in a military cemetery of that nation.

When Elie Wiesel, in a phrase that became famous, told the president, "That place [Bitburg] is not your place," the emotional impact was amplified by a consciousness that the Jews had been a displaced people for too long—lacking their own place or haven until the establishment of Israel in 1948. If the soldiers buried in that German cemetery had won the war, the Jews would have disappeared from the face of the earth, and unlike the Wehrmacht or Waffen SS buried there, no place could have been found to honor them. Close to six million did perish, many in unmarked mass graves. "Here rest a thousand dead," one of the signs reads in the Bergen-Belsen memorial site. The Jews were to be remembered only in Nazi histories, where their extermination would be, Himmler said, "the most glorious page" in the annals of the Third Reich.

No wonder a sense of shock and betrayal swept the Jewish community. The head of a country that had given refuge to so many victims of the Nazis—a country they trusted and where, all thing considered, they felt at home—did not seem to have a real sense of their history. Veterans' groups too protested, as did many church-related organizations with a more troubled view than the president about who had the right to forgive. Many pointed out with columnist Lance Morrow that "forgiveness to the injured doth belong." Unfortunately, Mr. Reagan compounded his error by explanatory statements that made no distinction between the fallen German soldiers and the murdered Jews; indeed, he suggested that both were "victims" of a Nazi oppression whose responsibility he limited by laying it upon the madness of "one man."[2]

Those who mock official Soviet distortions of history must have been embarrassed. This interpretation, surely, was equally bad, however benevolent its motive. Good intentions do not guarantee good history, any more than do revengeful ones. "1985," then, is not so far from "1984," despite the fact that George Orwell was evoking the danger of totalitarianism: how it would distort history and by its "newspeak" flatter and flatten the mind. Nor all that far from "1914," when Walter Lippmann foresaw that out of the unrest of democratic liberties there comes not disciplined thought but a penchant for easy and hopeful solutions. The "real American," he wrote, in *Drift and Mastery*, was actually a dreamer seeking a "Golden Age in which he could drift with impunity." But "this habit of reposing in the sun of a brilliant future is very enervating. It opens a chasm between fact and fancy, and the whole fine dream is detached from the living zone of the present."

That detachment in the president, that optimistic ability to overlook certain things in the past and so to counter drift by an appearance of mastery, is what everyone felt. Some were grateful; many were offended. A sense of history is particularly important in the era of the Holocaust. It was a vicious propaganda in the form of history that, if it did not bring Hitler to power, certainly helped to justify his excesses once in power. A similar libel comes today from the Soviet sphere, which sees the Holocaust as a conspiracy of Zionists and Nazis to create the conditions for the founding of Israel. There exists, moreover, a crude revisionism that claims that the death camps with their gas chambers and crematoria were merely unpleasant work camps (more like Gulags, say). Finally, a more subtle revisionism is all around us that mitigates the horror of the camps, not by denying it but by using equalizing comparisons. So Vietnam or the bombing of Beirut is dubbed a "holocaust." The exceptionality of the Holocaust is diminished by such liberal yet vague analogies.

It should therefore be stated very clearly: Even if "nothing human is alien to us," the burden of the Shoah cannot be overcome because it cannot be reduced to familiarity. The Holocaust remains human and alien at the same time. The worst attitude we could take is to persuade ourselves that it might not happen again *or* that it is something that happened before—that the Holocaust was one catastrophe among others.

It is true that such a perspective divides history by positing a caesura more decisive than a theophanic event. It makes of the Holocaust a *novum* (as Emil Fackenheim, among others, has argued); so that, for the time being, which may last some time, all that went before and all that presently befalls us must be seen in the ominous light of that destruction. The history of the Jews, Nikolai Berdyaev wrote, presents nothing but a perpetual crucifixion. This very fact, however, helped to deceive and decoy Hitler's victims, as Raul Hilberg has shown in his classic *The Destruction of the European Jews.* The Jews were used to pogroms, accustomed to those terrible yet temporary turns of fortune. Elie Wiesel has said of his youth: "Somehow I accepted persecution as a law of nature. I was convinced that this was how God created the world, that once a year we had to avoid being in the street because on that winter evening, or on that day in the spring, Christians attacked Jews. It was clear, it was normal. I didn't even protest." But the Nazi terror aimed at a "Final Solution."

In witness accounts by Holocaust survivors two phrases recur: "I saw it," and "I could not believe what my eyes have seen." It needs a particular courage not to overcome the past but to live with it still. Historians, we are told, instruct us in the uses of the past, yet it is hard to see what that means when the Holocaust is the issue. Education, in this case, cannot be equated with enlightenment. The universe of death we call the Holocaust or Shoah creates, as Claude Lanzmann has said, its own sacred and isolating wall of fire. The very fact that it happened repels us. Yet it also makes us aware how painful it is to stay with a knowledge that is about evil rather than about good, and so tempts us to simplify what happened or commemorate it merely ritually.

I personally learned that despite the attention the Holocaust had received (at least since the TV series "Holocaust" was screened), one could not count on the facts being known or their significance being understood. Publicity, media exposure and Days of Remembrance have been less than successful in conveying the enormity of the Shoah. "Bitburg" disclosed that what understanding there was at the highest level of government led not to sensitivity, but only to sentimentality. For even if Mr. Reagan was being shielded from too close a contact with the emotional side of things, the straight historical truths also were not getting through; and this meant an astonishing ignorance or lack of interest on the part of his advisors.

Although journalism during the Bitburg episode was of very high quality, too many letters in the papers repeated charges about Jewish attempts to claim a monopoly on suffering. This makes me doubt that Holocaust studies have affected more than a very small portion of the public. My work with the Video Archive for Holocaust Testimonies at Yale suggests the same conclusion. There has to be a will to talk, but also a will to listen. The survivors are finally talking, but are we ready to listen?

An anecdote can illustrate the difficulty of speaking about the Holocaust experience—or taking it in. I had addressed a small group of survivors for some fifteen minutes, setting forth the reasons why they should give their testimony. When I finished an old—a very old—woman turned her arm over, disclosing the bluish tatoo, and said simply: "I was there."

It comes to that, first and last, to that evidential, sorrowful "I was there" spoken by those who were in the camps. I felt unnecessary, and yet I had to be "there" myself as a belated witness to that act. Those who complain about the attention the Holocaust is receiving are right that no one should make a platform out of the suffering of others. And we have seen young people with political ambitions who are falling into that temptation, and whose rage in denouncing Mr. Reagan's mistake gave the impression of seeking a constituency.

Yet the political brouhaha does not excuse those who say, Enough. They have forgotten two things. That the survivors must be heard now, if at all; and that for a long time they were not heard, or not believed. The Holocaust is such Bad News that even now teachers and researchers who take up the task of telling what they know face all kinds of psychological obstacles. The bereaved too are not always exempt from subtle forms of denial, as Primo Levi tells us in his remarkable "The Memory of Offense." We have to reconcile ourselves to the fact that an utterly inhumane event like the Holocaust occurred, before we demand another kind of reconciliation—a forgiving spirit on the part of those who survived, and who represent not only themselves but their murdered families.

Mr. Reagan's initiative, as William Safire pointed out, at least had the virtue of eventually adding thoughtfulness to ritual. He was led by an invisible "pedagogical hand." The initiative, in other words, did the opposite of what it intended, and so gave us a chance—however unfortunate the occasion—to think matters through more honestly. It produced, for example, a speech by Richard von Weizsäcker (president of the Federal Republic of Germany) that is really a public confession never before uttered at that level. Yet from the letter-debate in the London *Times*,[3] it was equally certain that the so-called Christian-Jewish dialogue had not advanced very far.

The letters suggested that Jewish ethical thinking is not known or appreciated, and that Christian attitudes about forgiveness approach at times old anti-Semitic stereotypes concerning the obstinacy and hardheartedness of the Jews. This is an unhappy theme. Clearly, ecumenical assemblies are not enough: it is time to broach more forcefully the issue of Christian anti-Semitism, and the related question of prejudicial Gospel texts from Matthew and John that remain an integral part of the lectionary. They support, and have done so for centuries, an anti-Jewish mentality and the idea of collective guilt. Vatican II's declaration, modifying the charge of deicide and collective guilt, at least officially recognized the problem without being as decisive a statement as one would wish. And it certainly has not sunk in. Claude Lanzmann's epic film *Shoah* contains a chilling sequence in which the filmmaker's patient questioning of people in front of a Polish Catholic church (a colorful ceremony honoring the birth of the Virgin forms its background) leads finally to a startling change of mood, as the crowd goes from good-hearted professions of ignorance as to why the Jews suffered the Holocaust, to excited explanations based on Matthew 15:27, with its climactic "His blood be on us and on our children!"

The Bitburg affair made American Jews feel vulnerable. Not because they doubted the soundness of the American system or the good will of the president. Yet they understood, again, their dependence on that good will—on how even in a democracy the tune is called on high, and "administration" means more than carrying out a mandate with efficiency. Those who do not see why there was so much agitation about Mr. Reagan's "modest symbolic gesture" are failing to analyze the immense importance that the impression of being fully in charge has in a pluralistic society. *E pluribus unum*: how is this unity to be maintained in so divided, so heterogeneous a country, without force, or the least amount of force? Think of the passions aroused by the silent or one-minute prayer controversy. An agreement on *symbols* is crucial if violent encounters are to be avoided. Hence there are no "modest" symbolic gestures.

Jews may be particularly sensitive to symbolic acts because they have often been humiliated by them. Forced baptism, forced gestures of obedience (Freud recalls his father's story of quietly retrieving his cap knocked into the gutter when a gentile wished him off the pavement) are among the more *benign* events of their history. The "forced reconciliation" of Bitburg, therefore, can suggest the possibility of further steps involving state power. The German philosopher Jürgen Habermas concluded that politicians cannot be trusted to exert spiritual or moral leadership. They will always engage in "forced reconciliation," or what Kenneth Burke, recalling Hitler's era—which we still ponder, however far we are from it—characterized as "sinister unifying."

In this situation, then, an honest appraisal seems better than words of false comfort. The questionings of Job suit an age that nevertheless reaches out in the hope of *tikkun*—a Hebrew word that suggests a mending rather than reconciliation. The Bitburg turmoil did sometimes provide such a mending in the form of new coalitions (whether or not they will prove to be transitory) in America and France. One especially moving development was reported by Henry Rousso. Though the French community's response, like that of their government, remained muted, Bitburg provided the occasion for a march and a manifesto that united young Jews and immigrant workers, including Arabs. They discovered a common cause in protesting racism, whether anti-Jewish or anti-Arab (the latter a growing problem in France), and issued an eloquent statement affirming that "there are wounds and acts which can never be effaced from the collective memory."

This mending, as Emil Fackenheim has reminded us, also extends to the question of our speech, and its involvement in symbols.[4] In 1985, and perhaps every year, we begin to think anew about the symbols that are supposed to unite us, yet, like Bitburg, often reveal deep and unresolved points of difference. The memory of offense cannot be eradicated by the magic touch of benevolence. Not in the private mind, and not in the general consciousness of those who have been through the Holocaust or suffered other crimes of the Nazi era. "Pity and Love are too venerable for the imputation of guilt," William Blake has one of his grand, self-deluding figures declaim. For he knows these virtues too must be open to scrutiny. What he calls "mental fight" continues.

As I write this, six months after Bitburg, there are some who feel that an unfortunate incident was inflated into a *cause célèbre*. Bitburg, they say, cannot retain its significance. Yet Bitburg was meant to be significant, was meant to create a symbolic occasion, and therefore relied on image-making and the media—on the very forces that exposed a flawed thinking. "Reagan: F in History," a French newspaper headline declared. The president and his advisors, however, were not alone in finding it difficult to "master" history. America, as Walter Lippmann suggested, is a land that has made light of the past and sometimes taken pride in shaking off an unnecessary burden. The American Adam is a figure both mocked and admired. There was nothing covert in what happened: the media simply reflected an iconomania that is creating a "generation without memory."

Both the Germans and the French, in this light, are closer to a past that keeps returning. Even the people called by Shimon Dubnov "the veterans of history" are finding it harder to bring their past into the collective memory. It does not help to quote Santayana, that those who refuse to learn from history are bound to repeat it. For history sends mixed messages. Dubnov, a great historian, said that the nineteenth century promised the emancipation of the Jews, the full restoration of their civic rights, despite ominous regressions toward the close of the century in Russia and Austria. Yet our time has witnessed a Holocaust that took Dubnov's own life even as he was recording the deadly scene.[5] How then can remembrance lead to redemption, as a famous Hasidic master, the Baal Shem Tov, thought? The memorials we multiply reflect a universe of death, of which history is the record. In this regard, the survivors of the camps become a crucial generation for us. They are, often, the history we would rather forget; yet their memories, though traumatic, did not entirely displace in them a tradition of learning transmitted for two thousand years.

Notes

1. The situation in France is much less clear. Even in talking about survivors, the word "déporté" is more common than "survivant," and Alain Resnais's famous *Night and Fog* avoids identifying the inmates of the camps as mainly Jewish. In an issue of the *Nouvelle Revue de Psychanalyse*, 15 (1977), entitled *Mémoires*, the Holocaust does not make an appearance.

2. Jean Améry writes: " . . . death in battle and the [camp] prisoner's death are two incommensurables. The soldier died the hero's or victim's death, the prisoner that of an animal intended for slaughter. . . . The decisive difference lay in the fact that the front-line soldier unlike the camp inmate was not only the target, but also the bearer of death." *At the Mind's Limits: Contemplations by a Survivor on Auschwitz and Its Realities*, trans. Sidney Rosenfeld and Stella P. Rosenfeld (Bloomington: Indiana University Press, 1980), 16.

3. Reprinted in *European Judaism* 19:2 (Spring 1985), 3–17. The controversy centered on a letter by Dr. A. C. J. Phillips, chaplain of St. John's College, Oxford, which contains the following sentences:

> . . . A theology unwilling to come to terms with the oppressors, however heinous their crimes, imprisons itself in its own past jeopardizing the very future it would ensure.

Bitburg

Without forgiveness there can be no healing within the community, no wholeness, holiness. The leopard cannot lie down with the kid. Indeed the opposite occurs. For failure to forgive is not a neutral act: it adds to the sum total of evil in the world and dehumanizes the victims in a way the oppressors could never on their own achieve.

In remembering the Holocaust, Jews hope to prevent its recurrence: by declining to forgive, I fear that they unwittingly invite it.

4. *To Mend the World* (New York: Schocken Books, 1982), especially chapter 4.

5. See Elie Wiesel, "In the Footsteps of Shimon Dubnov," in *Against Silence: The Voice and Vision of Elie Wiesel* (New York: Holocaust Library/Schocken Books, 1985).

Five

The Voice of Vichy

In case you did not know it, we are living in a thoroughly depressing time. Books, reinforced by the media which keep the information hot, tell us of past and present atrocities. There is no escape from the massacres in Bosnia, the violence accompanying a power struggle in Somalia, assassinations and the violation of human rights in Haiti, state-sponsored terror or random killings almost anywhere. I open my newspaper today (November 10, 1993), the morning after Kristallnacht, and learn that the number of refugees in the world has swollen to forty-four million. In a single week, or so it seems, books are published that remind us that since the 1960s over a hundred thousand Guatemalans have been killed, many of them Mayan Indians, and that between 1941 and 1945 Vichy helped to deport 76,000 Jews, of whom only 2,500 survived. Newsworthy novels, films and stories appear regularly to thrill, entertain or horrify with accounts of ruthless regimes, or they pick at the memory-scabs growing slowly around the deep wounds of the Holocaust, the Vietnam War, and the Cambodian genocide.

What makes these renewed confrontations, these seemingly honest words and images, even more depressing, is a perception growing in us, and twisting guts as well as eyes, that this hyperknowledge about both perpetrators and victims, this wish to disclose and expose everything, may be no more remedial than the conspiracy of silence that used to exist. After yet another shooting in an Ulster Pub, this one killing six Catholics and a Protestant, the *New York Times* reported that "Ordinary people were plunged into a kind of flattened despair," a condition that an administrator of one of the groups working for peace called "compassion fatigue."

I don't know what will happen if our psychic defenses, ordinarily fairly successful in absorbing traumatic stress, should begin to give way entirely, rather than occasionally malfunctioning and producing new versions of the original torment or aggression. Without turning into a partisan of silence, I feel it is important to raise the question of what we learn from the assault of bad news—from this *kakangelic* drive made possible in liberal democracies by the real-time reporting of the electronic media.

It may be, of course, that the public memory now being created, which

The Voice of Vichy

is more sulfurous in its contents than any hell-obsessed preacher of old, will reveal—precisely because it has removed willful blindness and superficial optimism—profounder strata of human persistence and courage.[1] Yet there are signs that all our just and justifiable research may simply reinforce a prior and very strong religious conviction about persistent human evil. This conviction always incites, when mixed with political and self-interested motives, a manichean terror of the other, of the potential enemy in the other— and so exacerbates the xenophobia we are so studiously seeking to prevent. That the ravages of the Holocaust, moreover, were planned in Germany, and abetted by so many in France—that the most civilized countries of that time tolerated criminal regimes—not only increases our own suspicion of western cultural pretensions, but subjects us to mockery even by those who are blatantly xenophobic because of their nondemocratic or fundamentalist doctrines.

In France, a self-protective silence, though punctuated by scandals and revelations, prevailed for close to fifty years after the Occupation, as if public memory could not tolerate the truth of French complicity in the persecution of the Jews. Until the 1970s even many French Jews did not differentiate between their fate during the Occupation and that of other citizens, and not till the early eighties—just at the time that the so-called revisionists were gathering momentum—did *Vichy France and the Jews*, by Paxton and Marrus, make it impossible to escape a further investigation of Vichy antisemitism and especially the role of the French police. It took another decade, till 1992, the fiftieth anniversary of the "grand rafle" in Paris, for conferences, journal publications, and ceremonies to catch up with the facts. I do not have to rehearse the entire story of the antisemitic policy of Vichy, of what was done to the stateless Jews ("apatrides") who had taken refuge in France and, eventually, to many French nationals ("les bons vieux juifs de France"). After the war most of the top officials responsible for this policy escaped prosecution, and sometimes pursued successful careers in government and business.[2]

The bad news is far from over. Richard Weisberg, founder of the Law and Humanities Institute, and who teaches at Cardozo Law School, is studying the behavior of his own profession during those years in France: how lawyers dealt with the *Statut des Juifs* of October 3 and 4, 1940 and June 2, 1941, ordinances harsher in their legal definition of Jewishness than Nazi racial laws. Not only those with three Jewish grandparents but persons with two Jewish grandparents when married to a Jew fell under the Vichy definition, which aimed to drive as many Jews as possible from the government, the professions and indeed out of public life altogether. Weisberg shows how rarely the doctrine of the *droits de l'homme*, proud heritage of the French Revolution, and pervading legal opinion since then, was used to contest, at any level, these illegal and persecutory statutes.[3]

It was to be expected that Xavier Vallat, the first "Commissaire général aux questions juives," should speak as follows in the preface to a typical broadside of a book written under the banner of what was sometimes called *rational antisemitism*:[4]

> "The French Revolution, the first, [Vichy, that is, is the second, a counter-revolution] was mad enough to consider Jews citizens like any other, and gradually in the next century-and-a-half, all governments successively committed the same error for fear of appearing to be 'reactionary.' . . . The Jew will want to be a naturalized citizen without this representing a desire to fix his roots in a particular place. Simply to enjoy the fullness of his rights as a citizen, there where he happens to be. . . . And the most curious character of this wandering race is that it wishes to take over, everywhere it travels. Its dream of universal domination attaches itself to each of its offspring, all of whom are conscious of belonging to the superior race . . . [Jews] have invaded the public and intellectual professions [*les professions libérales et intellectuelles*], the press, the radio, the movies, the higher administrative offices and politics, that is, everything that serves to govern a democracy. France was stricken with a Jewish brain fever [literally, flux to the brain, *transport juif au cerveau*] of which it almost died."[5]

Yet this type of rhetoric is topped in its pseudo-objectivity by a Sorbonne thesis for which André Broc received his "Docteur en Droit" the same year. Entitled *La Qualité du Juif: Une notion juridique nouvelle*[6] it claims, just like Vallat, that the Jews would never be assimilated to the nations among which they lived, despite the earlier effort of Rome under Caracalla and the French at the time of their revolution. To apply to Jews the doctrine of the *droits de l'homme* was an error. "From the fact that the Jews were men, it did not logically follow that they should have been citizens of the country in which they found themselves, but the equivocation that called 'emancipation' their naturalization spread and perpetuated itself." Moreover, notably in France, Broc continues, "the influx of foreign Jews as well as their propensity to play a role in our internal and international politics inspired by their own interests, has restored to the Jewish problem globally a relevance it had lost." He concludes by assuring us that none but technical legal considerations are his subject: he intends to analyze efforts to provide a definition for Jewish specificity from a perspective characterized as "de pure technique juridique."

Such instrumental reasoning, or "bureaucratic culture," has long been identified (first by the Frankfurt School) as an essential factor in the creation of writing-desk murderers and the industrialized efficiency behind the massacres of the Holocaust. It is important to stress that people like André Broc are bystanders in civil society, who collaborate without the threat of martial law. The pressures in Vichy France on lawyers, academics, and intellectuals generally came from their wish to continue in their career, to protect their opportunities (increased by the removal of talented Jews), and to make "discourse as usual," that is, to talk in terms of "problems" and "solutions" and "technique." Zygmunt Bauman, in his book on *Modernity and the Holocaust*, and Claude Lanzmann in *Shoah* also make a strong case that the ethos of bureaucracy and its technical jargon contributed to enervating the human and moral sensibility of the writing-desk murderer.

However, it is difficult to attribute the collaboration, active or passive, of so many bystanders and civil servants simply to opportunism, even when strengthened by fear, professional deformation, and a deceiving distinction between what Maurras characterized as "antisémitisme d'état" in contrast to a vulgar "antisémitisme de peau." For there is often a note of idealism, or utopian politics, mixed in with what we would prefer to depict as a cynical, xenophobic, or profitable antisemitism. Already in the 1930s, a disgust with party politics, and sometimes with parliamentary democracy as a whole, led to an ideal of "sinister unifying" (Kenneth Burke, in a 1930s essay on *Mein Kampf*) which sought to suppress divergent and dissident voices. Add a disenchantment with a corruptible human nature that was felt to require a virile discipline and leadership in order to function collectively, add the rejection of cosmopolitanism as an unrealistic and anti-national doctrine, add an aversion to both communism and finance capitalism, and fascist philosophies gain in credibility. They become, in Eric Voegelin's words, "political theologies"; they promise, like religions themselves when church and state have not separated, a justified and orderly community, a *Volksgemeinschaft* with a common purpose—an ideal that proves to be even more seductive when national pride is humiliated, as was the case with Germany, or national power is felt to be waning, as in the case of France.

When I asked previously, what we could learn from the imagery of violence and the evidence of injustice and persecution that follow us into the most pastoral places, I meant to imply that knowledge of the worst, while it produces flashes of righteous anger, can also incite deep feelings of powerlessness. Imagine now that you are exposed to daily spectacles of *force majeure* and anti-Jewish propaganda. In such an atmosphere, if there is no countervailing thrust, it is all too easy to side with power, to blame the victim who is made to look degraded, and to accept a relentlessly manichean picture of politics and the world. What we glimpse here is an unpredictable factor in our new-won realism, our global knowledge of "political wretchedness" (Terrence des Pres) as disclosed by the media. The good side of this information explosion is that we cannot not know; the problematic side is that the power of the media is such that the world of appearances and the world of propaganda can be made to merge—a total encompassment that became obvious for the first time in the Nazi era.

My purpose is not to explain in order to forgive, or to mitigate in any way the shameful aspect of collaboration or its cover-up. But often when I remember what happened a sense of incredulity rises in me. The danger of allowing that feeling to persist, without analyzing it as well as the facts that cause the feeling, is that it may lead us into easy denunciations, into judgments that cost nothing in terms of self-reflection and which distance us from that era. Yet that era has not entirely passed away, when we look at our position as bystanders. Are we not still in the constant presence of images and reports of terror and injustice, obliged to endure them impotently or to give them a certain talky spin? Who has not experienced a contemporary form of the incredulity with which we regard the Vichy or Nazi past? For we suffer at the present time not only from compassion fatigue but also from a sense of unreality that is specifically our own. It is as if the news we turn to with a certain eagerness were a kind of show, an electronic spectacle whose images hover in museal or virtual space. It is hard to define that sensation precisely, but it too, this sense of the unreality of our own world, will have to be faced rather than evaded.

By this detour I come finally to the negationists. The principal movers among them are, without a doubt, blatant antisemites; but that does not explain how they get away with their tactics, how they think they can deny the documented and overdocumented facts: the archives, the historians, the witness of the survivors, the witness of the perpetrators, the witness of the bystanders. It is true that the negationists nuance their denial in various ways, by saying that, yes, Jews were killed, yet not in the numbers claimed or by the use of gas. But this pretense of weighing the facts like regular historians always results in the same negative conclusion: there is no evidence of a Holocaust, that is, of a systematic "Final Solution" that intended to exterminate all Jews. Many Jews were victims, but because of the war, and not a war against the Jews—though, it is alleged, the understandable animosity of true citizens toward these rootless and war-mongering nomads made then a special target. Thus the victims are blamed, and doubly so: for it is also charged that they have inflated their casualty figures into a Holocaust in order to demand compensation and embezzle the moral conscience of the world. Moreover, they have been successful in this not because the evidence supports them but because they still control the media.

You have doubtless noticed that this argument can only be persuasive if it taps into a double distrust: of the Jews and of the media. That convergence is essential; but even it would not work unless the negationists or those targeted by them did not suffer from a deep and basic anxiety: that seeing is no longer believing; that the world of appearances and the world of the media can be made to merge; that an old-time solidity has disappeared, and now unreality, manipulation, forgery are taking over. It is surely no accident that Faurisson first tried to make his reputation by proving that we were the victims of a literary mystification or forgery; and that Maurice Bardèche, together with Robert Brasillach (rabid antisemite and brilliant writer, the only intellectual executed after the war for a journalism deemed to be treasonable), authored a first and still very important *Histoire du Cinéma.*

Bardèche and Brasillach, certainly, had a love affair with the movies and a complex understanding of that new and magical medium which, they said, gave "l'éternité à l'éphémère." This paradoxical formula betrays a consciousness as impressionistic, aesthetic and hedonistic as Walter Pater's. The medium which reduces us to watching glittering shadows also serves the authors' eudaemonic desire for recording and preserving the passing moment. Their "Verweile doch" combines reality-hunger, the wish of the diarist to inscribe time, with a nostalgia about a time that is always already past. The link between the fixating power of the medium (even though these are "movies") and the mutability of the historical moment, which Susan Sontag described in her book *On Photography* as "the innocence, the vulnerability of lives headed toward their own destruction," is clearly anticipated. In Brasillach, and especially his novels, this vulnerability becomes almost voluptuous; while in Bardèche, as in the arch-antisemite Drumont, there is a fierce conviction that the old order, "la France d'alors," always seen as a pastoral organic community, is not just passing away but being actively destroyed.

What is alleged is that here too the Jews have spoiled everything. It is they who are said to have commercialized the cinema and created an industry in which "pleasing the public" would override all other considerations. "Les marchands de tapis juifs, roumains ou hongrois, des aventuriers de tout ordre, qui s'étaient rendus maîtres d'une partie du cinéma, aggravèrent la situation par les procédés qui auraient menacé l'avenir de n'importe quelle autre industrie, et qui naturellement poussèrent vers la médiocrité définitive presque toute la production et en particulier la production française."[7]

It is disheartening to multiply instances of the sad and vicious utterances of Bardèche and other negationists, or of self-styled "rational antisemites" such as Brasillach and Charles Maurras, or of the nasty, instinctive sort like Léon Daudet and Céline. It is enough to show that they sought to project an image of the Jew as, in Richard Wagner's words, a "plastic demon of decadence": that is, as the very principle of the non-solid, of what is essentially groundless, rootless, shape-shifting, cerebral, cunning, and abstract, and—like money in distinction to landed property—an agent of perpetual displacement and dissolution. That stereotype existed before a second, specifically modern sense of spookiness, associated with the cinema as a dangerous if seductive simulation of reality, reinforced it. For the antisemite the assimilated Jew is but another uncanny and tricky simulation.

The older stereotype is often exemplified by Maurras, and nowhere more crassly than when he celebrates the new racial laws in *La seule France* (1941). He asserts that it is the right of the French to keep the Jews out of the professions because "we are the masters of the house our fathers have built and for which they have given their sweat and blood. We have the absolute right to impose our conditions on nomads whom we receive under our roof." Gloating over the castles, lands, apartments, art objects, and collections left behind by the Rothschilds and other fugitives, he suggests that they should be sold off to alleviate the heavy peasant debt. That seems to him an ingenious way of doing justice, of compensating for what the Jews did against the peasant, or against the French earth itself:

> Those who do not have French soil on the soles of their boots, in the final analysis lived off this good earth that our race alone made fertile. The loud-mouths [batteurs d'estrade] who unleashed against this soil the ravages of war and did not want to face the consequences, had begun by stripping and fleecing it by means of the usury and speculation which permitted them to amass an anonymous and vagabond fortune. . . . May the eternal laborer of this mother-earth be better compensated in this way for his hard work. [Que l'éternel travailleur de cette terre mère soit ainsi mieux payé de son dur travail.][8]

The Voice of Vichy

There is something too eloquent and overindulgently classical here. A high style feeds on the easy and vulgar stereotype it ornately varies. We can separate *fond* and *forme* as in a well-conducted "explication de texte"; but since this is not a school exercise but the very Voice of Vichy on which lives depend, we glimpse the tragic fact that not the Jews but calumniators like Maurras are out of touch with reality. Yet every reality-loss is blamed on the Jews. Baudrillard, who extends Benjamin's insight on how technology invades sensibility, suggests that the later negationist obsession with challenging the historical reality of the Holocaust is only another expression of our growing sense of unreality. This unreality fuses our horror of the Holocaust with an incredulity that comes from the awareness that we now live more and more among simulacra. We have reached, Baudrillard writes, in *The Transparence of Evil*, "the impasse of a hallucinatory *fin de siècle*, fascinated by the horror of its origins, for which oblivion is impossible. The only way out is by denial or negation."

Allow me to add a short epilogue. What I have said is relatively devoid of the pathos that comes when we think of Auschwitz as unrepresentable, or, in Jabès's words, "the indestructible memory of a void." The work of mourning, which cannot yet be limited in the case of the Shoah, will necessarily join itself to prior—adequate or not—symbols of grief and desolation. We test those symbols. A "cry without a voice" rises up in Henri Raczymow, a second generation writer. Or a survivor who visits the Warsaw ghetto shortly after its liquidation hears a "woman's voice calling from the rubble," an unidentified, ghostly sound, recalling Rachel lamenting her children or the Shechinah who accompanies Israel into exile. There are, also, the orphaned tongues Jabès calls from the void—all those questioning and quarreling rabbis, including the marvelous names they bear. They constitute a post-Holocaust tradition from which a sort of midrash rabbah might be drawn.

But instead of showing how writing and mourning are related, or how the Holocaust renews that dark connection, I have turned to those who live in denial, and suggested that they too are haunted by a loss for which they seek an explanation, a specific cause; and the Jew often becomes that cause. They also are mourning, but with a vengeance. Bardèche, in the remarkable and unrepentant pages of *Nuremberg, ou, La Terre Promise*, though he acknowledges the existence of concentration camps and of German crimes against the Jews, denies all French responsibility for their deportation and death in words whose sense of loss and laying of blame beggar even those of Maurras:

> We have ceased to be a great nation today, we have even perhaps ceased to be an independent nation, because [Jewish] wealth and influence have made their point of view prevail over that of the French who are attached to the conservation of their land and who wanted to preserve the peace. . . . And still later, we found them heading the persecution and calumny directed toward those of our comrades who had sought to protect them from the severity of the Occupation in this country, where we have been settled far longer than they have, where our parents were settled, and which the men of our race turned into a great land. And they say that today they are the true husbandsmen of this earth which their parents did not know, and that they understand better than we do the wisdom and mission of this land of which certain among them scarcely know the language: they have divided us, they have exacted the blood of the best and purest among us, and they have rejoiced and still rejoice in our dead. The war they desired, it has given us the right to say that it was their war and not ours. They have paid for it, as one pays for every war. We have the right not to number their dead with ours.[9]

Many will see in this nothing but a meretricious defense of Vichy's policy of collaboration, and a repetition of the most common antisemitic clichés. Yet as an exercise in rhetoric, as an exemplary piece of classical prose, this is "French" to the core.[10] What is mourned here, in the very style, is the passing away of a language and culture identified with the nation and its classical past. In short, a *civilized* fear of alienation, which we all share to a degree and which has intensified in the age of electronic simulacra, is contaminated by a *savage* antisemitism that preceded the Holocaust and continues today, and not only in the negationists.

Notes

1. I read each week two or three truly moving analyses and admonitions by honorable and conspicuous people like Václav Havel that spell out political and moral truths of the first importance. Are such fine statements more than a balm that covers, as if with grass, another mass grave recently exhumed? Through them, at best, we clutch at hope, at a renewal of our resilience, while secretly fearful of every green spot remaining on earth or in our minds.

2. See Michael Marrus and Robert O. Paxton, *Vichy France and the Jews* (New York: Basic, 1981). Paxton's *La France de Vichy* and Ophuls's *Le chagrin et la pitié* had punctured the silence earlier. By now the role of Vichy in the "Final Solution" has been well docu-

mented in important works by Serge Klarsfeld, André Kaspi, and (especially on the "silence" after the war) Henri Rousso.

3. See Weisberg, "Legal Rhetoric under Stress: The Example of Vichy," in *Poethics: And Other Strategies of Law and Literature* (New York: Columbia University Press, 1992). For an overview of the missing initiative for institutional self-examination, see the special May 1992 number of *L'Esprit*, "Que faire de Vichy?"

4. See, e.g., Robert Brasillach in the *Je suis partout* of April 15, 1939, as quoted in *Morceaux Choisis*, ed. Marie-Madelaine Martin (Genève-Paris: Editions du cheval ailé, 1948), 114: " . . . nous pensons aussi que la meilleure manière d'empêcher les réactions toujours imprévisibles de l'antisémitisme d'instinct, est d'organiser un antisémitisme de raison" (we believe also that the best way of preventing the always unforeseeable reactions of an instinctive antisemitism is to organize a rational antisemitism).

5. Gabriel Malglaive, *Juif ou Français: Aperçus sur la question juive* (Paris: Editions C.P.R.N., 1942), 6–8. How ominous, in retrospect, is the metaphor of "transport" used here by Vallat! For Vallat, see especially Marrus and Paxton, *Vichy France and the Jews*, chap. 3. In his trial after the war, Vallat defended himself against charges of collaborating treasonously with the enemy by saying that his antisemitism had nothing to do with the Nazis, but was indigenously French.

6. Paris: Presses Universitaires de France, 1943, 6. The "*dépot légal*" is given as December 31, 1942.

7. *Morceaux Choisis*, 30–31. In Iris Barry's translation of the book, explicit references to the Jews fall away, and Poland is substituted for Hungary: "Itinerant carpet vendors, strange men from Poland and Rumania, adventurers of every sort who had already gained partial control of the cinema. . . . " *The History of Motion Pictures* (New York: Norton, 1938), 374. The impressive side of Bardèche and Brasillach is that they are candid about the mediocrity of most film production and insist that it is an independent art that must develop its own aesthetic. They regret the passing of the silent movies and a highly stylized visual poetry.

8. Charles Maurras, *La seule France* (Lyon: H. Lardanchet, 1941), 197 and 198.

9. *Nuremberg, ou, La Terre Promise* (Paris: Sept Couleurs, 1948), 188–90 (my translation). One can set beside this Paul Claudel's article "Les morts de la déportation" in *Le Figaro* of May 3, 1952, addressed to the Grand Rabbin of Paris. Referring to the State of Israel, asking it "to associate itself officially with the mourning of offended humanity," Claudel writes: "Ses morts sont les nôtres et les nôtres sont les siens."

10. Jeffrey Mehlman in *Legacies: Of Antisemitism in France* (Minneapolis: University of Minnesota Press, 1983) shows the latency of this murderous nostalgia in Giraudoux and other classical authors of modern French literature.

Six

The Cinema Animal
On Spielberg's *Schindler's List*

As a film that conveys to the public at large the horror of the extermination, *Schindler's List* is entirely successful. The mass scenes are heart-rending: the liquidation of the ghetto, the enticement and deportation of the children from the camp, the mothers rushing the convoy, and later, the exhumation and burning of the bodies (a scene from hell). The scale is deliberately varied: from the brilliant opening, matching the smoke of the extinguished candle and the smoke of the locomotive, to Schindler's hilltop observation of the exterminating action, to the close-ups in the apartment buildings (the chaos of terror made physically painful to the viewer's eyes by handheld, unsteady cameras, as if the eyes had to be punished for what they could not feel). Then back to the hilltop and the extraordinary glimpse of the little girl in the red coat wandering alongside and apart from the murders and roundups, as if on an ordinary kind of walk. Then the heartbreaking effort of the boy to find a hiding place, ending in the sewer. The sheer assault on the lifeworld of the Krakow Jews as well as on their persons could not be rendered more effectively than when the contents of the suitcases are emptied, first at the deportation center, where the spoliation is clear, then during the ghetto's liquidation, when even spoliation ceases to matter, and the contents and then the suitcases are contemptuously thrown over the banisters.

We have learned that technique is never just technique: it retains a responsibility toward the represented subject. This link of responsibility distinguishes Spielberg here. The difference between close-ups and long shots is utilized again and again: uncomfortably but tellingly we sometimes see the action as if through the telescopic sights of Goeth's (the Nazi commander) murderous rifle. The imperative to make everything *visible* is not modified by such distancing; rather, the viewers' eyes are more fully implicated. We are made aware of our silent and detached glance as spectators removed in time and place. Neither the creator of this film nor its viewers can assert, like the chorus in the *Oresteia*: "What happened next I saw not, neither speak it."

Yet, as I realized later, the premium placed on visuality by such a film made me deeply uneasy. To see things that sharply, and from a privileged position, is to see them with the eyes of those who had the power of life and death. There is no convincing attempt to capture a glimpse of the daily suffering in camp or ghetto: the kind of personal and characterizing detail which videotestimony projects record through the "lens" of the survivors' recollections.

Nor is there an attempt to explore the behavior of the main protagonists. Spielberg has been commended for not making Schindler transparent or seeking to illuminate the mystery of his compassion. While we do not need or want an "explanation," both Schindler and Goeth remain stylized figures that fail to transcend the handsome silhouettes of the average Hollywood film. The madness of Goeth is made believable simply by the madness of the war and particularly this war against the Jews; and there is no conversion or turn in Schindler that is expressly highlighted. Seeing the brutal liquidation from the hilltop may have played its part; but it is only when "his" Jews are fated to be sent to Auschwitz that he shifts decisively from making money to spending his money to buy them back. The scene in the cellar between Goeth and Helen Hirsch, and in Goeth's house between Schindler and the drunken camp commander on the subject of power, are psychologically credible, but their frame remains a crude and deadly game of power.

Goeth's offhanded, as if casual murderousness, moreover, especially when he toys with sparing the young boy who has sinned against cleanliness (the neurosis is barely hinted at), can be perversely humanizing. Against our will, we are made to identify with the hope that something in this man is redeemable, and that the boy will be saved.[1] The pathology against the Jews, moreover, is always expressed in actions rather than words, as if no argument or introspection were needed. Only in defense of Schindler, imprisoned for kissing a Jewess, does Goeth trot out some garbage about the spell cast by those women, which betrays his own acted-out fascination with Helen Hirsch. The film's pace remains that of an action movie which tolerates no diversion except to increase suspense: it "clicks" from shot to shot, from scene to scene, with the occasional mechanical failure symbolizing a chance for human feelings to reenter the sequence.

Spielberg is always precise, with a special ability to translate history into scene and synecdoche. Yet his tendency toward stylization is both distancing and disconcerting. The wish to encompass, through the episode of "Schindler's List," the enormity of what happened in Krakow and Plaschow, leads to moments approaching Holocaust kitsch. The SS officer playing the piano during the liquidation of the ghetto, and the "Is it Bach? No, Mozart" comment of the soldiers who hear him, is an unnecessary touch; I feel the same about the scene with the "Schindler women" in the showers at Auschwitz, which is melodramatic and leaves the audience confused (like the terrified prisoners, in that crucial moment of uncertainty, when the lights go out) about the issue of disinfecting showers and gas showers. The episode, however, in which Goeth vaunts that he and his troops are making history, because the Jews who settled in Krakow six centuries ago will have ceased to exist by day's end, is important, and recalls Himmler's Poznan speech.

Poster effects, that make this very much a Hollywood film, will show through even more with the passage of time. While a certain flatness in the characters may be inevitable in a panorama of this kind, and strengthens the mass scenes and "actions" that convey so ferociously Nazi callousness and terror, the focus on Goeth on the one hand and Schindler on the other is too clean, like the killings themselves, which are quick and neat, though always shocking in their coldblooded nature. Two of the three endings of the film are also Hollywood: the farewell scene in the factory is stagey, and Schindler's breakdown (concerning his not having saved enough Jews: had he only sold his car, his gold Nazi pin, etc.) detracts rather than adds; the survivors walking en masse toward the sunset with "Jerusalem the Golden" sung by an angelic offstage chorus (in Israeli showings of the film, I understand the song was changed to "Eli, Eli"), while giving a certain comfort after all those scenes of mass victimization, is again Hollywood or fake Eisenstein. This sentimentality is redeemed only by the final sequence: it takes us out of docudrama, and presents the survivors, the Schindler remnant, together with the actors who played them, as they place a ritual pebble on Schindler's tombstone in the Jerusalem graveyard.

Claude Lanzmann takes a radical position in a comment on *Schindler's List*, writing that the Holocaust, "is above all unique in that it erects a ring of fire around itself. . . . Fiction is a transgression. I deeply believe that there are some things that cannot and should not be represented."[2] I too believe in the possibility of reticence: that there are things that should not be represented. Yet because our modern technical expertise is such that simulacra can be provided for almost any experience, however extreme, it is more today a question of *should not* rather than *cannot*. What should not be represented remains a moral decision; a choice that does not have to be aggravated by a quasi-theological dogma with the force of the Second Commandment.

It is true that the more violence I see on the screen, through real-time reporting or fictional re-creation (all history sooner or later returns as film, to use Anton Kaes's phrase), the more I rediscover the wisdom of a classical poetics that limited direct representations of violence or suffering, especially on the stage, and developed instead a powerful language of witness or indirect disclosure. The idiom of violence should not be routinized and become, as so often in the movies, an expectation, even a default setting. Though genius may breach any decorum and overcome our abhorrence, as Shakespeare does when he shows Gloucester's blinding on stage, it is clear that repeated depictions of *to pathos*, as Aristotle names those bloody scenes, will desensitize rather than shock, especially when art enters the era of mechanical reproduction. The Rodney King tape, shown over and over again, turns into an icon, a barely expressive metonymy.

In short, Spielberg's version of *Schindler's List* can be faulted on two counts. One is that it is not realistic enough. It still compromises with Hollywood's stylishness in the way it structures everything by large salvational or murderous acts. The stylishness, in fact, leads often to stereotype and visual cliché. But the second is that the very cruelty and sensationalism of the event, reconstructed through a spectacular medium, exerts a magnetic spell that alone seems able to convey the magnitude of the evil. Viewers of this powerful film are surely troubled by the question that Adorno has renewed concerning the pleasure we take in tragedy; or they may wonder how its spell, so close to voyeurism, could have been modified. The "ineluctable modality of the visual," with its evacuation of inwardness, fixates imagination more than the formulas of oral tradition. Artists have always, in one way or another, rebelled against the tyranny of the eye.[3]

A self-conscious commentary intruded into such a movie is no solution: it would merely have weakened its grip as docudrama, or postmodernized the film. Spielberg has created a fact on the screen, and the moral challenge passes to the viewers. Can we, either during the movie, or as those images recall themselves in the mind, become like the Percivale of legend, who must decide what to ask or not to ask of an extraordinary sight? There is no guarantee, of course, that the questions we ask—not only about how the Holocaust could have happened, but what is to be done now that it has happened—will be redemptive.

In the debate about this film the major issue becomes: What are the characteristics of an authentic depiction of the Shoah? "Authentic" is a heartfelt, yet slippery word. I will have to rephrase the question: How should we value a graphic, cinematic realism of Spielberg's kind, seemingly unconscious of itself (that it remains a fiction of the real) and which elides (except for the last scene) the passage of time and the relation of memory to reality?

To answer this question I seek the help of two other well-known films about the Holocaust. Claude Lanzmann in *Shoah* rejects all archival images or simulacra: he keeps the film in the present, the time of composition, reuniting survivors and the original (now deceptively peaceful) scene of their suffering. He animates that scene by an action of the survivors' own memory, and even—as in the case of Bomba, the Auschwitz barber—by using props to assist a painful return of the past. In this radical and principled work, the presence of the past is evoked primarily through human speech, through testimony; and so the film is anything but archival, or a historical simulacrum.

Lanzmann too is very much, in his presence, a part of this present. His questioning can become, not just with the perpetrators but also with the victims, a pressured interrogation. Occasionally this creates a problem. For he does not appear to be all that interested in the survivors' life or afterlife: the way their daily reality is still affected by a traumatic past. Instead, with relentless directorial insistence, he recovers and communicates every detail of *how* the "Final Solution" was implemented, every aspect of the death-machinery's working, of the technological Mammon that demands its sacrifice. That is the "reality" he brings home in all its technical and bureaucratic efficiency. Stunning, disconcerting, obsessive, and either hypnotic or tedious, *Shoah* is a film that does not entirely spare Lanzmann himself, who is shown to be—in the service of his cause—ironic, manipulative, and anything but likeable. To his credit, however, he does not seek to explain the obscene facts by a Marxist or any other thesis. "There is no Why here," he quotes (in a later comment on the film) a concentration camp guard's welcome, recorded by Primo Levi.

In Haim Gouri's trilogy that opens with *The Eighty-First Blow*, precisely what Lanzmann rejects is the very base of the representation. Reality is depicted exclusively through archival images. But individual memory does enter, through the voice-over of survivors who comment on the events—a tangle of voices with its own richness and variation, and in no simple way subordinated to the photomontage. These images and voices have to speak for themselves: though sequenced, there is no other effort to bring them into compositional time, which Lanzmann never departs from. Yet the director's didactic if invisible hand remains palpable. In *Flames in the Ashes*,

The Cinema Animal

for example, the part of Gouri's trilogy that deals with resistance, the issue of why Jews did not put up more fight is "answered" by footage of defeated Russian soldiers, columns of them stretching to the horizon in an endless line, utterly dejected, guarded by very few Germans, and scrambling abjectly, like animals, for cigarette butts or food.

Neither Gouri's nor Lanzmann's films are *primarily* about memory in its relation to reality. Although Lanzmann composes his film as an oral history, his interviews are used to reconstruct exhaustively and exclusively one aspect only—the most terrible one—of the Shoah: its end-phase, the "Final Solution," together with the technology and temperament that made it possible. Gouri's focus is more varied, less obsessive, but he must compose the visual track mainly in the "idiom" of the perpetrators, since most of the photos at his disposal (especially in *Flames in the Ashes*) were made by the Nazis themselves for propaganda or documentation.[4]

The very format of voice-over adopted in Gouri's trilogy is reminiscent of newsreels shown in the old movie theaters. Goebbels's propaganda machine exploited the format blatantly in such films as *Der Ewige Jude*. But in Gouri the excited and triumphant monologue of the announcer has given way to a spirited montage of voices. His documentary gains its integrity from the fact that it invents or reconstructs nothing. It struggles, rather, with a mass of received materials: utterances, images, musical score.[5] They are all "clichés." Gouri is symphonic, a conductor rather than a director; and though his emphasis remains on reportage, the structural gap between visual footage and voice-over makes the film both less unified in its realism and more interesting from a formal point of view. A picture, here, is not worth a thousand words but *requires* these words (the voices of the survivors, in their timbre as well as their message) to humanize it, to rescue it from voyeuristic hypnosis.

Yet Gouri never develops his technique in order to portray memory as either its own place, evolving its own stories or symbols, or in a competitive situation. The relation of cinematic image to voice-over (*voix-off*, the French say) is not problematized as in Alain Resnais's and Marguerite Duras's *Hiroshima, Mon Amour*. Different lifeworlds—that of the Japanese man and the French woman, that of the aftermath of the atomic bomb and the aftermath of the Nazi occupation—are juxtaposed in that film; while soundtrack and image are sometimes at odds. Today, as we recede from the original event, and identity—personal or collective—is increasingly based on publicized memories, there is bound to be an ever greater tension between different "cultures." These are now defined by what is rescued from oblivion or singled out for remembrance, by modes of representation, reception, and transmission.

However different their films, both Lanzmann and Gouri avoid an invasive technological gaze. We have become painfully aware of that gaze since Vietnam, Biafra, Somalia, Bosnia, Rwanda.[6] For it is no longer unimaginable that some of the terrible scenes reconstructed by Spielberg might have been filmed in real time—as if that present were our present—and piped almost simultaneously into our homes.[7] Those who watch *Schindler's List*, therefore, face the dilemma I have already mentioned. How do we respond to such sights? In our very impotence, do we protest and turn away, or find some other defense? Have we no choice but to demand that these representations be labeled unpresentable? How can we morally accommodate the fact that "what others suffer, we behold"?[8]

Schindler's List has not only achieved popular acclaim but is being prepared for widespread use in the schools. This suggests that all my reservations and questions have missed a very basic point: as the Greeks (though not the Hebrews) maintained, a clear picture of what is feared can moderate that fear. It may be fundamentally affirming to "sing in the face of the object" (Wallace Stevens) as Spielberg incredibly seeks to do.

Yet even Spielberg cannot pass beyond the limits of realism. Though there is a bona fide attempt to follow the facts and to be accurate about the Jewish milieu depicted (how much his errors or compromises detract from the overall picture will remain in dispute), so much in the movie is structured like a fiction, so much is like other action films, though based on documented history, that the blurring between history and fiction never leaves us free from an interior voice that murmurs: "It is (only) a film." This happens not simply when the film is most vulnerable—when it is not about the Holocaust at all but stages a homoerotic psychodrama, scenes of tense mutual jockeying between Goeth and Schindler—but also when episodes like the liquidation of the ghetto force us into a defensive mode by the sheer representational power displayed. Visual realism can induce an "unreality effect." Hans Jonas is reported to have said that "At Auschwitz more was real than is possible."

Though Spielberg's gaze seems to me problematic, we should explore the questions it raises. And while I prefer Gouri's and Lanzmann's alternate modes of representation, almost the obverse of each other and more respectful than Spielberg of the action of memory and the issue of presentability, there is no need to insist dogmatically on a single type of "realistic" depiction. I want to describe briefly other exemplary modes, especially those that respect the action of memory.

In the case of Aharon Appelfeld (whose novels have not yet been filmed) memory is an absent presence. We are made to feel the scorching flame that animates his characters but we never see it consciously displayed as a haunting or unbearable force. We know something has displaced their life or basic trust or vital faith, yet memory's "fire," as Appelfeld calls it, is subject to a perpetual curfew.

His novels stand out, in fact, for not singing in the face of the object; he does not describe the Shoah directly, only the before and after. The survivor is often his theme, but not the specificity of Holocaust memory. He refuses the slightest hint of melodrama, focusing instead on the daily life of human beings who have difficulty living in this world after what they have gone through, yet cannot escape into political or religious mysticism. They want to do something with a life, their life, that was spared, but continue to feel guilty and out of focus.

Like Helga in *The Healer*, there is always a sick person who seems to take on herself the symptoms of an obscure illness; but that illness is intermittent, cut across by an extraordinary earthiness and a horizon where that earthiness is not opposed to faith. Yet there has been a fatal separation between faith and feeling, orthodoxy and assimilation. Jewish emancipation has not fulfilled Jewish needs. If we ask, given his characters' lack of orientation, where are they going, it is tempting to answer with Novalis: "Immer nach Hause," "Always home." That underlying nostalgia is too close to a death-drive.

A sense of spiritual waste emanates from Appelfeld's stories, exacerbated by the shiftless biological energy his characters display, and by strong, though discontinuous moments of physical pleasure in nature, in just being alive. There is no purposeful dying but also no rebirth. Yet it is rebirth that is at the horizon of all this aimless wandering. The irony in many Appelfeld novels, from *Age of Wonders* and *Badenheim* on, is that a post-traumatic condition, which requires no extreme effects of art to represent it, begins to resemble the human condition as a whole. So the insouciance or innocence of his assimilated Jewish characters (a trait that makes them sleepwalkers in an increasingly hostile environment) is not unlike that of camp inmates who have passed through the worst. Both groups display a hypnotic alertness, where everything is registered by the senses yet meaning and affect seem rarely to get through. A movie in their mind (which we cannot see) makes the survivors wander about restlessly, up and down, back and forth, ever wakeful though wishing to sleep it off. In the case of the assimilated, pre-Holocaust Jews, the restlessness seems to come from a haunting lack of memory: they are described as "ego floating on the surface of consciousness." For both groups, then, getting away from the past, its fullness or emptiness, is not enough: they crave a distraction—even an ecstasy—as deep as nature itself, or an anti-selfconsciousness principle as subsuming as art.

Often, therefore, Appelfeld evokes a magical but recuperative sleep, midway between amnesia and gestation. Of the youngsters who finally reached Israel, he writes: "After years of wandering and suffering, the Land of Israel seemed like a broad, soothing domain, drawing us into deep sleep. Indeed, this was our desire: to sleep, to sleep for years, to forget ourselves and be reborn."[9] An extended psychic absence is the necessary prelude for healing, for a rebirth that has a distinctly aesthetic dimension, in that empathy returns to what was previously merely observed.

"We must transmit memory," Appelfeld has written, "from the category of history to that of art." A question arises concerning that program: do his novels veil historical memory too much or do they save the specificity of art in an age of brutal realism? The problematic reaches beyond Holocaust-centered representations. A film like Resnais's *Last Year at Marienbad* is distinguished by its deliberate, stylized entanglement with the absence rather than presence of memory—with memory-envy. In its chill and elegant way, it parallels Appelfeld's distancing: a decisive event is presupposed, a virtual *lieu de mémoire* that cannot be brought to life, that refuses to become a living encounter.[10] Yet that there was, once, a place and a time of real encounter continues to exert its seduction. The French classicism of the film is, by way of both the sterile setting and the actors' deportment, a protest against another kind of seduction, that of contemporary realism. At the same time, it succeeds in starkly shifting the focus to a man and a woman who must perform their minuet with little to help them except a memory that is more unreal than real: memory here remains the mistress of illusions.

In a similar yet also startlingly different way, the German filmmaker Alexander Kluge refuses to allow the "forces of the present"—our programmatic realism—"to do away with the past and to put limits on the future."

The Cinema Animal

His movies come to terms with the past and its continuing pressure by incorporating images of ruined or deserted Nazi architecture. These negative *lieux de mémoire*, once glorified by Nazi films, serve as a reminder of the "eternity of yesterday." Symptoms of a fatal collective dream that has not really passed away, they play on in the *Kinotier*, the "cinema animal" (Kluge's phrase) we have become.[11]

What is to be done with that cinema animal: how can it be nurtured, but also trained? Memory and technology have become correlative themes. If, by a new fatality, everything returns as film, then not only is the present endangered as a site of experience, but also the past. The Soviet joke that "the past is even less predictable than the future" takes on a broader significance, one that encompasses us too. The authenticity of past and present are imperiled not only by Enlightenment philosophies of progress, which elide everything for the sake of the future, nor just by the selfishness of each Now Generation, but also by a subversive knowledge that information technology can infiltrate and mediate everything, so that our search for authentic or unmediated experience becomes both more crucial and desperate.[12]

That context strengthens the importance of a new genre of representation, the videotestimony, which is cinematic and counter-cinematic at the same time. Formally, videotestimonies make a double claim: they convey "I was there," but also "I am here"—here to tell you about it, to take that responsibility despite trauma and pain, despite the divide between present and past. The "I am here" is the present aware of the past but not seeking its grounding there—for it finds not a ground but a destabilizing abyss, a murderous ditch like the one victims were forced to dig for their own corpses. Thus the position of the Holocaust survivor expresses a much more difficult juxtaposition of temporalities than past and present. In the survivor, aware of new generations, aware of his own decimated community, truth and transmissibility enter into conflict. Some such tension has always existed: Gershom Scholem senses it in the veiled procedures of the mystic, and Walter Benjamin in the peculiar world of Kafka's imagination. But this time we know from photos, from film, from documents, very precisely what happened, and what makes the story so difficult to tell. The chilling facts, however, are not the only thing the witnesses seek to give, or what we want from them. Rather, their "I am here" balances the "I was there" and recalls the humanity of the victim who has to survive survival. There was life in death then, there is death in life now: how is that chiasmus to be honestly recorded?

It is here that technology both helps and hinders, and we see a new genre emerging. The video-visual medium has its hypnotism, but it becomes clear, when one views the testimonies, that its effect is, in this instance, more semiotic than hypnotic, that the medium both *identifies* and *differentiates* persons who have been through a wasting and dis-identifying experience. Every time we retrieve an oral history in this form, even when, tragically, it tells of Treblinka or Auschwitz, technology helps to undo a technology-induced sameness. For the more fluent we become in transmitting what we call our experience, the more similar and forgettable the experience becomes. What had previously to pass through the resistant channels of tradition is now mediated by a superconductive technical process that seems to promise absence of friction and equal time (equal light) for everyone. Hence a subversive feeling about the interchangeability and replication of experiences—a replication implicit in the technological means of their transmission.[13]

Testimonies are, as a genre, not limited to recording witnesses of the Holocaust: "testimonial video" is a more general contemporary phenomenon that links memory and technology in order to rouse our conscience and prevent oblivion. But the relation between memory and technology is especially problematic when the experience to be transmitted is traumatic. As I have indicated, the more technically adept we are in communicating what we call our experience, the more forgettable the latter becomes: more interchangeable and easily simulated. Yet Holocaust testimony, in particular, uses video to counter a video-inspired amnesia. A homeopathic form of representation is being developed.

While not exempt from error and unconscious fabulation (especially forty and more years after the events), these audiovisual documents allow occasional spontaneous access to the resurgence of memory as well as to significant *details* of daily life and death, which history as *histoire événementielle* displaces or passes by. Memory is allowed its own space, its own flow, when the interview is conducted in a social and non-confrontational way, when the attempt to bring memories of the past into the present does not seek to elide a newer present—the milieu in which the recordings took place. Since the period in which they will be viewed is not the period in which they were recorded, just as the period of recording is not the time of the original experience—a pattern challenged by "real-time" video, or "The Assault of the Present on the Rest of Time"—a temporal complexity is created very close to the dimensionality of thought itself, and which undermines the attempt to simulate closure, or any kind of eternity-structure.[14]

Let me give an example of that temporal complexity, inseparable from the rhythm of memory when expressed in words. In one of the Yale video-testimonies a woman tries to describe her state of confusion during a Nazi "action." She wraps her baby in a coat, so that it appears to be a bundle, and tries to smuggle it by a German guard who is directing the Jews to left or right. She says she holds the bundle on her left side, thinking she will rescue it that way; but that memory is already a confusion, showing the strain she was under in making choices. As she passes the guard, the baby, who is choking, makes a sound; the guard summons her back, and asks for "the bundle."

At that point in her story she utters a "Now," and creates a distinct pause. It is as if by that "Now" she were not only steeling herself to speak about what happened next, but seeking to recapture, within the narrative, the time for thought denied her in the rushed and crucial moments of what she had lived through. She goes on to describe her traumatic separation from the baby: she wasn't all there, she claims, or she was numb, or perhaps, she implies, she is imagining she had a baby—perhaps she has always been alone. Even Jack, her husband, she says, later on—slipping to another now-time as the camera pans to him (and for a moment we think she is saying that even with Jack she has remained alone)—even Jack didn't know her story, which she revealed to him only recently, though he too is a survivor. When, just before this moment, she admits she gave the officer the baby, she does not say "the baby" but "the bundle" (a natural metaphor, sad and distancing, yet still affectionate, perhaps a Yiddishism, the "Paeckel"): "He stretched out his arms I should hand him over the bundle and I hand him over the bundle and this was the last time I had the bundle."[15]

I remember in a shadowy yet haunting way a moment in one of Resnais's films (I believe it was *Muriel*, set in the period of the Algerian war and revelations of torture by certain elements of the French army), when a home movie is inserted, and the muteness of the medium seems to heighten our sense of the mutilation (physical, psychological, or both) inflicted on the woman who is its subject. Emptied of sound those scenes screamed all the more. I also remember them in black and white, and contrasting with the color film; but I may be wrong about that. The crude tape was like a play within a play, and I thought of the mime in *Hamlet*, that serves to catch the conscience of the king. Here as there the irruption of an archaic medium takes us out of the temptation to smooth over or aestheticize what happened. Breaking the frame suggests that a crude form of realism may be closer to the truth than its sophisticated version. Silenced memories live on silently.[16]

That Spielberg shoots in black and white has an archaizing effect and could have been a temporal distancing, but it seems post-color, so rich a tonality is achieved. Spielberg made the right choice; yet the film needed also an *internal* contrast to relieve what I have called its invasive technological gaze and to respect unglossy aspects, the graininess and haltings of memory. So Gouri, at the end of *Flames in the Ashes*, presents an epic array of photos, creased rather than glossy, and in a static flow of images quite unlike the film's erratic though fluent montage up to that point. But Spielberg seems always in a hurry, or in love with mimesis, with the motion and hugeness of a medium that has retained its magic, and which he stages, whatever the subject, for the sake of the child in us—for the children whose murder, though not directly shown, is his most terrible and poignant theme.

It is the child in the adult which remains Spielberg's theme even here: the abused and disabused child. Cinema addresses that sin against the child—not only, as in *Schindler's List*, by terrifying us with pictures of a mass infanticide, but also, in general, by reviving a structural link between the adult memory and the childlike imagination.[17] For our increased ability to recover the past through historical research or psychotherapy is abetted by technology's proficiency with simulacra. Yet Spielberg's art is not primarily retrospective, because the child and the adult differ as "cinema animals."

The child (in us) still learns through wonder; for young people, the past can never catch up with the future, with freedom, with possibility. Who can forget, in Spielberg's *Close Encounters of the Third Kind*, the boy's face when his toys spontaneously light up, start up, come alive? That mixture of innocence and wonder, of an expectant gaze that says "I always knew you were real, you were alive" is unforgettable. Whatever our age, when we enter the cave and become "cinema animals," we also reenter a realm of possibility. Our feelings are freed—even for the sinister subject, for a film like *Schindler's List*, which reconnects them with a knowledge we had desensitized or relegated to footnotes. But the adult, as distinct from the child, is a "cinema animal" also in a more disturbing way.

Now the ability to reproduce simulacra, or to think we *see* memories, to call them up and project them onto the wall of the cave, can make us their prisoner. They are no longer toys, companions, comforters, masks endearing rather than frightening, whose silent smiles or grins disclose, ever so intimately, a mysterious realm. In a society of the spectacle, strong images are what property or the soil is often said to be: a need of the soul. If the incidence of recovered memory seems to have increased dramatically in recent years, it may be that images of violence relayed hourly by the media, as well as widespread publicity on the Holocaust that leads to metaphorical appropriations (Sylvia Plath is a famous case), have popularized the idea of a determining trauma. It is understandable that many might feel a pressure to find within themselves, and for public show, an experience equally decisive and bonding, a sublime or terrible identity mark. The wound of absent memory may be greater than the wound of the memory allegedly recovered, and which, however painful, recalls a lost intensity, a childlike aura.

In a powerful and precise essay, "La mémoire trouée" or "The Memory That is Full of Holes," the French writer Henri Raczymow speaks of a double vacancy that affects his identity as a Jew.[18] There is the loss of traditional Judaism, which Bialik captures in his poem "On the Threshold of the House of Prayer."[19] The Haskalah or Jewish Enlightenment had already created, before the war, a diaspora within the diaspora: many Jews could participate only intellectually and nostalgically in a communal life which, viewed from a threshold that was never crossed, seemed warm and appealing. This loss is made more rather than less acute by the realization that the mourned reality was a sentimental construct, and could not now be expressed except in fiction, or "by sewing scraps together." But the second loss for Raczymow's generation (for the children and grandchildren of the survivors) is what Nadine Fresco has called "the diaspora of ashes": the physical and cultural destruction of Jewish communities, especially in Eastern Europe.

Raczymow, whose family came from Poland, does not seek to impose his sense of an absent or ashen memory on anyone else. But the way he situates himself as a writer helps us to think through the fact that Spielberg too must be situated. There is no universal or omniscient point of view, however objectifying the camera-eye may seem to be. So the brilliance of *Schindler's List* reflects a specifically American kind of optimism. This optimism does not make a statement about human nature (presenting Schindler as a hero need not cancel out Goeth or atrocities never before depicted so vividly) but rather a statement about *film* as a technology of transmission which differs from *writing* as Raczymow conceives it.[20] For Spielberg the screen must be filled up; he brings to life what we know of the documented history—in that sense he does not "recover" memory at all but enables its full transmission as imagery. Raczymow, in contrast, both as a Jew and a writer, lives the paradox of having to express a double void, and becomes, in the words of Maurice Blanchot, "the guardian of an absent meaning":

> My books do not attempt to fill in empty memory. They are not simply part of the struggle against forgetfulness. Rather, I try to present memory *as* empty. I try to restore a non-memory, which by definition cannot be filled in or recovered. In everyone there is an unfillable symbolic void, but for the Ashkenazic Jew born in the diaspora after the war, the symbolic void is coupled with a real one. There is a void in our memory formed by a Poland unkown to us and entirely vanished, and a void in our remembrance of the Holocaust through which we did not live. We cannot even say that we were *almost* deported.[21]

Notes

1. This insidious optimism is reinforced by the structuring theme of the film. J. Hoberman points out in a symposium on *Schindler's List* in the *Village Voice* (March 29, 1994) that Spielberg chose a story in which the meaning of the camps' deadly selection ritual is reversed: "The selection is 'life,' the Nazi turns out to be a good guy. . . . "

2. *Manchester Guardian*, March 3, 1994, 15, translated from *Le Monde*.

3. In this and the next paragraph I anticipate Chapter 10, "Holocaust Testimony, Art, and Trauma."

4. An exception is footage of the Eichmann trial in Jerusalem, which deeply influenced him (see his *The Man in the Glass Booth*), as well as many of his compatriots.

5. In Alain Resnais's *Night and Fog*, one of the early (1955) if not the earliest attempt to work with archival footage (much of it familiar now, through that film), what one feels most is the dilemma: what can be done, morally, visually, with such atrocious images? In Resnais's "essay," then, scenes appear sometimes too composed, and the recited monologue that serves for voice-over too poetic, even if deliberately so.

6. " . . . this is what the white ones cannot understand when they come with their TV cameras and their aid. They expect to see us weeping. Instead they see us staring at them, without begging, and with a bulging placidity in our eyes." "I opened my eyes for the last time. I saw the cameras on us all. To them, we were the dead. As I passed through the agony of the light, I saw them as the dead, marooned in a world without pity and love." From the *New York Times* op-ed column of January 29, 1993, by Nigerian novelist Ben Okri.

7. According to journalist Richard Schickel, Spielberg said that he "wanted to do more CNN reporting with a camera I could hold in my hand"; he also reportedly told his cast "we're not making a film, we're making a document," *Time* (December 13, 1993): 75.

8. See Terrence des Pres, *Praises and Dispraises*. An unsparing use of archival footage can also, of course, raise that question, as in Resnais's *Night and Fog*. But this seminal movie intended to shock viewers out of their ignorance or indifference. Its assault on the viewer is only modified by an "essayistic" effect, achieved by Resnais's formal virtuosity of composition and Jean Cayrol's voice-over.

9. "The Awakening," in *Holocaust Remembrance: The Shapes of Memory*, 149. Also Appelfeld *Beyond Despair*, introduction and Lecture One. In the case of survivor immigrants to Israel, the "sleep" was induced by a suppression from without as well as a repression from within: Zionist ideology had, on the whole, contempt for Old World Jews and insisted on refashioning them.

10. Appelfeld's American contemporary, Philip Roth, refuses to fast in the French way—which remains quite sumptuous—and does not give up anything of his own art and comic gift, because the Holocaust is not his theme. He manages to endow Anne Frank with an alternate life as Amy Bellette, the focus of Nathan Zuckermann's fantasies in *The Ghost Writer*, just as he transposes Kafka into a Czech refugee who outlived his work and becomes an unknown Hebrew school teacher in New Jersey. See the fine article of Hana Wirth-Nesher, "From Newark to Prague: Roth's Place in the American Jewish Literary Tradition," in *What is Jewish Literature?*, ed. H. Wirth-Nesher (Philadelphia: Jewish Publication Society, 1994).

11. See the presentation of Kluge's thought in "The Assault of the Present on the Rest of Time," *New German Critique* 49 (1990): 11–23.

12. Gertude Koch observes, in the *Village Voice* symposium (March 29, 1994), how even the "realism" of *Schindler's List* is mediated by film history: "he recycled every little slip of film that was made before to produce this film." She thinks Spielberg tricks us into believing—through this "rhetoric" which presents so powerfully what we seem to know or have actually seen before in other Holocaust movies—that it happened exactly like this. But this is a problem with every realistic film, although it can be argued that the stakes here are higher. I prefer to treat this problem as one concerning Spielberg's elision of the perspective of personal memory.

13. Critical thought, therefore, looks for residues of technology in every product, in case the truth has been modified to achieve transmissibility. The era of simulacra is necessarily an era of suspicion. Walter Benjamin is the literary source for these reflections, extended by Guy Desbord and Jean Baudrillard.

14. On testimonial video generally, see Avital Ronell, "Video/Television/Rodney King: Twelve Steps beyond *The Pleasure Principal*," in *differences: A Journal of Feminist Cultural Studies*, 4 (1992): 1–15.

15. Bessie K., Holocaust Testimony (HVT-205), Fortunoff Video Archive for Holocaust Testimonies, Yale University. See also Lawrence L. Langer, *Holocaust Testimonies: The Ruins of Memory* (New Haven: Yale University Press, 1991), 49.

16. Since writing this, I was able to see *Muriel* again. The home movie projected in the film is indeed silent, but it does not show Muriel's torture directly. Bernard (the French soldier who has returned from Algeria) narrates the abuse as a voice-over that accompanies images of the daily life of the soldiers, as they fight or train, mingle with civilians, mug for the camera. A powerful and typical Resnais counterpoint is created between two incompatible memories: a series of harmless images, picture postcards in motion, and a hauntingly absent—fantasized or covered up—reality. It is interesting to recall that this film, subtitled "Le Temps d'un Retour," and with a screenplay by Jean Cayrol, was released ten years after *Night and Fog*.

17. Historians like John Boswell in *The Kindness of Strangers* have begun to document the prevalence of infanticide. They make us aware how deeply the love of children is accompanied by a fear and resentment of them. Deborah Dwork, in *Children with a Star*, records the pain of children caught up in the Holocaust, but also the love that saved them, and establishes the importance of the oral history of child survivors. Judith S. Kestenberg's "International Study of Organized Persecution of Children" is creating an important archive. Finally I might mention Jean-François Lyotard's *Lectures d'enfance*,

The Longest Shadow

which are basically meditations on the *infans*: on the relation in the human being of the mute to the representable, a relation that can never satisfy a haunting "debt" contracted at birth.

18. Originally presented as "Exil, mémoire, transmission," and translated from "La mémoire trouée," *Pardès* 3 (1986): 177–82, as "Memory Shot Through with Holes," in *Yale French Studies* 85 (1994): 98–105.

19. The word "Beit Hamidrash" in Bialik's title means "House of Study" as well as "House of Prayer" and points to an integration which is among the things now lost.

20. The concept of writing, in Raczymow, is certainly influenced not only by the post-war "New Novel" (which he mentions) but by a longer genealogy that includes Mallarmé and Proust. The *cultural* revolt in French literature against realism—and often within it—was more programmatic and consequent than in England and America. Moreover, several important authors, some Jewish, some not—they include Blanchot, Jabès, and Derrida—link the integrity of writing to its "Hebraic" questioning of (realistic) image-making.

21. Raczymow, *Yale French Studies* 85 (1994): 104.

Seven

Public Memory
and Its Discontents

I want to raise the issue of how to focus public memory on traumatic experiences like war, the Holocaust, or massive violations of human rights. You might think this is not an issue at all; that we are, in fact, too absorbed in such painful matters. I have often heard objections which say that the study of the Holocaust, in particular, is displacing among Jews a learning-tradition two thousand years old. There may be some truth to that charge; it is easy to become fascinated with cruelty and violence, with the mystery of such extreme inhumanity. But we cannot turn away from the world in which this happened; and the question of what impedes our focus is complicated by the very efficiency of modern media, their realism and representational scope.

The substantial effects of film and telecommunications are having their impact. An "information sickness," caused by the speed and quantity of what impinges on us, and abetted by machines we have invented that generate endless arrays, threatens to overwhelm personal memory. The individual, we complain, cannot "process" all this information, this incoming flak: public and personal experience are not being moved closer together but further apart. The arts, it used to be said, aspire to the condition of music; now the "total flow" of video seems to dominate. Can public memory still be called memory, when it is increasingly alienated from personal and active recall?

Among the symptoms of this malady of our age are philosophic discussions about the existence or nonexistence of a "post-humanist subject," a conference on "The Uses of Oblivion," and the fear, openly expressed, that "our past will have no future in our future" (David Rieff). Even as our senses are routinely besieged, the imagination, traditionally defined as a power that restores a kind of presence to absent things, has its work taken away, and is in danger of imitating media sensationalism. It becomes, as Wallace Stevens said, a violence from within pressing against the violence from outside. In the midst of an unprecedented realism in fiction and the public media, there is reason to worry about a desensitizing trend, one that keeps raising the threshold at which we begin to respond.

How do we keep our sensitivity alive, when such vivid and painful events become our daily fare? How do we prevent denial or indifference from taking over? We have known for a long time that there is great suffering in the world, suffering impossible to justify. Such knowledge must have been with us at least since the Book of Job was written. But we also know from the time of Job's so-called friends to that of Holocaust negationists, that suffering is explained or rationalized against all odds.

Today we have entered a new period. Until recently, perhaps until news from Bosnia reached the screen, we clutched at the hope that had the indifferent masses in Germany or America known what was going on in the concentration camps, known with the same graphic detail communicated today by TV, surely the atrocities could not have continued. There would have been an outcry of the popular conscience and so much protest that the Holocaust would have had to stop.[1]

Yet right now we are learning a new truth about human indifference. As the media make us bystanders of every act of violence and violation, we realize that this indifference or lack of focus was not so incomprehensible after all. For we glimpse a terrible inertia in ourselves and can even find reasons for it. We register the fact that no event is reported without a spin, without an explanatory or talky context that buffers the raw images; and we realize that pictures on TV remain pictures, that a sort of antibody builds up in our response system and prevents total mental disturbance. Even while deploring and condemning the events, we experience what the poet John Keats called "the feel of not to feel it," as we continue with everyday life.

It is not my intent to add to our already considerable sense of guilt or powerlessness. My point is that the media place a demand on us which it is impossible to satisfy. Paradoxically enough, their extended eyes and ears, so important to informed action, also distance the reality of what is perceived. Terrible things, by continuing to be shown, begin to appear matter-of-fact, a natural rather than manmade catastrophe. Zygmunt Bauman has labeled this the "production of moral indifference."[2]

For our sensibility, however compassionate, is not superhuman: it is finite and easily exhausted. Sooner or later coldness sets in, whether we admit to it or not. We remain deeply engaged, however, because official morality does not cultivate that coldness. This is an important difference between our situation and that of Germans under the Nazi regime, so that viewer reaction splits schizophrenically into responding passionately to images of global misery and an exhausted self-distancing. Those images, for all their immediacy, become too often electronic phantoms.[3]

A desensitization of this kind (Robert Lifton calls it "psychic numbing") was already noticed by Wordsworth near the beginning of the Industrial Revolution. He complained in 1800 of a "degrading thirst after outrageous stimulation" which was blunting "the discriminating powers of the mind" and reducing it to "a state of almost savage torpor." People were losing their ability to be moved by ordinary sights and events, by "common life," because of "the great national events which are daily taking place, and the increasing accumulation of men in cities, where the uniformity of their occupations produces a craving for extraordinary incident which the rapid communication of intelligence hourly gratifies."[4] Wordsworth created, in response, a minimalist poetry, a "lyrical" ballad which reduced the narrative or romance interest to near zero, and urged the reader to "find a tale in everything."

Since Wordsworth's time psychic numbing has made considerable progress. The contemporary problem is not Bovaryism or Quixotism— seeing the real world (defensively) with an imagination steeped in romance—but looking at whatever is on the screen as if it were unreal, just an interesting construct or simulation. Actuality is distanced by a larger than life violence and retreats behind all those special effects. While Adorno discerns an "obscene merger of aesthetics and reality," it is not surprising that art historian Robert Rosenblum should defend what he calls Warhol's "deadpan" by claiming that it reflects a "state of moral and emotional anaesthesia which, like it or not, probably tells us more truth about the realities of the modern world than do the rhetorical passions of *Guernica*."[5]

But if the present has now less of a hold, if abstractness and psychic numbing have indeed infected us, how can we remain sensitive to the past, to its reality? Spielberg's *Schindler's List* won its acclaim in part by getting through to us, by lifting that anxiety—though not without deploying spectacular means.

Consider a related problem intensified by the media: whether we can trust appearances. Because our technical power of simulation has increased, but forgetfulness has not decreased—the speed with which events fall into "the dark backward and abysm of time" has, if anything, accelerated—the greatest danger to public memory is *official history*. Even the dead, as Walter Benjamin declared, are not safe from the victors, who consider public memory part of the spoils and do not hesitate to rewrite history . . .

or re-image it. Milan Kundera in the opening episode of *The Book of Laughter and Forgetting* recalls how a discredited Communist leader was airbrushed out of a famous historical photo—so readily is history falsified and public memory deceived.

You may have seen a movie that is set in Argentina under the military dictatorship. It could also have been set in Eastern Europe during the time of Soviet domination. Puenzo's film, *The Official Story*, tells a tragic and typical narrative of public deceit and personal discovery. It is the story of a mother who learns that her adopted child was stolen from a "disappeared" Argentinian woman. At first she does not suspect the truth, but a small doubt punctures the basic trust she has in the system: that doubt grows and grows, the search for the truth grows and grows, until—as also in *Oedipus the King*—a hidden past is revealed. But, tragically, her resolute pursuit of the truth breaks up the family and endangers the child.

What I have described comes close to being a universal kind of plot, as old as the historical record itself. What is the difference, then, between past and present? The contemporary difference can be summed up in a famous phrase of Emerson: "We suspect our instruments." The very means that expose untruth, the verbal or photographic or filmic evidence itself, is tainted by suspicion. All evidence is met by a demystifying discourse or charges of manipulation. The intelligent scrutiny to which we habitually submit appearances becomes a crisis of trust, a lack of confidence in what we are told or shown, *a fear that the world of appearances and the world of propaganda have merged through the power of the media.* To undo this spell and gain true knowledge would then be more tricky than in gnosticism, which distrusted nature and tried to gain a knowledge of the true god behind the god of nature.

What I have argued is that there is a link between epistemology and morality, between how we get to know what we know (through various, including electronic, media) and the moral life we aspire to lead. My account has been rather pessimistic: it implies that the gap between knowledge and ethical action has not grown less wide for us. The pressures to be politically correct, to say and do the right thing, have increased, but neither our thinking nor our actions have adjusted to the challenge so clearly stated by Terrence des Pres, who said that, after the Holocaust, "a new shape of knowing invades the mind," one that opens our eyes—beyond the Holocaust—to the *global extent* of political misery.[6] In a democracy, moreover, and once we are in the electronic age, while there is more realism, there is also the liability that goes with that: a gnawing distrust of public policy and official memory. The free speech that is one of the foundations of truth in the democratic "marketplace of ideas" leads to a continual probing, testing, and even muckraking that has an unexpected effect on the integrity of the public life it was intended to assure.

Indeed, the more that official history is disputed by scholarship or media-journalism, the more an insidious and queasy feeling of unreality grows in us. What are we to do, for example, with all the speculations about Kennedy's assassination that parade as investigative journalism or docudrama? It is as if the political realm, and possibly all of public life, were inauthentic—a mask, a Machiavellian web of continuous deception.[7] This negative insight also undermines the gravity and uniqueness of lived events, and encourages a deep skepticism about the world—or a relentless, compensatory belief in something fundamental and unfalsifiable, a something which often takes the form of nationalistic or religious fanaticism.

My aim in raising this issue of the relation of morality to knowledge in a democratic and electronic age is, frankly, moralistic. I seek to draw some conclusions, not only to describe as clearly as possible a contemporary dilemma. Terrence des Pres, again, states that dilemma with the precision of a proverb: "Thanks to the technological expansion of consciousness, we cannot not know the extent of political torment; and in truth it may be said that *what others suffer, we behold*."[8] The triumph of technology has created two classes which can coexist in the same person: those who suffer, and those who observe that suffering. This fact cannot be touted as moral progress, but there is one gain from it. Given our new eyes for the pain of others, and given that "we cannot not know," all monopolistic claims about suffering no longer make sense.

"What others suffer, we behold" is like a second fall from innocence, a second bite of the fatal apple. It removes all excuse by taking away our ignorance, without at the same time granting us the power to do something decisive. Often, therefore, we fall back on a religious feeling, as President Reagan did at Bitburg, though in his case it served the bottom line of NATO policy. At Bitburg, Mr. Reagan's reconciling memorial perspective equated fallen German soldiers, including Waffen SS, and the civilians they killed, many of them Jewish victims. This "dead" perspective shortcircuits reflection on a torment des Pres called political, because of its manmade rather than inevitable nature.

Even when the politics are not so obvious, skeptical contemporary thought sees them everywhere: in religion, in memory, in art. But that insight too has no activist or redemptive value. It simply confirms des Pres's hellish vision of universal political torment. When we ask, haunted like Tolstoy by such suffering, "What is to be done?" no course of action proposes itself as entirely credible. Rather, the ethical impasse breeds, I have suggested, desperate and manichean solutions, post-Tolstoy fundamentalisms, whether religious or political.[9]

A related reaction is cultural revolution and its instrument, the politicized memory. In flight from human and hermeneutic complexities, this kind of politics saturates everything with ideological content and claims redemptive power for a purified vision of the past. I have previously mentioned the role of official history, promoted by the apparatus of state. It manipulates memory like news.

Now it is true that a war is always going on to modify memory, and we all wage it in ourselves first: who does not remember moments of altering (or rationalizing or shading) experiences painful to self-esteem? When waged publically, however, such warfare leads to an institutionalized and bogus recollection, a churlish denial of the history of others (covering up, for instance, at Theresienstadt and Auschwitz, the Jewish identity of most of the victims), or an artificially inseminated perspective. A single authorized narrative then simplifies not just history but the only *active* communal memory we have, made of such traditional materials as legends, poetry, dances, songs, festivals, and recitations, the sum of which helps to define a "culture," when combined with various interpretive traditions.

Art as a performative medium—art not reduced to official meaning or information—has a chance to transmit *this* inheritance most fully. When art remains accessible it provides a counterforce to manufactured and monolithic memory. Despite its imaginative license, art is often more effective in "embodying" historically specific ideas than the history-writing on which it may draw. Scientific historical research, however essential it is for its negative virtues of rectifying error and denouncing falsification, has no positive resource to lessen grief, endow calamity with meaning, foster a vision of the world, or legitimate new groups.[10] But art remains in touch with or revives traditional materials that satisfy our need for community without repressing individualist performance.

We start indeed with a cultural inheritance, yet that cannot be fixed as immutably as doctrine is in theology. Memorial narratives asserting the identity of nation or group are usually *modern* constructs, a form of anti-memory limiting the subversive or heterogeneous facts. Invented to nationalize consensus by suggesting a uniform and heroic past ("O say, can you see . . . "), they convert "great memories" into political theology. Cults and myths do not go away in modernity; on the contrary, revolution, national rebirth and the drive for political legitimation make blatant ideological use of paradigms from the past. So Marx objected in *The Eighteenth Brumaire* to the French Revolution's historical masquerade: its archaic revival of symbols from the Republican phase of the Roman Empire.[11] This tendency, taken to its extreme, views the culture of a community not as its "nonhereditary memory" but as a pristine essence to be repristinated, a foundation with biological or mystical force that determines history.

What is viable, then, in the notion of collective memory tends to be artistic rather than nationalistic; and unless we keep in mind this link between art and memory—recognized when the Greeks made Mnemosyne the mother of the Muses—national or ethnic politics will reduce culture to a tyrannous and frozen difference, a heroic narrative demanding consent.

A sense of the nation as vital to cultural memory arose in Romanticism. Throughout Europe, artists and scholars tried to free literature from the yoke of "foreign" classics by retrieving (and counterfeiting if necessary!) a native tradition. This literary nationalism was often a reconstruction, motivated by visionary nostalgia. "A people who lose their nationality create a legend to take its place," Edwin Muir wrote about Walter Scott's attempt to carry on a tradition that had lost its continuity. The ideal culture, according to Romantic historicism, was produced by the spirit embodied in a people, a spirit of the folk (*Volksgeist*) which expressed the true, distinctive voice of each nation among the nations.

Collectors and antiquarians hunted for old stories, songs, and ballads: relics of a past now disappearing too quickly, and to which popular or archaic strength was imputed. A lively interest arose for anything regional rather than cosmopolitan: the buzz words were "local attachment," "local romance," even "local superstition." Hence Wordsworth's "Hart-Leap Well," a self-consciously recreated ballad, typical of a return to stories represented as an emanation of particular places—places impressed on the collective memory and still part of the imaginative life of ordinary people.[12]

These legends about place stretch back to the Bible and seem to reflect traces of a popular memory. Being topocentric (subordinating time to place) they also lessen our anxiety that the ancient rapport between singer and audience, or artist and community, may have broken down. "We have no institutions," Alasdair MacIntyre declares, "through which shared stories can be told dramatically or otherwise to the entire political community, assembled together as an audience, no dramatists or other story tellers able to address such an audience. . . . Our audiences are privatized and dispersed, watching television in homes or motel rooms. . . . " This panicky view shows how deep the nostalgia for a collective memory runs. Since it is indeed difficult to humanize modern urban spaces, to invest them with a historically charged sense of place, the picture arises of a storyless modern imagination moving from non-place to non-place, and even enjoying the anonymity of highways, airports, large hotels and shopping malls. It looks as if each sacred memory-place (*lieu de mémoire*) is emptied out to become what Marc Augé defines as a nowhere-place (*non-lieu*).[13] Yet the old myths die hard: Michael Kammen in *Mystic Chords of Memory* notices "the remarkable way in which local events can be conceptualized to conform to paradigms of religious tradition or to the totally secular needs of a modern state struggling for existence."

Before I discuss three recent literary ventures that respond to the challenge of reattaching imagination to the collective memory, or creating a communal story under modern conditions—conditions described in the introductory part of this chapter—let me add a few words to define contemporary *public* memory in its difference from the traditional *collective* memory.

Maurice Halbwachs, killed at Buchenwald, viewed the collective memory as a "living deposit" preserved outside academic or written history. "In general," he writes in his posthumous book, "history begins only at the point where tradition ends, at a moment where social memory is extinguished or decomposes. . . . [T]he need to write the history of a period, a society, even of an individual does not arise until they are already too far removed in the past" for us to find many living witnesses.[14]

Although these lines were probably composed in the 1930s, they already seem dated, for today we feel a need to record everything, even as the event is occurring; and the media not only make this possible but encourage it. It is this nervous effervescence that marks modern experience and the rise of public memory in distinction from collective memory. The loss or subsumption of the past in the present, a present with very little presence beyond the spotlight moment of its occurrence—which wearies itself out of the mind by its violence or is almost immediately displaced by another such moment, sound-bite, or instantly-fading image—this self-consuming present, both real and specious, vivid and always already a trace, is curiously like the collective memory in that it has, to quote the historian Yosef

Public Memory and Its Discontents

Yerushalmi, "not the historicity of the past but its eternal contemporaneity." (Yerushalmi offers the example that in Jewish liturgy the destruction of the First and Second Temples is conflated, as if it were the same *hurban*; and the Holocaust is often assimilated as the third *hurban*.) Of course, public memory is also utterly different: it strikes us as a bad simulacrum, one that, unlike the older type of communal or collective memory, has no stability or *durée*, only a jittery, mobile, perpetually changing yet permanently inscribed status.[15] Hence my opening question on what *could* focus public memory on the traumatic events it is busy recording.

Halbwachs's observation that we are motivated to write things down only when they are in danger of fading entirely can be made relevant to his own project: today the collective memory is in this danger. Doubly so: It is weakened because public memory, with its frantic and uncertain agency, is taking its place; and because a politicized collective memory, claiming a biological or mystical permanence, tries to usurp the living tie between generations.[16]

With this remark we return to literature. One reason literature remains important is that it counteracts the impersonality and instability of public memory, on the one hand, and on the other the determinism and fundamentalism of a collective memory based on identity politics.[17] Literature creates an institution of its own, more personal and focused than public memory yet less monologic than the memorializing fables common to ethnic or nationalist affirmation. At the same time, because today the tie between generations, the "living deposit" or "passé vécu," as Halbwachs calls it, is jeopardized, creative activity is often carried on under the negative sign of an *absent memory* (Ellen Fine) or *mémoire trouée* (Henri Raczymow).[18] A missed encounter is evoked, through a strenuous, even cerebral exercise of the imagination, as if the link between memory and imagination had been lost.

I turn first to Toni Morrison's *Beloved*. Its epigraphs suggest not only a comparison between the political suffering of blacks and Jews but also that the pathos and the covenant have passed to the former. One epigraph is a dedication: "Sixty million and more." The second alludes through a New Testament quote to the concept of the Chosen People: "I will call them my people, which were not my people; and her beloved, which was not beloved" (Romans 9:25).

It is no exaggeration to call *Beloved* that people's *zakhor* ("Remember!"). Where in black history is there something comparable to a genealogy of "begats," or the millennia of myths, chronicles, scriptures, and scriptural interpretations that characterize the collective memory of the Jews? (Concerning the begats, Julius Lester reminds us, on the dedication page of *To Be a Slave*, that "The ancestry of any black American can be traced to a bill of sale and no further. In many instances even that cannot be done," and John Edgar Wideman prefaces *Damballah* with "A Begat Chart" and a "Family Tree.") African American memory remains to be recovered. But more important still, where is *the conviction of being loved that makes memory possible?* What kind of story could have been passed on, or who stayed alive long enough to remember a suffering that destroyed those who might have been tradents, a suffering that allowed no development of person, family or ethnic group? "Anyone Baby Suggs knew, let alone loved, who hadn't run off or been hanged, got rented out, loaned out, bought up, brought back, stored up, mortgaged, won, stolen or seized."

Between Baby Suggs, or Grandma Baby as she is also called, and Beloved, the little girl killed by her mother, there is no growth or normal history or significant genealogy. The child whose life was aborted at less than two years old, and who preternaturally reenters the mother's house as a young woman (now able to talk and carry on conversations of the most affectionate kind), is a ghost from folklore who expresses hauntingly the unlived life, a love that never could come to fulfillment except in this fantasy-form. Morrison's startling use of the *revenant*, the spirit-figure that returns in many a romantic ballad (a genre that itself needed "revival"), challenges us to a suspension of disbelief. Not so much, I would suggest, disbelief affecting the preternatural return of Beloved—for that partly pagan, partly Christian myth has "a foundation in humanity," as Wordsworth would have said—but disbelief concerning the atrocities suffered by African Americans, *that* ghost which we have not entirely faced.

African American history discloses, then, in a novel like Morrison's, a special difficulty concerning its "absent memory." The subject of that history, the black community, is so scattered by suffering, so "disremembered and unaccounted for," that the story to be passed on "is not a story to pass on," and Morrison can only represent it by a ghostly "devil-child," a fantasy-memory of the love or election this people has not known. In search of that reversal of fate, *Beloved* becomes a *Song of Songs*, the Shulammite's scripture.

My second example of absent memory is very different. The postmodern work of art, to which I now turn, cultivates that absence and does not seek to recover the very possibility of memory itself—of "rememory" as Morrison names it. Raymond Federman, for example, tries to do without resonant

Public Memory and Its Discontents

names and local romance in *To Whom It May Concern*, though he too, like Morrison, subverts an unfeeling realism. He uses gimmicks (as he admits) to fight "the imposture of realism, that ugly beast that stands at bay ready to leap in the moment you begin scribbling your fiction." He renounces realism even in a novel that recalls the great roundup and deportation of Jews from Paris in July 1942, and its impact on two children who escaped. His self-defeating venture takes courage from experiments, starting with Sterne and Diderot, which portray life as an infinite detour rather than a punctual drama or epiphany: as something less than heroic, composed of accidents, small gestures, and simple, even insignificant words. Thus the *non-lieu* gains a sort of authenticity. "The grim story of Sarah and her cousin should be told without any mention of time and place. It should happen on a timeless vacant stage without scenery. No names of places. No decor. Nothing. It simply happened, sometime and somewhere."

Federman is indebted to the New Novel that evolved in postwar France, and such films as *Last Year at Marienbad*. They depict memory as a mode of seduction—as a narrative of past encounter suggesting that the human condition is so empty or forgetful, so deprived of sacred space *(lieu de mémoire)* and therefore so needy, that it cannot be redeemed except by the construction and imposition of an imaginary history. This deliberate recourse to a perhaps fictional past returns us, of course, to the province of the collective memory, except that *Marienbad* seeks to erode the latter's historical and nationalist pretensions (the Versailles-like decor in the film is meant to be only that, a decor) in favor of the private, imaginative needs of one man and one woman. Federman, like Resnais or Robbe-Grillet, refuses to give his characters more memory than they have. The wound of an absence remains. In this he speaks for an entire postwar generation that lost parents or relatives, while they themselves missed the brunt of the war. "They suffered from not suffering enough," he writes of his escaped children.

My last example is a genre that in documentaries such as *Eyes on the Prize* or Lanzmann's *Shoah* or the witness-accounts in Yale's Video Archive for Holocaust Testimonies is also oriented toward an "absent memory." Personal testimony has long been a significant part of both religious and secular literature, and is usually considered a type of autobiography. Videotaped oral testimony, however, is partly a creation of modern technology and so has a chance of influencing that environment. As history it seeks to convey information, but as oral witness it is an act of remembrance. And as this spoken and more spontaneous mode, which can be recorded without being written down, it contributes to a group biography through highly individual yet convergent stories. The collective memory thus becomes a collected memory (James Young), at once a private and a public legacy, and through video itself counters video's dispersive flow.

Each testimony is potentially an act of rescue, as the Israeli poet, Haim Gouri, observed when covering the Eichmann trial: a rescue "from the danger of [survivors] being perceived as all alike, all shrouded in the same immense anonymity." Moreover, by recording an experience collectively endured, by allowing anyone in the community a voice—that is, not focusing on an elite—a vernacular and many-voiced dimension is caught.[19] Memory collected this way is too plural and diverse to be politicized or sacralized. But I can characterize the genre of these testimonies best, and the Archive of Conscience they are building, by saying that they accept the *presence* of memory, however painful, rather than its absence.[20]

The amnesia that invades characters in postmodernist fiction (think of the difference between Beckett and Proust), creating a limbo in which the tape of memory starts and crashes, again and again—this amnesia may reflect a public memory that has become primarily space instead of place, anonymous and occupied by impersonal networks of information. As memory, then, it is purely virtual if not absent. In oral testimonies, however, a burdened recollection asserts itself and fashions a complex relation to the rupture between the positivism of historical experience and the symbolic stores of collective memory. Not only do memory's informative and performative (or ritual) functions try to unite again, but time present, in these testimonies, becomes more than a site of loss or nostalgic recuperation: more than the place which reveals that our capacity to experience has diminished, or that the past must be forgotten to be survived.[21]

Even if memory, as Rimbaud said of love, has always to be reinvented, this does not alter the truth that some kinds of memory are better than others. Though Plato suggested that writing would be harmful to recollection, it proved essential for transmitting thought, both in manuscript and print. Writing a thing down meant passing it on, for a communal or generational recipient. But who is the addressee of the new electronic writing, with its capacity for near-instantaneous reception and transmission? Every TV program is implicitly addressed "To Whom It May Concern," which begs the question of who *must* be concerned.

Videotaped oral history is an important compromise, because it comes on the cusp between generations, addresses those still growing up, and at a time when the collective memory is fading into the quasi-timeless, panoramic simultaneity of public memory. From Abel Gance and Walter Benjamin to Jean Baudrillard, this impact of technology on memory-institutions such as art and history has been a subject of intense reflection. I have emphasized the difficulty, moral as well as cognitive, of responding to the images before our eyes in a critical or affective manner when the audio-visual mode becomes ineluctable and bypasses or floods time-bound channels of personal memory.[22]

I have also suggested that there is such a thing as memory-envy. It shows itself in writers who seek to recover an image of their community's past—a past deliberately destroyed by others or which was not allowed to form itself into a heritage. Memory-envy also touches a generation that feels belated: the "generation after" which did not participate directly in a great event that determined their parents' and perhaps grandparents' lives. Memory is lacking in both cases as a basis for the integrity of person or group. At the level of the collective, moreover, memory-envy can take the form of foundation narratives, myths of origin that fortify group identity. Some of these decisive but also imposed identity-fictions must be labeled false memories.

Increasingly, politicized and simplified aspects of the collective memory take over from an actual artistic heritage. We still have the arts, and literature in particular, to recall that each of us is a being made of many beings, and that the heritage of the past is pluralistic and diverse. But as the collective memory weakens, political religions (Eric Voegelin's name for totalitarian regimes) falsify the complexity of the past and cultivate an official story that seeks to reawaken ancient hatreds. This falsified memory, with its foundation myths, or fundamentalist notions of national destiny and ethnic purity, is the enemy. We cannot allow it to masquerade as history, as is happening with the Pamyat movement in Russia, the attempt to rehabilitate Tissot in Slovakia, and nationalistic nostalgia, whether in Bosnia or the Middle East. The outbreak of unreal memory can be fought, but only if younger bystanders, whether artists or scholars, bring testimony of their own, ballads of their own, before our eyes. And only if, like the Carribean poet Derek Walcott, they accept the scarred rather than sacred, the fragmented rather than holistic nature of what he names "epic memory," which has to be recomposed—performed—again and again. For oral tradition, however monumental its aspiration, remains an art of assemblage. To reconstruct "this shipwreck of fragments, these echoes, these shards of a huge tribal vocabulary, these partially remembered customs" needs a special love. "Nothing can be sole or whole / That has not been rent," Yeats's Crazy Jane tells the Bishop. "Break a vase," says Walcott, "and the love that reassembles the fragments is stronger than the love that took its symmetry for granted when it was whole."[23]

Notes

1. The shock factor seemed greater during the Vietnam War, the Biafra famine, and even occasionally before that. In 1941, filmed Japanese atrocities in China, or, in the 1960s, pictures of southern brutality against blacks during the Civil Rights movement, caught the attention of the American public.

2. See Bauman, *Modernity and the Holocaust* (Ithaca: Cornell University Press, 1989). The context of his discussion is Nazi bureaucracy and Hannah Arendt's thesis on the banality of evil. Concerning immediate media coverage of the Bosnian conflict, Slavenka Drakulic asks in the *New Republic* (June 21, 1993): 12: "here they are, generations who have learned at school about concentration camps and factories of death; generations whose parents swear it could never happen again, at least not in Europe, precisely because of the living memory of the recent past. What, then, has all the documentation changed? And what is being changed now by what seems to be the conscious, precise bookkeeping of death?"

3. No wonder many in the younger generation, who are the most susceptible, are drawn to the unreality of fiction, to horror movies and other artificial plots, ever more crude, gothic, and violent: one can pretend that these, at least, are mere fantasy.

4. Preface to *Lyrical Ballads.* Compare Goethe's notation circa August 8, 1797, in his *Reise in die Schweiz*: "Sehr merkwürdig ist mir aufgefallen, wie es eigentlich mit dem Publikum einer grossen Stadt beschaffen ist; es lebt in einem bestaendigen *Tummel von Erwerben und Verzehren*." (It seems to me very peculiar and worthy of notice, the quality of public life in a great city; it is marked by a constant tumult of acquiring and consuming.) (Cf. Wordsworth's famous line, "Getting and spending, we lay waste our powers. . . . ") He goes on to mention, in particular, theater and the inclination of the reading public toward novels and newspapers as the major distractions. These early symptoms of a consumer culture show that, from the outset, sensations are among the commodities being produced and consumed.

5. "Warhol as Art History," in *New Art*, ed. A. Papadakis, et al. (New York: Rizzoli, 1991). Henri Lefebvre's theory of "everydayness" diagnoses a "generalized passivity" that accompanies the increasing uniformity of everyday life (itself a functionalist result of the industrial and electronic revolutions) and is often veiled by the surface of modernity. "News stories and the turbulent affectations of art, fashion and event veil without ever eradicating the everyday blahs. Images, the cinema and television divert the everyday by at times offering up to it its own spectacle, or sometimes the spectacle of the distinctly noneveryday, violence, death, catastrophe, the lives of kings and stars—those who we are led to believe defy everydayness." For Lefebvre, see *Yale French Studies* 73 (1987): 7–11. Or cf. Gianni Vattimo on what he characterizes as a "growing psychological dullness": "Technical reproduction seems to work in exactly the opposite sense to *shock*. In the age of reproduction [the reference is to Walter Benjamin's essay of 1936 on that subject], both the great art of the past and new media products reproducible from their inception, such as cinema, tend to become common objects and consequently less and less well

Public Memory and Its Discontents

defined against the background of intensified communication." Gianni Vattimo, *The Transparent Society*, trans. David Webb (Baltimore: Johns Hopkins University Press, 1992), 47–48.

6. Des Pres, *Praises and Dispraises: Poetry and Politics, the 20th Century* (New York: Penguin, 1989), Prolog.

7. The result of this can also be comic: think of the energy some expend on seeking to prove that Shakespeare was really Francis Bacon or the Earl of Essex, or consider that even children's literature is beginning to exploit this revisionism, as in "The True Story of the Three Little Pigs" by Alexander T. Wolf.

8. *Praises and Dispraises*, Prolog (my emphasis). That which "we cannot not know" is "the real," according to Henry James.

9. Such as blaming the "white devil" or the Jew for the world's suffering, or the notion of an evil empire. One of the few treatises to take up the possibility of ethics in a technological age, Hans Jonas's *Das Prinzip Verantwortung* (Frankfurt a/M: Insel, 1979) argues that our sense of technological power has led to utopian expectations: that it is all too easy to conceive of action on the pattern of technical progress, and that we need, therefore, a new "modesty" as the basis of moral activism: "In view of the quasi-eschatological potential of our technical processes, ignorance about ultimate consequences becomes itself a ground for responsible hesitation—a second-best quality, should wisdom be lacking." In America, at the same time, televangelism spawns its own sublime simplicity: the sinful past can be overcome by turning to a savior figure. The sense of universal suffering conveyed (painfully) by the media is here relieved (painlessly) by the media.

10. Indeed, Jean-François Lyotard defines our "postmodern" condition as "incredulity toward metanarratives" produced by progress in the sciences. There is often a rupture, then, between the increasingly scientific history of the historians and the culture of the community, that is, collective practices structured by group memory. In Judaism this separation from communal ways of remembering becomes painfully clear after the Holocaust. The command *zakhor*, "remember!" that resounds throughout the Bible and Jewish tradition, used to refer to observances that stressed, in Yosef Yerushalmi's words, "not the historicity of the past, but its eternal contemporaneity." Today the same "remember!" documents in volume upon volume a genocide that has weakened Jewish continuity. A form of memorizing rather than remembrance, and information rather than performance oriented, it is very different from the liturgical memory, the collectively recited lamentations, petitions and hymns, or the scripture study, by which Jews as a community healed or at least integrated the catastrophes in their past. Amos Funkenstein reintroduces the notion of "historical consciousness" to show that the split between historical and liturgical memory is not, today or in earlier times, as absolute as Yerushalmi represents it: see "Collective Memory and Historical Consciousness," *History and Memory* 1 (1989): 5–27.

11. Two more contemporary examples. (1) East Germany's foundational cult, centered on the prewar Communist leader Thaelmann. Thaelmann may have been brought to Buchenwald and executed there toward the end of the war. To magnify Buchenwald as the symbol of German resistance to fascism, the East German government identified the cell where he was killed, made it a cavernous shrine and used it to initiate young devotees of the youth movement. The Thaelmann cult excluded all perspectives on the Nazi era except that of heroic Communist revolt, and became a sterile and self-exculpatory "god-term" for East Germany, one that allowed its inhabitants to transfer guilt for fascism and war crimes exclusively to the citizens of the *other* (West) Germany. (2) The rebirth of Israel, as Saul Friedlander and Alan Mintz (among others) have shown, acti-

vated a "paradigm retrieval" which had long ago linked catastrophe and redemption. "The national historian," Funkenstein writes, "who in the nineteenth century enjoyed the status of a priest of culture, and whose work, even professional, was still read by a wide stratum of the educated public . . . even created some of [the symbols], some almost from nothing, such as the legend of Hermann, the victorious Cheruskian hero of early Roman-Germanic encounter." "Collective Memory," 21.

12. The stories often crystallize or cluster around proper names, especially place-names (Hart-Leap Well; Beth-El; Wessex; Balbec; Paris, Texas; Ole Kentucky; Chelm; Homewood). Some of these are fictional places; but such is the power of art that names outlive in our imagination referents they may never have had.

13. Pierre Nora, Les lieux de mémoire: La République. La Nation. (1984-) and Marc Augé, Non-Lieux: Introduction à une anthropologie de la surmodernité (Paris: Seuil, 1992). The conception of non-lieu plays with the legal term by which courts refuse to receive a complaint or nullify its basis in law. Cf. Claude Lanzmann, "Le lieu et la parole," in Les Cahiers du Cinéma, 37 (1985). He describes there how he develops a technique to overcome the "non-lieu de la mémoire." For MacIntyre, see After Virtue: A Study in Moral Theory (Notre Dame: Notre Dame University Press, 1984).

14. La mémoire collective, 2nd ed. (Paris: Presses Universitaires de France, 1968), 68–69. Halbwachs's "collective memory" is a broader concept than "communal memory": no memory, according to Halbwachs (in the wake of Durkheim and Marc Bloch), is purely individual but always depends, to be a memory, on an "affective community" (which need not be religious or ritual). Edward Shils in Tradition (Chicago: Chicago University Press, 1981) makes the case that there is a sense of the past which is inculcated early and which is important as a general "sensibility to past things" as well as for its specific contents.

15. "Commentators on American culture note that a sense of historicity is shifting away from singular stories that are forever true—away from story-lines that are hero-oriented and confrontational. There are fewer authentic moments of 'catastrophe time.' . . . " Don Handelman on "media events," in Models and Mirrors: Toward an Anthropology of Public Events (Cambridge: Cambridge University Press, 1990), 266ff.

16. Jacques Le Goff, in describing the work of Pierre Nora on memory-places, and a new history "which seeks to create a scientific history on the basis of collective memory," does not entirely confront this difference between public and collective memory in his rather optimistic assessment. "[T]he whole evolution of the contemporary world, under the impact of an immediate history for the most part fabricated on the spot by the media, is headed toward the production of an increased number of collective memories, and history is written, much more than in earlier days, under the influence of these collective memories." History and Memory, trans. Steven Rendall and E. Claman (New York: Columbia University Press, 1993), 95.

17. Cf. the description of what J. Assmann names "das kulturelle Gedächtnis," which seeks a stability beyond the saeculum of oral history and the span of Halbwachs's collective memory. "Kollektives Gedächtnis und kulturelle Identität," in Kultur und Gedächtnis, ed. Jan Assmann and Tonio Hölscher (Frankfurt a/M: Suhrkamp, 1988). Funkenstein, "Collective Memory," sees the difference between a purely liturgical memory and a more dynamic, heuristic collective memory emerging in the historical consciousness. The latter, according to him, appears in the hidushim (new insights) of rabbinic (halakhic) law-finding, as well as in literature—but he does not provide us with a conceptualized understanding of the difference between "the liturgical incantations of a dynasty of tribal leaders" and "the poetry of Homer or the Book of Judges."

18. See Ellen S. Fine on post-Holocaust Jewish writers (especially the children of survivors) in "The Absent Memory," *Writing and the Holocaust*, ed. Berel Lang (New York: Holmes & Meier, 1988). Also Nadine Fresco, "Remembering the Unknown," *International Review of Psycho-Analysis*, 11 (1984): 417–27. For Henri Raczymow, see 95–96, above.

19. Videotape adds to that dimension by allowing the recording of "stylistic" and "prosodic" features, such as gestures, visually accented pauses, etc. As in photography generally, more detail previously thought of as incidental or accidental is included. This increases oral history's movement away from *histoire événementielle*.

20. Claude Lanzmann, in "Le lieu et la parole," *Cahiers du Cinéma* (1985), goes so far as to say that his film seeks an "incarnation." "Le souvenir me fait horreur: le souvenir est faible. Le film est l'abolition de toute distance entre le passé et le présent" (374) (Recollection disgusts me: it is so weak. The film aims at the abolition of all distance between the past and the present).

21. I must leave aside, here, the more general issue of the revival, through history or art, of memory-places. For the sensibility, for example, that joins Wordsworth to Milton in understanding memory-place, see *Paradise Lost*, IX, 320–29. In terms of academic transmission the *lieu de mémoire* becomes a "topos"; but the boundary between discourse, on the one hand, and poetry and even living performance, on the other, is quite porous, as was shown by E. R. Curtius's magisterial book on the way the classical tradition reaches modern European literature, and by the famous research of Parry and Lord on the formulaic compositional methods of Yugoslav bards. For Halbwachs's interesting treatment of "Religious Space," see *La mémoire collective*, 145–46 and 160–65. Monuments too are *lieux de mémoire*, involving, like stories, real or legendary places.

22. For Hegel it would have needed the entire history of the world, together with an intellectual odyssey of millennia, before mind is mind, free of its *subservience* to sense-perception, and able to retrieve all its memory-stages in the activity of thought. Meanwhile (i.e., in everyday rather than visionary temporality) interesting makeshift solutions are found. I have mentioned Alexander Kluge; Claude Chabrol's recent *L'oeil de Vichy* (1993) raises the spectator's consciousness of visual dependence by creating a film purely out of archival propaganda images, countered only by a dry historical commentary placing them in context. And Wilfried Schoeller has written: "Every museum, every monument, every memorial site recalling the Nazi era should reserve a moment of discretion, should leave something open and perhaps even claim the status of ruin or artifact, so that the imagination can still be active toward something in it."

23. Walcott, Nobel lecture, "The Antilles: Fragments of Epic Memory," in the *New Republic*, December 28, 1992: 27. However, in emphasizing the performative dimension we need to distinguish between an opportunistic recomposing of the collective memory, motivated by identity politics, and the creative-heuristic use of its traditions in art. Such notions as Schiller's "aesthetic education" may provide a beginning for theorizing that difference. The formalist's deinstrumentalizing emphasis on what is distinctively literary also responds to the need for a critical perspective.

Eight

The Book of the Destruction

The point was not, of course, to produce the biggest and saddest coffee-table book ever. Would it, in any case, have been a book? It is said that a museum, filled with replicas of the vanished life, especially the burnt and plundered temples, also exhibited a Scroll of Fire. Our sages of blessed memory and fertile wit pondered whether that scroll was really a book, and if so what kind of fire had inscribed it. One of them said in the name of a man "from Czernowitz" that it was written in black fire on black milk. Another claimed that it was written with dying embers that could only be seen at night.

> Asche.
> Asche, Asche.
> Nacht.
> Nacht-und-Nacht.

Reb Jabes, son of Jabes, said that the Scroll of Fire was that pillar by which the Blessed and Merciful One redeems the impurity of the night every single dawn. It burned without smoke and turned mourning into morning. But Abel, Kajis, and Ish-Chanit said that in those days history returned and everything was seen again, illumined by a strange cold flame. The pagans Mozart, Napoleon, and Van Gogh, as well as a certain Nazarene, returned that way. Going from light to heavy, even the Haman of that time, may his name and image be erased, would have come back like a vampire whose coffin can never be secured, however many curses nail it shut. Reb Idel taught there was such a book in a form beyond letters; witness the *remez* in Samuel and Joshua to a missing *sefer hayashar.* There surely existed a Book of the Destruction but it was not meant to be found. And to what may this be compared? To a king who made himself sick reading and reading, and decreed that there be no more accounts of the destruction. He appointed seventy elders to draft a single volume, a *sefer hashoah* that would be consecrated in a great convocation and recited to the people. After a year and a day the elders came and said to him: O King, whose mercy is like the rays of the setting sun, we cannot do what you have commanded. You yourself must gather it together, in your wisdom and strength. For we are inspired only by fear and awe, that bring discord rather than unity. The dead cannot praise, but in this matter the living cannot praise either. Such a book would need six hundred thousand margins, one for each soul at Sinai, if the Covenant is to hold in the face of the slaughter. The king answered, like the Holy One that sits and roars when he remembers his children in distress among the nations: You have endured only two watches of the night, come back when you have sat all three. He also said, Names and Testimonies, Testimonies and Names: not praise, not blame, not commentary. In a year and a day the elders appeared once more at the foot of the throne, fearful as a woman on the birthing-stool, and said, O King, whose mercy et cetera, we cannot do as you have decreed. For the names and testimonies stretch to the very end of the world, and whenever we choose one rather than another, or tell the thousands as a single tale, pain mingles with satisfaction. Silence is better: O let not the Accuser snuff the smell of mortal change. Have you not taught us, through the hand of your servant, in the Pirkei Hayim Nizokaim: to wrest pleasure from pain is forbidden, or to throw fodder to Gath and Ashkelon.

My latter-day parable is meant to be more than an expression of reader's insomnia. It is hard to give up the idea that a *Yizkor* or memorial book will emerge with something of biblical strength, one that could be read and understood by all. The very idea of such a book, at the same time, might produce a deceptive sense of totality, throwing into the shadows, even into oblivion, stories, details and unexpected points of view that keep the intellect active and the memory digging. Every ambitious writer, nevertheless, projects a work of that kind, or a poetics leading to it—though the idea of the Great Book is receding, and with it that of a canonical work about the Shoah.

We have been asked to probe the limits of representation of an event that is different in kind or degree from other catastrophic turns of history. I want to insert this topic into the field of literary studies. The question of the limits of representation has been important to poetics. The *genera dicendi* determined the level of style and prescribed what was fitting for each literary kind. Voltaire objected to the phrase the "blanket" of the dark in Shakespeare's *Macbeth* as too low an expression for tragedy. In French neo-classicism, which promoted such limits rigorously, it was as if everything were potentially to be shown at court, in the king's presence. That decorum prevailed as an ideal. Before pursuing a line of inquiry that might seem archaic, let me say a few words about what has happened to the limits of literary representation in the modern era.

Contemporary literature and art have almost total freedom of expression. When rules or norms enter, they do so mainly as a foil, in order to be breached. My first thought, therefore, is that even in the case of the Shoah there are no limits of representation, only limits of conceptualization. Though our technical capacity for depicting the extremest event is in place, it has outstripped the possibility of thinking conceptually or in terms of decorum about those representations, despite the growth of a literary and cultural criticism that wishes to overcome the intelligibility gap. Critical thought is somewhat desperate these days because the representations have multiplied and increasingly assume the force of fact. We are made to run after images (or between them, like the hero of the film *Enemies: A Love Story*), images whose aim seems to be a humiliation of the mind in favor of megareality or megafantasy.

Technique and the increasing gap between representation and conceptualization are of special relevance to the Shoah. Claude Lanzmann repeats Primo Levi's story of an SS man's welcome to KZ prisoners: "Hier ist kein Warum" ("There is no Why here"). Lanzmann himself will not probe the Why in his film, only and relentlessly the How—the how of technique, how exactly it was done, how many were processed, how long it took. Or, what did you know, hear, see, do? His questions avoid the one question that haunts us: Why?[1]

Perhaps the SS man was merely parroting what he had heard directed at himself during his own training. But he had also been compensated for the dismissal of all undisciplined and idle thoughts. For him a new motivation was provided by the *Weltanschauung* or master narrative Hitler promulgated as fundamental; whereas this same world view totally negated the victim's human status and right to live. Even the right to die in a human way: Jews were exterminated like dangerous or diseased animals. One difficulty in interpreting what happened may be related to the expulsion of the Why, which we might be willing, perhaps were willing, to relinquish, but cannot do so after this action of the murderers.

In every realistic depiction of the Shoah, the more it tries to be a raw representation, the more the Why rises up like an unsweet savor. We describe but cannot explain what happened. Could "unrealistic" depictions, then, alleviate the disparity? Is it a certain type of mimesis that troubles us, so that a more abstract or mythical art might escape our discontent—those works, precisely, whose artifice we most admire, or which seem to embody a reflection on representational limits? I could mention Celan, Appelfeld, Fink, Pagis, Grossmann, Ozick, Louis Malle: their art makes us feel there is something that cannot be presented, or—to quote Jean-François Lyotard's definition of the modern project—their technique "presents the fact that the unrepresentable exists."[2] The works I have mentioned release us from the presumption that realism can be absolute.

Yet Lyotard goes further. He does not view the gap between representation and the unpresentable as a defect but as a value. To harmonize them is to transgress a limit. He turns Kant's analytic of the sublime in a new direction. Kant linked the emotion of the sublime to a dynamic conflict between the faculty that conceives and the faculty that "presents": whereas feelings of beauty arise when an object gives pleasure without our having a conceptual understanding of that pleasure, so that we fall back on "taste" to validate it, sublime feelings arise when we conceive, for example, of the absolutely simple or the infinitely great, without being able to find an object or sense-presentation to make them rationally communicable. In the sublime there is at most a "negative presentation," as in Malevich's "white" squares or what is hinted at by the Bible's commandment against graven images. An aesthetics of the sublime, therefore, "will enable us to see only by making it impossible to see; it will please only by causing pain." The postmodern differs from the modern not essentially but by projecting "the unpresentable in presentation itself . . . [it] searches for new presentations, not in order to enjoy them but in order to impart a stronger sense of the unpresentable." According to Lyotard, this brings art and philosophy closer, for it is the business of both "not to supply reality but to invent allusions to the conceivable which cannot be presented" (*The Postmodern Condition*, pp. 79ff).

I want to read Lyotard's emphasis on unrepresentable reality in the specifying context of the Holocaust. He has the courage to attempt a post-Holocaust aesthetics. Usually the aesthetic as a dimension of culture is first to be targeted in moments of crisis or catastrophe: Adorno's "to write poetry after Auschwitz is barbaric" has become notorious. Yet, recontextualizing Lyotard, we can speculate that it is possible to save the aesthetic as an aesthetics of the sublime. The mental blockage characteristic of the Kantian sublime is now said to arise not from a sense of nature's greatness or the idea of an absolute magnitude but from what Saul Friedlander has called the "modes of domination and terror at [the Holocaust's] very core."[3] These modes baffle the mind, not so much as historical realities, for the Final Solution, horrendous as it is, is comparable *at that level* to other large-scale massacres. It is when domination and terror become absolutes, that is, when they are *ideologized* and *totalized*, that we cannot discover in ourselves a possible scenario to explain what happened. We want to say, "It is inconceivable," yet we know it was conceived and acted upon systematically. We continue to harbor, therefore, a sense of improbability, not because there is any doubt whatsoever about the Shoah as fact but because what was lived through, or what we have learned about, cannot be a part of us: the mind rejects it, casts it out—or it casts out the mind. We are forced to admit that something in human behavior is alien to us, yet that it could be species-related. As Habermas has written, "A deep stratum of solidarity between all that bears a human countenance was touched."[4] I will return later to that "human countenance."

The Kantian sublime has a second movement, in which the blocked reason rebounds, and even feels uplift. That would seem impossible here. *This* trauma, even when experienced indirectly, requires a lengthy process of silence, mourning and recuperation. Shoshana Felman describes that process as an "impossible witnessing," and Eric Santner as a disruption of the economy of narrative pleasure. Any elation, then, can only be a nervous reflex: the head still smiling, for the fraction of a moment, after it has been cut off. Yet I will argue, at some risk, that Lyotard's work in this area, as well as our own work as historians, witnesses, writers, is itself *eine Art Schadensabwicklung:* the undoing of a blockage, a necessary *intellectual* response, more like the upbeat movement in the dialectic of the sublime than a nervous tic.

Lyotard's subject, even when his focus is on art, is really political anthropology: the nature of man as political animal and specifically, in the light of the Shoah, the nature of consent. The issue of consent becomes crucial after the Hitler era because our bafflement centers not only on the criminal actions of the regime but also on the deceptive consent of the bystanders (a similar kind of consent was overturned almost fifty years later in eastern Europe), the loyal or statutory consent of the perpetrators (which the courts and research such as Christopher Browning's have probed),[5] and a disabling of the consenting faculty in the victims, the substitution of automatism for autonomy. Lyotard extends to political theory Kant's remarks on the possibility of aesthetic judgment by drawing from the analytic of the sublime a *différend* (between what is conceivable and what is presentable) that always challenges unanimity, or the harmony achieved by eliminating dissent. He adopts, at the same time, Kant's refusal to sideline the issue of taste and art, since a consensus about the aesthetic does not lie beyond or below rational judgment. If the discourse of reason can be maintained in matters of art, there is—precisely through heeding the example of art—a hope for such discourse in politics too.[6]

Yet faith in a consensus achieved by reasoning together is modified by Lyotard's awareness of the limits of reason, an awareness made acute by history itself, where that reason—bureaucratized, instrumentalized—has turned into amoral technology and raison d'état. No wonder he is attracted, like the Frankfurt School, to the Kantian mode of critique rather than to Hegel's totalizing schema. He understands that in the past, and catastrophically in the recent past of the Nazi era, the price exacted for political stability and apparent consensus has been too high. The price was coercion and terror, and the result uniformity.

There are many unusual things about Lyotard's post-Holocaust aesthetics. Not least among them is that the representational limits of postmodern art turn out to be the limits of reason in Kant's aesthetic judgment. We breathe a double sigh of relief: art is reasonable (not irrational, myth-mongering, obscurantist), and art contributes by its *peculiar sublimity* or *différend* to an appropriate political philosophy after the Holocaust. It haunts us, it does not leave our mind, that after the Shoah we need a representation of the "human countenance" that would remove the distortion that countenance has suffered and strengthen its glance. This retrieved humanism is also the high argument of Emmanuel Levinas.

Though such words as *high* and *sublime* have become difficult to use ("No word intoned from on high," Adorno wrote, "not even a theological one, exists rightfully after Auschwitz without a transformation"), the terror of the Shoah required a response which we cannot but depict as heroic. Acts of resistance, whatever their motive, are destined to be part of a monumental narrative. We understand them philosophically as a withholding of consent, as a rejection of the legitimating master narrative of the persecutors. After the fact, then, it is appropriate to ask whether that refusal was based on a narrative of its own, that is, a self-presentation or collective vision that was not fully articulated, but could have been deeply engrained as an ethos. If there was such a narrative, there is an obligation to represent it and keep it from disappearing into a vague sublimity. We need it to shore up our own resolve.

Yet the very fact of its appearing to be heroic given these circumstances, rather than ordinary as it might be in the conduct of daily life, makes us consider the conditions of its possibility. If we recall the self-intoxication of

Nazi oratory, its "elated clichés," we quickly come to the conclusion that a counter-elation would be compromised from the outset. The retrieved narrative cannot be ordinary yet also cannot be sublime in the nazified sense. It is here that an extracanonical representation emerges, suspended between history and memory, suspended also between literature and documentary, whose subject is consistently the daily response to terror, and which provides the lineaments of that sublime yet ordinary story that is a necessity and not an indulgence if we still believe in educating the imagination. I refer to the genre, or rather the collective archive, of survivor testimonies, and I want to say something about its value.

For the survivors of the Holocaust, simply to tell their story is a restitution, however inadequate. Ordering one's life retrospectively brings some mastery, and so relief, to the unmastered portion. Yet that factor is less crucial than something that goes back to the special nature of their agony. In the camps they were systematically deprived of foresight: though they saw all too forcefully what was before their eyes, their ability to discern a normal pattern that could eventually be expressed in the form of a story was disrupted or disabled. Few could hope to make sense of the events, could hope to hope, could link what they had learned in the past to what now befell them. The promise of extending experience from past to future via the coherence of the stories we tell each other, stories that gather as a tradition—that promise was shattered. To remember forward—to transmit a personal story to children and grandchildren and all who should hear it—affirms a desegregation and the survivors' reentry into the human family. The story that links us to their past also links them to our future.

Whether survivor testimonies, especially the less rehearsed, oral kind, create a new text—a narrative representation significantly different—cannot be considered here at length. Lawrence Langer explores that aspect in *Holocaust Testimonies: The Ruins of Memory*, and his book involves the legitimacy of oral documentation as a whole, what sort of value it has as an account of those events. But we do know of shifts in the form of representation over the course of time. One such shift, described by Hayden White, takes us from annals to chronicles; another, less centered on chronology and more on character, has given dreams a language and created a new representation of reality on the basis of Freud. Thus the coherence of many novels, films, and biographies depends today on the explanatory power of dream and flashback. With or without recorded dreams, individual life is often construed like a Freudian dream. Do survivor testimonies signal another shift in the history of representation? If so, have previous shifts been triggered by collective traumatic experiences? How should we classify survivor narratives: what kind of text are we faced with?[7]

Such questions may sound overly scholarly, but their aim is respect for these documents. The memoirs of survivors are sometimes so vivid in their focus on detail, so condensed and overdetermined in their idiom, and so apocalyptic in their imagery, that whether or not we accept them as history they cast a shadow on all previous fiction that claims to depict human existence *in extremis*. Video testimonies are, in addition, countercinematic: a talking head, another talking head, a few awkward questions by an interviewer, are all that appears on screen. No theatricality or stage-managed illusions. Humiliating pictures shot for propaganda purposes by the killers are replaced by oral "photographs" told from the survivors' point of view. They constitute a roll-call of voices and dispel the anonymity of victimage.

The difficulty of seeing these accounts as representations comes only from the fact that they do not, like historical discourse, make the real desirable (if only as an object of knowledge), or the desirable real, in the manner of fictions. What is real here is not desirable; indeed, it is so repugnant that it may affect the will to live on. And what is desirable was once, in the camps, so removed from actuality that even now, recalled in the space of memory, it reveals an attaint that phantomizes the survivors' life and speech.

My long excursus, I am not ashamed to admit, is to assure survivor testimony a place in the Book of the Destruction. But I have not forgotten the question of limits as it affects art after the Holocaust. Even if, like Lyotard, we save aesthetics, and even if we avoid, in art or the discursive genres, a false sublimity, what limits representation of the Shoah is already expressed in survivor testimony as a sense of unreality that affects their past and present life. This question of "reality" is central, and the multiplication of facts in historical discourse or the sheer rate of publication of Holocaust-related films and books will not of itself contribute to belief or to quality of assent. It is not the disbelief of the revisionists alone that should concern us but also a limit of sensibility which surfaces here, and which the archaic rules of poetics I mentioned at the start have tried to respect.

Lyotard's phrase about "the conceivable which cannot be presented" should lead to the question: "Cannot be presented to whom?" In the aftermath of the Shoah silence about the audience is not just a refusal to overspecify. Let us complete his phrase to read "which cannot be presented to a society that considers itself civilized." As Ignacy Schipper wrote from Mai-danek: "Nobody will *want* to believe us, because our disaster is the disaster of the entire civilized world."

Schipper's statement goes beyond acknowledging that we don't like to hear bad news about ourselves. It suggests a disbelief that is strangely sym-metrical with Jewish disbelief of the *good news* that converted Christ's death into a redemptive event. It is now the Christian and "civilized" world that seems to adopt and even mock the Jews' prior disbelief; this turnabout makes Faurisson's proclamation of the "good news" that the gas chambers never existed all the more obscene. But the Holocaust threatens a secular as well as a religious gospel, faith in reason and progress as well as Chris-tianity. It points, in that sense and that sense only, to a religious upheaval. It challenges the credibility of redemptive thinking.

So threatening was the Shoah that disbelief, as I have mentioned, touched the survivors themselves and added to the silence of the world. When speech returns, two phrases stand out in their testimony: "I was there" and "I could not believe what my eyes had seen." The second phrase is not purely rhetorical. Appelfeld writes, "Everything that happened was so gigantic, so inconceivable, that the witness even seemed like a fabricator to himself."[8] The nature of what was experienced and could scarcely be believed needs our attention; it has a similarity to what transpires in Shake-speare's Troilus when he sees before his eyes Cressida's infidelity and is tempted to renounce his eyes rather than give her up. Such trauma leads to a splitting of the image which is like a splitting of identity: we too could say, of our tainted civilization, "This is, and is not, Cressid."

Through film, moreover, one of the high points of technological achieve-ment, the eyes have found a dominant form of representation, and this only increases the conflict between what was seen and what is believable. The thought of a limit to representation comes here from the very fact that through technical progress it *is* possible to provide a mimesis of everything, however extreme. The momentum of film, in fact, goes toward that ex-treme, as if the eyes had compulsively to test their own reality. This com-plicates Holocaust representation in the following manner.

Previously, the limits of representation were linked to social decorum and to the limitations of a particular art medium. So Lessing's *Laocoon* ar-gued that the distortion inflicted by pain on the human form was present-able in the temporal medium of poetry without transgressing art's law of beauty but not in the spatially static medium of statuary and painting. The thought here is not a squeamish one but expresses rather a sense of the vulnerability of civilized life, as if that sense were tied to a canon of physical

The Book of the Destruction

beauty or, more precisely, as if the slightest sign of creatureliness, visible pain, and mortality could puncture—unless framed in the right manner—a dearly achieved complacency. The highest kind of art may "invent allusions" to our damaged life, to our mortality and persistent creaturely condition, but it may not present them as such. Voltaire's comment on Shakespeare's breaches of style points to the danger of a breach in consciousness itself, to a sense of the cosmetic rather than constitutive presence of what passes for civilization. It is possible to say, smugly, that all this neoclassical fuss reflects the density of a defensive psychic structure, and that we no longer avert our eyes that way. But this would be to ignore our persistent averted-ness, even before the Shoah occurred. The neoclassical rules are gone; but their "alienation effect" may have been more realistic than we knew in their estimate of what will move rather than overwhelm or incite disbelief. We rediscover here Aristotle's criterion of probability. That the truth can offend probability is the dilemma of the artist who must follow truth without renouncing art.

It is not frivolous, therefore, to ask for a rethinking of poetics after the Shoah. Although Aristotle's treatise is but a series of notes, one senses in the importance it assigns to tragedy a shift of representational modes obscure in origin yet involving a different balance of human and divine, of human agency and a Dionysian sensibility. It is this shift Nietzsche reconstructs in *The Birth of Tragedy*. Are we living through another shift of this kind, and is it related to the Shoah?

These questions could be considered premature, and they require in any case a new Aristotle. I can but offer sketchy notes of my own. Concerning the continuing relevance of tragedy as a genre, Isaac Deutscher expresses his conviction in "The Jewish Tragedy and the Historian" that the passing of time will not lessen our sense of having been confronted by "a huge and ominous mystery of the degeneration of the human character," one to "forever baffle and terrify mankind." Yet Deutscher allows that "a modern Aeschylus and Sophocles" might cope with it, "on a level different from that of historical interpretation and explanation."[9]

The odds against this rebirth of tragedy are formidable, however, unless an older, pre-Enlightenment attitude returns. Deutscher, resolutely atheistic, won't look in that direction; he covers himself against the imputation of a return to myth or religion by choosing two of the greatest of ancient artists, who somehow transcend the issue of religious belief. Yet a host of questions remain. Did Aeschylus and Sophocles owe their ability to produce tragedies—so powerful that we continue to read and perform them two and a half millennia later—to their art or to their myths? Can we even distinguish between their art and their religious beliefs? Further, if we manage to isolate what enabled them to represent catastrophe, is their method transferable to the Holocaust era? In brief, is it a new or an older type of tragic art we are seeking?

We cannot wait on mystery to resolve mystery. Even should genius arise, it is unlikely to yield the secret of its art. Moreover, the relation of art to audience, which made those ancient tragedies effective public testimony—a contract, as it were, with the collective memory—that relation has changed. The religious matrix, which embedded the Greek tragedies and gave them exposure, no longer prevails. And for any emerging art I do not discern a contemporary audience strong or constant enough to maintain a similar relation. For by pluralizing the curriculum and opening the canon, we have intensified the problem of consensus. Should a great work arise it could not be transmitted without a religious or parareligious reception.

Though I respect Deutscher and the way he has put the question, he is more radical about the limits of historical discourse than he is about art. The issue of whether tragedy can be an adequate interpretation of the events of the Shoah, or whether, to go beyond Deutscher, "the worst returns to laughter" in some new, as yet unrealized, form closer to the grotesque[10]— these are by no means idle questions, yet they do not go to the heart of the matter. Beyond genre, I have suggested, the very rule of probability has suffered a shock, a rule that cannot be relinquished without giving up art's crucial link to verisimilitude: to a mimetic and narratable dimension.

What threatens the mimetic is, to put it bluntly, the infinity of evil glimpsed by our generation, perhaps beyond other generations. Though the Shoah proved finite, and the thousand-year Reich lasted but a dozen years, a limit was dissolved and an abyss reopened. How do we find a bridge over that abyss, a representation more firm than Apollonian form or neoclassical rules? Is there, for example, a "plausible narrative representation" of that evil, in art or historical emplotment?[11] Should we turn to the leprous itch, the epidemic of figures, the disorderly excess of signifier over signified in Shakespeare's carnivalesque drama of errors, or to the opposite strictness of Greek hemistichs in dialogue, verging on the disclosure of unspeakable truth? Or is the mad, postmodern perspectivism of Syberberg the best we can do?

The trouble with infinity of any kind is that it dwarfs response and disables human agency. We feel compelled to demonize it, to divest the monster of human aspect and motivation, to create the stereotype of an evil

The Book of the Destruction

empire. We romance ourselves into a psychically secure and ideologically upright posture, simplifying the representation of evil and the entire issue of mimesis. What is required, however, is a world that still has enough plausibility to represent what was almost destroyed: the trustworthiness of appearances, a consistency between the "human form divine" and what goes on within it, shielded from the eye.

The hurt inflicted on appearances—on a (harmonious) correspondence between outer and inner—is so acute that it leads to a stutter in the representational faculties. That stutter in verbal form is akin to poetry like Celan's, and in visual form it distorts, or simply divorces, features that once were kind. When Wordsworth as a young man hears for the first time the "voice of Woman utter blasphemy" (that is, a prostitute cursing), his reaction describes an ominous breach in the idea of the human, one that opens the possibility of deceptive look-alikes and, since the human form is not radically affected, drives a wedge between outward appearance and inner reality. It is as if the baffled eyes, unable to read the soul from a physical surface, were forced to invent an anti-race or dark double:

> I shuddered, for a barrier seemed at once
> Thrown in, that from humanity divorced
> Humanity, splitting the race of man
> In twain, yet leaving the same outward Form.
> (1850 *Prelude*, 7.388–391)

This troubled, ambivalent moment could breed either a deep compassion or a demonization of the other race. If the sense of evil gets the upper hand, scapegoating becomes inevitable as a way of marking the evil, of making its hidden presence biological and photogenic. The correspondence between inside and outside is saved, but a group is ritually excluded from the human community to bear the stigma of what is evil and markedly inhuman.

The demonization of the Jews by the Nazis was a representation of this kind. Nazi propaganda seized on Wagner's characterization of the Jew as a "plastic demon of decadence." The demon is a shape-shifter, cold, vicious, unchangeable inside, yet on the outside able to mimic (assimilate) any national character or cultured facade. An entire subindustry invaded German education to aid a differentiation that would not have been necessary if Jews had the gross features which caricatured them. The notorious children's book *The Poisonous Mushroom* was based on this same need to identify the "plastic demon" or deceptive look-alike. In short, the designation *Jew* allowed a demonizing solution to the dilemma of distinguishing appearance from "reality" when an overpowering sense of the indistinguishable presence of evil rendered useless ordinary skills of telling good from evil, or what was trustworthy from what was treacherous. The SS became "blade runners," and turned into the very androids from which they thought they were saving mankind.

If I stress visual representations it is because they environ us, and because the critic's search must be to separate kitsch from an authentic imagination of evil in the wake of the Shoah. The proliferation in science fiction of a manichean war against uncanny robotic enemies that no longer wear uniforms but have the metamorphic power to infiltrate as look-alikes may express in new coloration a very ancient fear. The challenge to visual representation, as I have said, does not come in the first place from lack of technique—we are still in the cinematic age and rarely talk about the limits of film—but comes principally from a doubt about the ethics of a certain kind of mimesis, or supermimesis. Just as the historical imagination often substitutes the violence of detail for the violence of violence, so the visual and cinematic imagination tends to save mimesis from a purely "negative presentation" by grotesquing what it touches, or surfeiting our need for clear and distinct identities. Hesiod said that fear of the gods was alleviated by giving them distinct shapes; so too our fear of the evil in human beings is alleviated by marking them like Cain, though not for their protection. Lyotard and also Wallace Stevens would like to believe that art makes things a little harder to see, yet the present, popular exploitation of Holocaust themes suggests instead a repetition of the imaginative and ethical error that defamed the victims.

I began with the statement that there are no limits to representation, only limits to conceptualization, to the intelligibility of the Shoah. Yet when we turned specifically to art a further limit did appear: as the experience of evil explodes into a sense of the infinite presence of evil, a precarious element enters the very act of representation. The material overwhelms art; the rule of probability suffers a shock. Let us say, simply, the human countenance is obscured. What is presented becomes an offense, an aggression, and may arouse such strong defenses that—in a profound way—we do not believe that what we are made to feel and see is part of reality. Even our insistence on the exceptionality of the Shoah may become an isolating maneuver rather than purely and strongly an acknowledgment. Moreover,

The Book of the Destruction

popular representations emerge that are uncomfortably close to fantasies that may have played their part in the genocide. Thus the problem of limits changes. It is not so much the finiteness of intellect as the finiteness of human empathy that comes into view.

Those limits of empathy are always being extended by art yet watched over by the rules of art. In classical tragedy, what Aristotle called *to pathos*, a scene of killing, wounding, and utmost suffering, was usually recited rather than shown. Survivor narratives are recitations of the kind and are far more bearable—despite the extremity of their *pathos*—than a modern sensationalism often bloodier than Jacobean tragedies or the terrible scene in *Lear* where Gloucester's eyes are torn out. Even a nonviolent representation, such as Cordelia's death, could be so painful as to have Dr. Johnson approve changing the ending and having Cordelia revive.

In this testing of the limits of our sensibility Claude Lanzmann's film is a powerful exhibit. *Shoah* blanches all other Holocaust depictions. It is an epic intervention that creates a rupture on the plane of consciousness like that of Auschwitz on the plane of history. By the authority of his art—the film is a judgment on previous art, as well as a documentary—Lanzmann places one issue at the center and marginalizes everything else, even the individual survivors and perpetrators who are made to talk. This single-minded concentration unifies the film but violates the privacy of those interviewed and exhausts the spectators. Primo Levi has written about the "incurable nature of the offense, that spreads like a contagion," affecting all who come in contact, victims as well as victimizers—and in *Shoah* it affects the artist too. The offense in question is not Lanzmann's direction, the obsessive honesty and ruthless irony that override every ordinary notion of decorum. For if the choice is between a precision that is traumatic and an imprecision that is obfuscating, then the choice must be for precision. The offense lies rather in the fact that the film, by a violence of its own, *forces* an act of recall, of anamnesis, from victim and victimizer alike, and forces it, in turn, on the spectator.

The interview genre, of course, as well as the recitational character of survivor testimony and Lanzmann's refusal to use archival footage, spare us from having to watch *to pathos* itself. There is an inbuilt and essential indirectness, despite which a question of limits arises. Is it not too much to have the narrative of extermination placed before our eyes so confrontationally and exclusively? The filmmaker has no interest in other aspects of the witness's life story. What is the purpose, then, of this massive film? The virulent stupidity of those who deny that death camps existed does not justify a production they would reject as they do all other evidence. Nor can the primary purpose be to instruct and move those who have remained ignorant: that goal would not have demanded such an outlay of spirit.

What then is Lanzmann's purpose? Though his film is a significant historical representation, it does not supply reality so much as it supplies art. The subject is hell itself: a state of victimage that had only been fantasized before the Shoah but then (as both Hannah Arendt and George Steiner have remarked) became totally real through the Shoah. And if that is the case, it is not crucial that this hell was "Made in Germany" and a product of Nazi ideology. Rather, it is important historically, but it is not what makes the film an authentic epic. The artistic purpose, which cannot for once be distinguished from the historical, is that reality has displaced fantasy; and this fact, at once terrible and incredible, means that myth and fiction may now have to be devalued to playthings, discarded in the light of their grim fulfillment. The rupture, then, involves story as well as history: the story of hell, of its representations. The unpresentable has been presented. Before Auschwitz we were children in our imagination of evil; after Auschwitz we are no longer children.

This representational shift is like a fall: "We cannot not know," Terrence des Pres wrote. The genocide makes us irreversibly aware of worldwide political torment. "Now a wretchedness of global extent has come into view; the spectacle of man-created suffering is *known*, observed with such constancy that a new shape of knowing invades the mind." Des Pres claims not that the world has changed but that we have changed as knowers, because of this "shift in the means of representation."[12]

Yet in such a world the problem of being a child, or more precisely, remembering that childhood exists, remains. Holocaust museums which try to educate visitors, leading them from relative ignorance to knowledge, must take that problem into account: they may not become, whatever the enormity of the destruction, a chamber of horrors. Lanzmann, as epic artist, has elided the entire issue of pedagogy and audience accommodation: he assaults the averted or childlike in us. Helen K. says in a Yale testimony, "I cannot believe what my eyes have seen," at the point when she describes children lining up to be gassed; "such little children."[13] Irving Greenberg asks whether we can still utter the traditional prayers and not be haunted by an image of the murder of more than a million children. Here is a limit that cannot be removed without psychic danger.

Which does not mean we cannot work effectively with or within this limit. Art has always known this. A picture, story, or poem that allows reflection and interpretation may be more crucial—if the aim is an active rather than

The Book of the Destruction

a passive response—than images that produce only shock and the defenses aroused by *to pathos*. The well-known Nazi photo of a Jewish boy, perhaps eight years old, with his hands in the air before armed German soldiers, is sad and eloquent enough: it can disclose the fact that no difference was made between children and adults in the Final Solution. Or read Günter Grass's *From the Diary of a Snail* and his account of its complex genesis in "What Shall We Tell Our Children?" Or recall Czeslaw Milosz's "Song about Porcelain," in which the poet admits he is moved more by the shards of "Rose-colored cup and saucer / Flowery demi-tasses" in a war-ravaged countryside than by the blackened, devastated field and its fresh graves:

> Of all things broken and lost
> The porcelain troubles me most.[14]

In the Book of the Destruction this lyric too has its place. An equation has formed in the poet's mind between that porcelain, nostalgic detritus of the bourgeois sensibility, decorated with roses, mowers, and shepherds, and the Pastoral as a healing mode of representation. The "small sad cry / Of cups and saucers breaking" suggests both the passing of an entire mode of life and the inadequacy of those fragile symbols. The fear, which I share, and on which I must close, is that what has been broken and lost is the pastoral sensibility itself, that the war and the Shoah have swept it away also. With it may have gone an art of obliquity that Milosz continues uniquely to practice. Our *sefer hashoah* will have to accomplish the impossible: allow the limits of representation to be healing limits, yet not allow them to conceal an event we are obligated to recall and interpret, both to ourselves and those growing up unconscious of its shadow.

Notes

1. Claude Lanzmann, in *Nouvelle Revue de Psychanalyse*, 38 (1988): 263. (In Levi's *Survival in Auschwitz* the context of this episode is a guard who snatches an icicle from the newly arrived and extremely thirsty prisoner.) When Lanzmann, in his film, does ask why of Polish peasants in the scene before the church in Chelmno ("Pourquoi toute cette histoire est arrivée aux Juifs?") the explanation of deicide surfaces collectively.

2. Jean-François Lyotard, *The Postmodern Condition: A Report on Knowledge* (Minneapolis: University of Minnesota Press, 1984), 78. It is interesting that Lyotard cites Diderot's half-fond, half-derogatory phrase, "ma petite technique."

3. Saul Friedlander, in *Writing and the Holocaust*, ed. Berel Lang (New York: Holmes and Meier, 1988), 68.

4. Jürgen Habermas, *Eine Art von Schadensabwicklung* (Frankfurt/Main: Suhrkamp,

1987), 163; in English, *The New Conservatism: Cultural Criticism and the Historians' Debate* (Cambridge, Mass.: MIT Press, 1989).

5. For an authoritative overview of public opinion in Nazi Europe see Michael R. Marrus, *The Holocaust in History* (New York: New American Library, 1989).

6. For Lyotard's most incisive reflections on the differend in relation to Kant and in terms of reasoning, witnessing, and consensus, reflections in which Auschwitz plays a decisive part, see his work of 1983 translated as *The Differend: Phrases in Dispute* (Minneapolis: University of Minnesota Press, 1988).

7. In thinking about the testimonies as representations I have been helped by Hayden White's *Content of the Form: Discourse and Historical Representation* (Baltimore: Johns Hopkins University Press, 1987), esp. chap. 1.

8. Aharon Appelfeld, in *Writing and the Holocaust*, 86. Primo Levi did not begin to write until two years after his release from the camps, at least in part because of that same sense of unreality.

9. See Isaac Deutscher, "The Jewish Tragedy and the Historian," in *The Non-Jewish Jew and Other Essays*, ed. Tamara Deutscher (London: Oxford University Press, 1968).

10. See Terrence des Pres, "Holocaust Laughter?" in *Writing and the Holocaust*, ed. Berel Lang.

11. The question in this form is most sharply posed by Saul Friedlander, especially in "Historical Writing and the Holocaust" in *Writing and the Holocaust*, and "The 'Final Solution': Unease in Interpretation," *History and Memory*, 1, no. 2 (Fall/Winter 1989).

12. Terrence des Pres, *Praises and Dispraises: Poetry and Politics, the Twentieth Century* (New York: Penguin Books, 1988), "Prolog."

13. Fortunoff Video Archive for Holocaust Testimonies HVT-58, Yale University Library.

14. See Czeslaw Milosz, *The Collected Poems, 1931–1987* (New York: Ecco Press, 1988). My attention was drawn to this poem by Robert Pinsky's essay in *Testimony: Contemporary Writers Make the Holocaust Personal*, ed. David Rosenberg (New York: Random House, 1989).

Nine

Learning from Survivors
The Yale Testimony Project

The Fortunoff Video Archive for Holocaust Testimonies at Yale University, founded in 1981, is dedicated to recording the experiences of those who survived the Holocaust and of others not directly persecuted who witnessed aspects of the genocide. Videotaping in England, France, Belgium, Germany, Greece, Yugoslavia, Slovakia, Israel, and Argentina as well as in the U.S., the Yale Video Archive is one of the largest audiovisual efforts of its kind, an "oral testimony" project that had gathered, as of March 1995, 3400 witness accounts. Acknowledging the educational value of television, the Archive is planning for the rest of the 1990s, the last decade in which those who had a direct knowledge of the events of 1933 to 1945 can be recorded.

An important reason for oral testimonies of the Holocaust is to allow survivors to speak for themselves. We should not speak for them; rather, we have a duty to listen and to restore a dialogue with people so marked by their experience that total integration into everyday life is a semblance—though a crucial and comforting semblance. One of the first things we learn from the taped memoir is that the survivor's language has an uncalculated poetry that won't fit in with most poetry as we know it, let alone most prose.[1]

I become aware, that is, how much of a monologue my own talk tends to be, and how important it is to let the voice of others come through. Not only because I am a single person and they, the survivors, are many; not only because, as I have mentioned, their very inarticulateness can be eloquent, affected by the extreme experience they—often for the first time in a public context—recount, but also because we who were not "there" always look for something the survivors cannot offer us. Though as a group survivors undergo the same pressures of mythmaking as we do, or a temptation not to speak the worst, the testimonies in the Yale Video Archive cannot be collectivized: they disconcert us, and alarm even the interviewers. Face to face with that world, it is our search for meaning which is disclosed, as if *we* had to be comforted for what *they* suffered. For us, who were not there, the classical axiom holds that "Nothing human is alien"; for them, "Nothing human is entirely familiar." The sense of the human has always to be restored.

Nor can we rejoice, as modernists have done, in the perspectivism of these witness-accounts; that is, in the interesting difference marking each story off through point of view and resonant detail. For the stories are also disastrously alike, repeating the same trauma, the same catastrophes. The Holocaust history that emerges from these personal accounts does not support the moralizers among us. If we learn anything here it is about life when the search for meaning had to be suspended: we are made to focus on what it was like to exist under conditions in which moral choice was systematically disabled by the persecutors and heroism was rarely possible.[2] That it occurred, as in acts of resistance like the Warsaw Ghetto revolt, is close to miraculous.

The term "oral history" to describe the Video Archive's effort suggests that although what is brought into view are individual testimonies, their purpose remains the documentation of a collective fate, the depiction through converging witness-accounts of a single event unparalleled in its murderous scope and with continuing, far-reaching consequences. Without the vast paper trail, of course, generated by perpetrators whose triumphalism was at once punctilious and absolute—without this mountain of evidence assembled and interpreted by academic historians, we would not be able to construct an adequate picture. Yet it would remain the picture of a self-documenting machine, of bureaucratic memos and orders of the day, of railroad schedules and administrative decrees, tons of masking jargon or "elating clichés" (Hannah Arendt, describing Eichmann's rhetoric). The victims would not be heard and would remain a presence only through humiliating or atrocious photos. Attention would continue to be displaced from them to a fascination with evil, power and indifference—to the enigma of the killers and the bystanders.

We occasionally find in the response of professional historians an attitude which shows commitment, yet is also surprisingly narrow. They say: These memoirs cannot be primary materials for history. For oral history is even less reliable than letters and diaries. Your belated testimonies seem to be spontaneous but are highly mediated: at such distance from the event memory fades or plays tricks or is contaminated by what the survivor has heard or read. When it comes to Holocaust history, moreover, the requirement to be exact is even more important, since slanderers who call themselves revisionists will pick on every discrepancy.

These objections have some validity, and I will return to them. It is important to have eyewitness accounts also closer to the events, and perhaps we will soon have more of them, with Soviet archives being opened. Yet we do not have to accept the opinion that oral and written history must coincide, with the oral part auxiliary to some great Book of Factual Truth. Certainly there are difficulties in remembering particular facts or thoughts as one moves away in time from an event; but may there not be compensations, including that very density or mediatedness of perception which the historian sees as problematic?[3] Obversely, can we be sure that the discourse of written history, so revised and contradictory, sometimes in matters of fact but always when it comes to interpretation, is any less mediated? Because "history" is written by one person, however well-informed, does not mean it has a truth-value transcending the heterogeneous chorus of voices, the being made of many beings, that is so present and alive in literary memoirs or oral documentation.[4] Recently, moreover, the conviction has grown that local knowledge, which speaks from inside a situation rather than from the outside in an objectifying manner, can provide a texture of truth that eludes those who adopt a prematurely unified voice. Research and criticism are best done, as Clifford Geertz, Michael Walzer, and Carol Gilligan have observed, by a "connected critic."

Even if pure spontaneity is an illusion—especially forty to fifty years after the event—it is bad faith to simply substitute the dry tones of the academic historian for the voice of witnesses. Few historians, actually, would deny this: and few non-historians would deny value to a written history that leads us through the mazes of confusing particulars by sifting all sources, including personal memories. We need that conscientious overview called history because, as Thomas Friedman wrote in the *New York Times*, covering the Demjanjuk trial: "The memory of evil, no matter how extreme, has its limits."[5]

Despite these limits, evil is a greater force in etching details on our memory than the good or ordinary life. The details themselves, of course, are by no means all about evil. Some camp inmates, knowing they faced annihilation, made their minds a scroll and recorded everything. Others were highly selective, or the choice of detail was done for them by personal factors that infuse and individualize their testimony. But the general accuracy of recall is astonishing: it has been suggested that in the absence of material remnants of their previous life (such as photos or personal items with associations), survivors treasured each fragment of memory. Deprived, moreover, of funerals and formal rituals, the very pain of their memories might often have become an identity mark important to the work of mourning, and which, necessarily incomplete in the camps, extended itself into the time after liberation.[6]

Oral memoirs, then, do not try to turn survivors into historians but value them as human witnesses to a dehumanizing situation. We cannot allow only images made by the perpetrators to inhabit memory. The records we are gathering intend to "open the book" of the survivor's mind: they are, at once, formal depositions, informal chronicles, expressive memoirs, and testimonies that look toward the establishment of a legacy. In a world increasingly deprived of oral tradition, they keep something of it alive. Those who collect these testimonies form small communities of transmission and help to alleviate the isolation of the survivors, as well as their own.

The distinction, in any case, between oral and written history fades out as we recall that nothing was meant to come from Auschwitz, written or oral. Auschwitz as a negation of Sinai was to be absolute. In its own terrible and unexpected way, however, the universe of the Holocaust did bring together, in a chain of places that were one place, the Jews of the diaspora. They beheld, as one victim put it, a black dawn. "I swear to you, it was not the sun, it was black. . . . "[7] A somber revelation of infamy comes to us still from that attempt to eclipse Sinai. I agree with those who say that to remember after Auschwitz is different from remembering before Auschwitz. Something has changed: we cannot "do history" as usual.

Through personal depositions, in a simple room that is not a courtroom, and heeding the ancient injunction "Thou shalt tell," thousands of survivors and bystanders have refracted the abstraction "six million" back into the fate of one person and then another, of one family and then another. Through this procession of individual testimonies the memory of evil—and sometimes of good—is made to extend its limits. Some barriers or limits remain, of course.

One limit comes from within the individual, whose physical survival had to be followed by a renewed contract with ordinary life, a psychic thrust into the future permitting relief and forgetfulness. Yet a remarkable degree of precision remains, because the memory of evil is first and last the memory of an offense, independent of the massiveness of the injustice suffered. So, at one point, a somber expression falls over the face of a witness, as he describes his schooling, just before his story reveals what causes that change of aspect. Even now, today, the pain of being hit by the teacher for the first time, just because he was a Jew, comes over him. (Jean Améry has described how devastating that "first blow" can be).[8] It is hard for me to forget, on another tape, a sudden ghastly grin as the narrator hesitates, then relates the sudden disappearance, practically overnight, of the entire gypsy population of the camp. The two events, the teacher's blow and the fate of the gypsies, may seem incommensurable, yet that they are not part of a statistical or impersonal narration, that we see the individual change as memory returns, makes them equally unforgettable. We understand better Jean Améry's protest against "the cold storage of history." "[N]o remembering has become a mere memory. . . . Nothing has healed. . . . Where is it decreed that enlightenment must be free of emotion?"[9]

Yet when scars are exposed and emotions are given so direct a representation by a thousand voices, do we not invest that group, and the further thousands each person stands for ("I am my town archive," one of them remarked) with a grim privilege? Is there an assumption, however tacit, that Jewish Holocaust survivors have a monopoly on suffering? And even if there is no such assumption, does the effect of their testimony tend in that direction? I hope not; but here a need for interpretation shows itself because of the immediacy of what is recalled.

There is something too forceful in every confession, irrespective of content. The difference between confession and testimony has still to be defined: I can suggest that the insistence on personal experience in *testimony* is not meant to silence us but to record and value a collectively endured history. The authority of testimony is linked to an immediacy that reinforces rather than displaces what can be generalized. It does not come from the singularity or even extreme character of what was undergone. For injustice has a universal structure: it arouses feelings of sorrow and indignation that can be shared, even when the actual experiences cannot.

Though it is the case that the Nazi-inspired Holocaust was unique in both conception and implementation—it instrumentalized the killing of all the Jews through camps and factories whose formal product was death—this horrible truth simply numbs both intellect and heart. We can respond to death only as we remember life: the livingness of a person, an hour before, or yesterday, how such a one looked, loved, would speak. To view these witnesses on the screen is not to exclude other suffering but to be reminded of every injustice, great or small, that wastes human life.

This point has particular importance because other persecuted groups could come to feel that Jews are seeking to exceptionalize the Holocaust at the expense of their own historical or continuing suffering. Toni Morrison's dedication of her novel *Beloved* to "Sixty Million and more," asks us to recall the sorrows of enslaved African Americans since the Middle Passage, their forced transportation to America in inhuman conditions. So it is crucial to stress that the claim of exceptionality refers to the implementation of an ideology that singled out the Jews for extermination solely because they were Jews. All were to be killed, whether by shooting, gassing, or working them to death—including the children. It is this fact, not numbers, which made the Nazis' war against the Jews an exceptional act of genocide, one we define by the special if inadequate term "the Holocaust."

Negroes, twinned with Jews in Nazi caricatures, were also considered a degenerate race in this sick ideology. Nazi racialism, presented as a science, established a pseudo-hierarchy of races: the Aryans were the masters, while those very low on the scale, Slavs, Negroes, etc., were doomed to be enslaved. The Jews, particularly dangerous because they might "pass," were to be driven out or killed; the conference at Wannsee in January 1942 confirmed and coordinated this policy of extermination.

I have said that the immediacy of these first-person accounts burns through the "cold storage of history." It gives texture to memory or to images that otherwise would have only sentimental or informational impact.[10] The difference between Holocaust and everyday experience remains, but now—as also in the way literature rouses the sympathetic imagination— emotion and empathy accompany knowledge. In fact, these personal narratives, though less shocking and fixating than many photos, could overwhelm viewers or arouse inappropriate defenses. This is especially true of the young: if they feel too vulnerable, if they draw the conclusion, however unconsciously, that their parents' protection is not reliable, they may defensively identify with whoever is more powerful.

Older persons too occasionally betray discomfort. Are you not, they ask, invading the survivor's privacy? The question arises even when it is known that each witness has come forward freely, perhaps after years of hesitation; and that, generally, the only pressure exerted is by the children of survivors who feel testifying is important, both for their parents' sake and the future. Those who express this reservation feel *their* privacy invaded by such intimate and painful recitals.

Why do we not complain about powerful and painful scenes in film, drama, or novel? Are these not equally an invasion of privacy? The reason is simple though not particularly praiseworthy: we fall back on the thought that this is fiction, a maneuver like closing the eyes when we can't look any more, or averting one's face internally. With survivor testimonies that sort of evasion is more difficult. If we wish to know what happened, to be in touch with realities, then we cannot turn away. When that same wish is shown to be hollow or halfhearted, then there is discomfort, even anguish.

Fiction is quite different in its effect. Our awareness of it as mimesis, as a reconstruction or recreation, encourages a more speculative and dialogic attitude: we can criticize, or talk freely with ourselves and others about it. While survivor testimony elicits its own kind of dialogue, it is only partly a dialogue with *us*. The survivors face not only a living audience, or now accept that audience rather than insisting on the intransitive character of their experience. They also face family members and friends who perished: the first book in English of oral documentation of the Holocaust, David P. Boder's interviews of survivors in displaced persons camps soon after the war, bore the title *I Did Not Interview the Dead.*[11]

It is the witnesses who undertake that descent to the dead. Though they address the living frontally, often using warnings and admonishments, they also speak (at some point in the testimony this is usually made explicit) for the dead or in their name. This has its dangers: to go down, as Vergil said, may be easy, but to come up again, *revocare gradum ad auras*, that is the hard task. "I am not among the living, I died in Auschwitz and no one notices it," Charlotte Delbo wrote.[12]

So they remember the dead, remember that they too were in these Houses of the Dead, yet they are not ghosts but truly back here addressing and instructing us. All this I cannot deal with except as it bears on the authenticity of a mode that may have the strength, if anything can have it, to counteract apathy as well as forgetfulness: an apathy that comes from emotional exhaustion but also from the media's false vitalism, or its repeated, competent, routinized and glossy display of extreme situations.

It is important not to sanctify witness accounts but to see them as a representational mode with a special counter-cinematic integrity.[13] When film is used for realistic purposes we remain aware that it is film: a simulacrum, something impersonated, artificial, and with the closure of traditional narratives. Documentaries too have a way of buffering realistic extremes: they are presented, and the narrator's patter induces a kind of distance.[14] Even sensational images—archival footage depicting humiliating parades, deportations, executions, charnel houses—often induce us to create a defense by thinking of all this as "events in the past." The past insulates those anonymous victims. But in video testimonies (or "testimonial video" generally)[15] there is nothing between us and the survivor; nor, when an interview really gets going, between the survivor and his/her recollections. The effect, therefore, can be extraordinarily intimate—it is hard not to cry. Those tears, when they come, are compounded of sorrow and rage: on the one hand, as Primo Levi has described his feeling at the moment of liberation, we would like "to wash our consciences and our memories clean from the foulness that lay upon them"; on the other, "nothing could ever happen good and pure enough to rub out the past . . . [we feel] that the scars of the outrage would remain within us forever, and in the memories of those who saw it, and in the places where it occurred, and in the stories that we should tell. . . . "(*The Reawakening*).

It is this very intimacy, then, as well as condensations or contingencies of recall, and what Lawrence Langer has called a "confusion of tongues"— the clash between the assumptions and vocabulary of the present world of survivor and interviewer and the word-breaking realities of the concentration camp universe[16]—which make each testimony a text in need of interpretation. Students of the arts have learned, moreover, that a degree of identification need not exclude a thoughtful, analytic response. In the classroom especially, given the charged nature of the testimonies, an introduction, a discussion, and a follow-up in the form of readings are appropriate. The reactivated connection between survivors and their experience, which the interview helps to foster, the courage shown by survivors in allowing themselves to recall a living death, should not place a contagious emotional burden on the viewers. Dialogue, not paralysis or secondary trauma, should be the result. Historical knowledge can reenter, and all sorts of hard questions about the How and the Why.

Let me give a single example of how indispensable interpretation is. A Belgian girl finds refuge in a Catholic home, and recalls her excitement when her father visits for the first time since their separation. The incident is so fraught with emotion that she wishes to do more with it in recollection than is possible. The result is a contradiction in the narrative: she tells us that she hid behind the door because she did not know who was coming, and she tells us she hid because she was so happy and wished to surprise her father. The contradiction, surely, is understandable; not only its emotional but also its imaginative side can be acknowledged. Since the dominant fact here is that she is in hiding, doubling the motive shows not only her mixture of fear and expectation but discloses the underlying theme of hiding within hiding.[17] The normal situation (the child jumping out to surprise her father) contrasts with the abnormal circumstances and suggests a deeper withdrawal.

The issue that looms so large in the objection to oral memoirs, especially those recorded some time after the event, is memory's susceptibility to be modified: by later reading, hearsay, or wishful factors. This issue should be faced. Testimony requires vigilance and the kind of methodical wariness we must bear toward all narratives, spontaneous or patently artful. There are always conditions that surround and influence the *prise de parole*.[18] Primo Levi divides the survivors into different classes of witnesses, whose knowledge was limited by their status in the camps or the moral burden of that status. He concludes: "the history of the Lagers has been written almost exclusively by those who, like myself, never fathomed them to the bottom. Those who did so did not return, or their capacity for observation was paralyzed by suffering and incomprehension."[19]

"Human memory," he also writes, "is a marvelous but fallacious instrument." This is the topic sentence of his first chapter in *The Drowned and the Saved*. Levi apologizes for the fact that his book is "drenched" in the "suspect source" of "distant memory." Yet none of this prevents him examining the past with a vigor born of a need for communication contracted in Auschwitz, and which remains with him, even forty years after liberation.[20] Many survivors mention their recurrent fantasy of finding someone to hear them out after liberation—a fantasy that, in most cases, was not satisfied, and led to their silence after an initial outpouring of narratives.

Just as the close study of scribal methods discovered such typical errors as dittography (skipping from a word in one line to the same word in another line, and omitting everything between), we observe parallel though more interesting lapses in the memory-work of oral testimony. Aside from inaccurate names and dates there is the Rashomon effect, possibly caused by the pressure of private associations; there are condensations similar to those described by Freud in dreams; there are colorful mistakes ("I took off my golden ears," says a woman, when she means the earrings that bought her, while in hiding, an egg for her birthday); there are simplifications which can be described as metonymies (every Auschwitz survivor seems to have gone through a selection by Mengele, as if he manned his post 24 hours every day); and there are moments that recur so frequently that they seem to be archetypal, whether literally true or not. Witnesses, for example, often quote a friend or relative who charges them, as the dying

Hamlet does Horatio, to tell his story. This last tendency, in particular, produces a "collective memory," a story typical enough for most to identify with. It is like being shown a group photo taken long ago and seeking to discover oneself in it. One is tempted to say "That's me," even though the image is so dim or different that one cannot be sure.[21]

Survivor testimonies recorded long after the event do not excel in providing *vérités de fait* or positivistic history. They *can* be a source for historical information or confirmation, yet their real strength lies in recording the psychological and emotional milieu of the struggle for survival, not only then but also now. It is no secret that when interviewers meet to discuss their work, they exchange interesting anecdotes about difficult cases. The survivors' identification with their lost companions can become an over-identification and produce a confusion between different if convergent destinies. The voice of the dead still calls the survivors to fulfill a promise. There have even been appropriations of the stories of those who perished, as if they were one's own story.

Another type of over-identification that affects the process of recording comes from viewers (or even interviewers) who are too protective. They do not always allow the survivors their voice. While interviewers acknowledge, of course, the terrible things that happened during the time of victimization, they often balance that by the fact of survival, which is then represented as more than accidental, indeed as a heroic outcome. There is nothing worse in this respect than talk shows where the host "oohs" and "aahs" over the terrible past and the brave, *so* remarkable person who can chat about it here on the show. Even at more sophisticated levels this search for heroic meanings is a need of the over-identifying listener rather than of the survivor. It is far from innocent, for the temptation to "launder" the behavior of people under extreme stress, and the lasting mark left by that stress, suggests that in terms of moral response we have not yet learned enough from the Holocaust.

By such laundering, by such defensively ennobling comment, we are expressing an anxiety that the survivor may be tainted. Primo Levi again speaks truly when he writes of the "awful privilege" of his generation that they have grasped the incurable nature of the offense imposed like a contagion on the human spirit. "It is foolish to think that human justice can eradicate it. It is an inexhaustible fount of evil; it breaks the body and the spirit of the submerged, it stifles them and renders them abject; it returns as ignominy upon the oppressors, it perpetuates itself as hatred among the survivors, and swarms around in a thousand ways, against the very will of all. . . . " To take away this kind of honesty from the witnesses is to treat them as patients rather than agents. But in telling their stories survivors are indeed agents: not heroic, perhaps even allowing the worst to remain unsaid, yet the strength required to face a past like that radiates visibly off the screen and becomes a vital fact.

There have been three periods when survivors of the Holocaust recovered their voice and an audience materialized for them. The first was immediately after the war, when the camps were disclosed. That period did not last: a devastated Europe had to be rebuilt, and the disbelief or guilt that cruel memories aroused isolated rather than integrated the survivor. What has been aptly called a "latency period" intervened.[22] A second opening was created by the Eichmann trial in 1960, and a third came after the release of the TV series *Holocaust* in 1978. So many lost their lives, will their life story too be taken away? was the complaint. Any survivor could tell a history more true and terrible in its detail, more authentic in its depiction.

Thirty-five years after liberation, moreover, the survivors and refugees living in America were fully settled, with grown families and a third generation in the offing. It was late: now if ever was the time to talk; they were no longer hesitant to be recognized and to pass on their experience as a "legacy."

A grassroots project developed in New Haven, Connecticut, when sensitive neighbors found they knew next to nothing about the survivors in their midst. By the time Yale offered its support, the "Holocaust Survivors Film Project," initiated in 1979 by Laurel Vlock, Dr. Dori Laub, and William Rosenberg, had pioneered the videotestimony idea and deposited 200 witness-accounts. The Video Archive for Holocaust Testimonies at Yale was founded in 1981 and opened its doors in October 1982.[23]

There is no reason why oral testimony projects like Yale's could not also collect the memories of other groups: those of Vietnam veterans, for example, or the historical experience of African Americans, Native Americans, or immigrants. The growth of journalistic television does not substitute for oral history because of its brief attention span; it cannot replace careful and sustained listening. The events in Bosnia should not have to wait thirty years to be documented in detail by the survivors.

If we had stopped to resolve all the questions surrounding our effort— including that of the exact value of oral history as history—we would never have proceeded beyond the first experimental tapes. But these proved so affecting, and the survivors were so supportive, that the film project continued, relying on a non-directive interview that encouraged spontaneity.

The principle of giving survivors their voice has been a sustaining one. Also that of giving a face to that voice: of choosing video over audio, because of the immediacy and evidentiality it added to the interview. The "embodiment" of the survivors, their gestures and bearing, is part of the testimony. It adds significantly to the expressive dimension. There was also our judgment that, in terms of education (though not in terms of politics and propaganda), Radio Days were gone. Audiences now and in the future would surely be audiovisual.[24] We decided to make video recordings of public broadcast quality, to build an Archive of Conscience on which future educators and filmmakers might rely. These living portraits are the nearest our descendants can come to a generation passing from the scene.

Let me emphasize that we are not filmmakers. We are gathering original depositions, as one gathers important manuscripts. (Many who testify did not have the chance for a higher, or even uninterrupted secondary education: this oral history, then, does more than duplicate or confirm what is already written down.) From that collection, which is being analyzed and indexed,[25] quotations are put together in montages of fifteen to fifty minutes and which are suitable for all audiences except young children.

I do not deceive myself into thinking that we have developed the perfect interview. There may be no such thing: the quality of oral history is influenced by the chemistry between interviewer and interviewee, and even by the day and place of filming. We have learned to accept that element of chance. One sometimes hears questions that seem wrongheaded or intrusive, yet surprisingly it does not always matter: once initiated, the flow of memory is so strong that such questions are swept aside or lead to a startling result. In a good interview the initiative remains with the person interviewed. The survivors' readiness is all, together with a conviction about the importance of giving public testimony and trust in the group that is providing the occasion. The interviewing process, in fact, creates an ad hoc community; and whether or not finally telling the story relieves traumatic stress, that communal dimension is certainly a comfort.[26]

Our edited programs have an educational purpose: for these montages young adults are part of the audience and pedagogy is crucial. After Claude Lanzmann—and his *Shoah* does divide the history of Holocaust representation into before and after—after Lanzmann, it is hard to think of communicating to children anything of that genocidal hell which made a point of killing children. When Helen K. says, "I cannot believe what my eyes have seen," she refers to children being exterminated, and—if anything could be worse—waiting in line day after day for that.[27]

Learning from Survivors

But the Video Archive does not set out to be an anatomy of genocide, or a relentless assemblage of each step in the extermination process. Using the interview in a compassionate way we gain a description of the everyday and psychological milieu of those caught up in the Holocaust, not excluding their life before or after the war in different countries.

The Holocaust is "eventful" history; it may even be an event that has ruptured our sense of what human nature is. Many expressive details of these witness-accounts belong, however, to the relatively non-eventful, non-dramatic story of men and women returning to ordinary life after extreme circumstances, and working their memories through.[28] "[T]he growing good of the world is partly dependent on unhistoric acts."[29] It is the entire person who is asked to speak, not only the one recalling terror and time of trial. In this, above all, the sociological or cultural value of the testimonies is clear.

Yet we refuse to "program" the interviews, declining to guess what special interests future generations might have. The welling-up of memories is crucial, rather than the imposition of a particular research interest, however important the latter may be for the overall picture. I will not claim that the interviewers do not have their own strong motivation and therefore an agenda.[30] They too, after all, belong to a specific memory-milieu: they create, in effect, a bridge or channel of transmission between generations by this timely, communal work. But in preserving a memory based on memories, on individual and multiple narratives, they renounce an omniscient perspective and allow the testimonies freer impact.

I have described what the testimonies are, as a mode of representation, a distinctive genre combining new and very old elements. My experience in recording the testimonies is similar to that of Lanzmann, while making his film. "There was an absolute break between the bookish knowledge I had acquired and what these people told me. I understood nothing any more."[31] I hope that everyone who views the testimonies will agree that breaking the silence is, for those who endured so dehumanizing an assault, an affirmative step, in part because of their very willingness to use ordinary words whose adequacy and inadequacy must both be respected.

Notes

1. Just one example: a woman tells of her experiences arriving at Auschwitz. The scene is notorious: bloodcurdling shouts, nightmare, the pajamas, the elegance of the

SS, dogs. After a journey already fatal for a part of the mass packed into the wagons, she tells us that at a certain moment she passed into "another state" (*un second état*) marked by dissociation and anesthesia. But when, exactly, did this happen? In the wagons, on arrival at the camp, at some point afterwards? She hesitates, then decides that it happened when her long and beautiful hair was brutally cut off. It was then, she says, that she experienced a "cut" (*une coupure nette*) between the person she had been and the camp prisoner.

2. The way the "recording imagination intersects with the will to interpretation," or "the memory of atrocity meets traditional moral authority, and they vie for the control of the narrative"—in the survivor but also in the interviewer—has been scrupulously analyzed by Lawrence Langer. See his "Interpreting Survivor Testimony," in *Writing and the Holocaust*, ed. Berel Lang (New York: Holmes & Meier, 1988) and, more comprehensively, *Holocaust Testimonies: The Ruins of Memory*.

3. Cf. Paul Thompson, *The Voice of the Past: Oral History*, 2nd ed. (New York: Oxford University Press, 1980), chap. 4, "Evidence." Marc Bloch, according to Bruce M. Ross, held that "faulty witnessing and the unreliability of memory testimony need not unduly worry historians, because . . . the historians' task is to understand the meaning of events, not their concrete representations. Understanding meaning is abetted rather than hindered by the complications of multiple causation of events." (*Remembering the Personal Past: Descriptions of Autobiographical Memory* [New York: Oxford University Press, 1991], 168–69.) Chapter 11 on Testimonies in *Les échos de la mémoire: Tabous et enseignement de la seconde guerre mondiale*, ed. Georges Kantin and Gilles Manceron (Paris: Le Monde, 1991) is a sensible discussion by teachers and witnesses of the "subjectivity" issue. One point made (p. 322) is that "Il serait important de relier le témoignage et l'écrit et d'insister sur cette nécessité de concevoir aussi les témoignages comme amenant à une rectification de ce qui est écrit, et pas seulement de rectifier les témoignages par les écrits" (It would be important to connect oral and written testimony and to insist on that necessity, understanding also that the testimonies may lead to a rectification of what is written, not only that the written be used to rectify them). A useful distinction was made between "reliability" (internal consistency of oral history narratives) and "validity" (conformity between the oral report and other primary sources) by Alice Hoffman, "Reliability and Validity in Oral History," Dunway and Baum, eds. *Oral History: An Interdisciplinary Anthology* (Nashville: American Association for State and Local History in Cooperation with the Oral History Association, 1988), 67–74. From a theoretical point of view, there is always a distance between saying and seeing; there would be no need for testimony if we could call up the event in its immediacy. The claim that a purely visual reconstruction is possible sins against that gap or interval, which is temporal, and may filter out a shock that belongs to the event and which questions "the monolithic integrity of the position of the witness." For a difficult but interesting account of the theoretical issue, see Bruno Tackels, "Ethik der Zeugenschaft," in *Bildstörung: Gedanken zu einer Ethik der Wahrnehmung*, ed. Jean-Pierre Dubost (Leipzig: Reklam, 1994), 130–47.

4. Paul Fussell describes, in *The Great War and Modern Memory* (New York: Oxford University Press, 1975), the struggle of war memoirists to find a perspective for experiences that are, as they occur on the battlefield, traumatic or senseless or both. At some distance from the Great War a kind of period style emerges, which Fussell characterizes as irony or "the abridgment of hope," and which then affects writing generally. To answer what type of stylistic coherence is emerging from the oral testimonies or the literary memoirs of the Holocaust is too ambitious for this essay. But if some type of coherence is basic to the possibility of narration, then temporal distance is not necessarily a disad-

Learning from Survivors

vantage. Fussell quotes Robert Kee, an RAF flyer in the Second War, on the relative unintelligibility of his diaries: "There's nothing you could really get hold of if you were trying to write a proper historical account of it all. No wonder the stuff slips away mercury-wise from proper historians. No wonder they have to erect rather artificial structures of one sort or another in its place. No wonder it is those artists who re-create life rather than try to recapture it who, in one way, prove the good historian in the end" (311).

5. Primo Levi, moreover, emphasizes in *The Drowned and the Saved* (trans. Raymond Rosenthal [New York: Summit, 1980]), how few camp inmates were "privileged" enough to gain an overview of events (see p. 141 above). The same caution is stated in *Les échos de la mémoire*: "Il n'existe pas de témoin du fait concentrationnaire dans sa globalité. Il n'y a que de faits quotidiens et partiels" (313).

6. See Anna Ornstein, "The Holocaust: Reconstruction and the Establishment of Psychic Continuity" in *The Reconstruction of Trauma: Its Significance in Clinical Work*, ed. Arnold Rothstein (Madison, CT: International Universities Press, 1986), 177ff.

7. Edith P., Holocaust Testimony (HVT-107), Fortunoff Video Archive for Holocaust Testimonies, Yale University Library.

8. See Jean Améry, *At the Mind's Limits: Contemplations by a Survivor on Auschwitz and Its Realities*, trans. Sidney Rosenfeld and Stella Rosenfeld (New York: Schocken, 1990). Originally published in German in 1966, and with a new preface in 1977.

9. Preface to the 1977 edition of Améry's *At the Mind's Limits*. Writing from the point of view of high school teachers, Annie Badower notes: "Il y a un problème de communication entre le monde de la déportation et le monde enseignant. . . . Il faut se donner les moyens, en rassemblant tous ces témoignages sur cassette vidéo, de sauvegarder cette possibilité d'un support emotionnel qui permet à l'intelligence des élèves de s'accroître." (There is a communications problem between the world of the deportees and that of the teachers. . . . We must find the means, by collecting all these testimonies on video, to safeguard this possibility of an emotional support which would allow the understanding of students to increase.) *Les échos de la mémoire*, 308.

10. This issue of how images, in a modern context especially, can be part of an emotional kind of education, one that does more than point in a cool and cognitive way (also important, of course) to a defining or traumatic event, is beginning to be more carefully considered. See James Young, *The Texture of Memory: Holocaust Memorials and Meaning* (New Haven: Yale University Press, 1993), and Don Handelman and Lea Shamgar Handelman, "The Presence of the Dead: Memorials of National Death in Israel," *Suomen Antropologi* 4 (1991): 3–17.

11. Urbana: University of Illinois Press, 1949.

12. "Je ne suis pas vivante. Je suis morte à Auschwitz et personne ne le voit." *Le convoi du 24 janvier* (Paris: Editions de Minuit, 1965), 66. A survivor of the Pol Pot regime, who has become blind without a clear physiological disorder, expresses a similar feeling. "Now, in her small dark apartment, she sometimes wonders if she is really alive or if she died in the rice fields; that is, she feels that the beatings she received caused her soul to be driven from her body, and she sometimes believes that it is back there." See Alec Wilkinson in "A Changed Vision of God," the *New Yorker* (January 24, 1994): 53.

13. They also intervene, as a representational mode, in over-objectified historical accounts, such as the chilling documentation of the perpetrators, "a field dominated by political decisions and administrative decrees which neutralize the concreteness of despair and death." (Saul Friedlander, in *Holocaust Remembrance: The Shapes of Memory*, 262.) Dan Pagis, an Israeli poet, and a survivor himself (he died in 1988), has written "Draft of a Reparations Agreement," which parodies the at once commanding and falsely con-

soling tone of such documents: "Everything will be returned to its place, / paragraph after paragraph. / The scream back into the throat. / The gold teeth back to the gums. . . . "

14. Narrator or anchor, that is, establishes an artificial and automatic mode of *address*. Whereas survivors of a traumatic experience often lose contact—cannot find a self in them to address, let alone one outside, while desperately and all the time hoping for a correspondent—the narrative that accompanies reportage simply assumes such a presence, the very thing that is absent or has been badly injured. There may be the punctual agony of flashbacks, of course, but these occur without—or with an arbitrary—addressee, and usually lack the sustained consciousness of the person who suffers them. The remarkable fact is, however, that artists have the capacity to *invent* or *restore* an addressee, an "I-Thou" relationship. Cf. Nanette C. Auerhahn and Dori Laub, "Holocaust Testimony," in *Holocaust and Genocide Studies* 5 (1990): 447–62.

15. For the term, see Avital Ronell's interesting work on the ethics of technology, especially "Video/Television/Rodney King: Twelve Steps beyond *The Pleasure Principal*," in *differences: A Journal of Feminist Cultural Studies* 4 (1992): 7–10. She thinks of testimonial video as a "bug or parasite" installed in television itself, and capable of producing the "ethical scream" that television "has massively interrupted."

16. See *Holocaust Testimonies: The Ruins of Memory*. Also Charlotte Delbo, who observes in *Days and Memory*, "not only the world but the word was split in two."

17. See Rachel G., Holocaust Testimony (HVT-139), Fortunoff Video Archive for Holocaust Testimonies, Yale University Library. Compare the overdetermination in Ezra 3:11–13, in which the writer describes a "great shout," first by doubling it as weeping and joy, then making that distinction indistinguishable because of the distance at which the shout, because it is so great, is still heard.

18. See chapter 5 in Michael Pollak, *L'Expérience concentrationnaire: essai sur le maintien de l'identité sociale* (Paris: Métailié, 1990).

19. Levi, *The Drowned and the Saved*, trans. Raymond Rosenthal (New York: Summit, 1988), Preface.

20. *The Drowned and the Saved*, 23, 34–35, 94.

21. For other pressures on memories, which makes them transmittable, see F. C. Bartlett, *Remembering: A Study in Experimental and Social Psychology* (London: Cambridge University Press, 1967); on the "effort after meaning," see James Fentress and Chris Wickham, *Social Memory* (Cambridge, MA: Blackwell, 1992). The Conclusions to Alice M. and Howard S. Hoffman, *Archives of Memory: A Soldier Recalls World War II* (Lexington: University of Kentucky Press, 1990), 144–54, came from a ten-year study of a "memory claim," its reliability and unreliability. The authors posit "a subset of autobiographical long-term memory which is so permanent and largely immutable that it is best described as archival." This subset has been consciously or unconsciously rehearsed, because its contents were salient and highly emotional. (By a "flashbulb" effect, subsequent events and otherwise unremarkable experiences can be incorporated and made permanent, if they are rehearsed along with the earlier memory, motivated by a sense that the earlier event was a turning point in the narrator's life.) The testimonies as oral history might seem to fall under what Jan Assmann calls "das kommunikative Gedächtniss" (communicative memory) marked by an interchangeability of roles ("Rollenreziprozität"). But as a potential legacy, with a strong commitment to maintaining this memory too, however painful— thus fulfilling the traditional commandment of *zakhor* in an unexpected and negative context—they also seek to enter "das kulturelle Gedächtniss" (cultural memory). There is an interesting tension, therefore, between the significant "small" (i.e., everyday) detail

of the accounts, which suggests the singularity (rather than interchangeability) of each witness's experience and the collective or assimilative aspects of their stories. Cf. Jan Assmann and Tonio Hölscher, eds. *Kultur und Gedächtnis* (Frankfurt a/M: Suhrkamp, 1988), 9ff.

22. During this time, however, because of the insensitive way the German Indemnification Law (passed in 1953) was administered, many survivors were subjected to an "enforced remembering" that "brought on a distinct feeling of renewed persecution, renewed interrogation, disbelief and degradation." See *Generations of the Holocaust*, ed. Martin S. Bergmann and Milton E. Jucovy (New York: Columbia University Press, 1990), 60ff.

23. My earlier account of the Yale Testimony project, "Preserving the Personal Story: The Role of Video Documentation," was published in the first issue of *Dimensions* (1985) and is reprinted in *The Holocaust Forty Years After*, ed. M. Littel, R. Libowitz, and E. B. Rosen (Lewiston: Edwin Mellen Press, 1989).

24. Financially it proved a difficult choice: what a single made-for-TV film costs is what the Yale Archive existed on the first four years. In 1987, Alan Fortunoff's generous gift to an endowment fund established by many donors guaranteed the archive a curator and a permanent place in Yale's Sterling Memorial Library. Till then the Charles H. Revson Foundation had been the main funding source of operations and it continues to support some projects.

25. This chapter focuses on the act of recording, and questions of memory and education; I do not describe the Yale Archive's method of providing intellectual access to the testimonies. For that aspect, see *Guide to Yale University Library Holocaust Video Testimonies*, 2nd ed. (New Haven: Yale University Library, 1994).

26. On this "communal dimension of trauma," and the case that "the traumatized view of the world conveys a wisdom that ought to be heard in its own terms," see Kai Erikson's sensitive "Notes on Trauma and Community" in *American Imago* 48 (1991): 455–72. On the "communité affective" (Maurice Halbwachs) that makes testimony possible despite the traumatization of the individual, Michael Pollak's *L'Expérience concentrationnaire: essai sur le maintien de l'identité sociale* is essential.

27. Helen K., Holocaust Testimony (HVT-58), Fortunoff Video Archive for Holocaust Testimonies, Yale University Library.

28. Because the life history details in the testimonies are neither impersonally micro-historic nor *fait divers*, they are difficult to categorize. We say too easily that they are comparable to the highly selective detail we find in literary constructs. For an important discussion of the testimonies' relation to a *histoire non-événementielle*, see Yannis Thanasseikos, "Positivisme historique et travail de mémoire. Les récits et les témoignages des survivants comme source historique," *Bulletin de la Fondation Auschwitz* 36/37 (1993): 19–39.

29. George Eliot, *Middlemarch* (final paragraph).

30. More interviewers have volunteered from the mental health professions than from history or sociology. Yet the way the interview is presented makes it a historical rather than therapeutic occasion. Martin Bergman remarks: "The danger of breakdown in the videotaped interview is less than would have been expected from therapeutic consultations with survivors. This may be due to the fact that the survivor whose story is filmed is not seeking personal help; he is called upon to bear witness. By being interviewed, he is entering history. He is doing his share in remembering. That such interviews are conducted because of the subject's involvement with the Holocaust gives the

interview the character less of a personal and more of a social and historical event."
Generations of the Holocaust, 320.

31. " . . . il y avait un décalage absolu entre le savoir livresque que j'avais acquis et ce que me racontaient ces gens. Je ne comprenais plus rien." In "Le lieu et la parole," *Cahiers du Cinéma*, 37 (1985): 374.

Ten

Holocaust Testimony, Art, and Trauma

And out of her mouth a stone passed
into my open mouth.
"This is the stone of witness," she said,
"that stops every heart."

—Allen Grossman, "The Ether Dome"

I begin, uncharacteristically, with an assertion. Today the relation of knowledge to the means of representation has changed. This is especially clear in the area of the Holocaust. We notice, on the one hand, an excess of knowledge, a plethora of detail about the "Final Solution" furnished by the techniques of modern historiography and the punctilious and overconfident record-keeping of the perpetrators themselves. On the other hand, powerful visual media are at our disposition to convert this knowledge into simulacra of the original event. Questions arise, therefore, about the limits of representation: questions less about whether the extreme event can be represented than whether truth is served by our refusal to set limits to representation.

It should not be assumed, in other words, that questions about representing the extreme are only technical in nature (how can we find *means* strong enough to depict what happened?) rather than scruples about the *end*, about the wisdom of recalling what happened. In the past this scruple was often declared formulaically. So Jewish chroniclers of the Crusades hesitate at the threshold: "In trying to tell of the wrath and the rage, not a heart has the strength, the hand fails on the page." We tend to forget this heart and this hand. Our endurance is taken for granted, as well as an inevitable prurience and curiosity; and the critique of realism, of its refusal to set limits, is left entirely to the dogmatists among us.

To take forms of representation seriously means to acknowledge their power to move, influence, offend, wound. That is why the conservative theme of representational limits is important, and why the issue has been central to poetics until very recently. At present the question of limits, in the media or in art, is raised only as regards children. It is assumed that adult eyes grow a thicker skin as experience inures them. The episode recounted by Augustine, about his friend Alypius in the Roman Circus whose first glimpse of blood-sport forever imprints him with the lust to see blood, must seem touchingly naive. But the question won't go away entirely because of a new and peculiar psychological stress exerted by the media's technological extension of eyes and ears.

This stress is due to the fact that the media have turned all of us into involuntary bystanders of atrocities, reported graphically and hourly. From this media-reportage of traumatic events, from this fluent and relentless transmission of violent images, a "secondary trauma" could arise, this time affecting the spectators of our own Roman Circuses. Though in the ordinary course of life everyone is exposed to sights of death and suffering, what is so worrisome is the routine exposure, one that habituates and fascinates and tends to produce feelings of indifference.[1]

It is not, then, the potentially traumatic impact of visual imagery that is, by itself, the problem. Yes, there *is* shock, and then, often, fascination; it is hard to expel from the mind the picture of kneeling Vietnam villagers being executed by a direct bullet to the head, or of naked Jewish women waiting to be killed, or photos of near-skeletons being dumped into mass graves after the liberation of Belsen, or of a headless body dragged away after the shelling of a marketplace in Sarajewo. But one must add to the fact of shock its routinization, the constant viewing of extreme pictures, their circulation as icons, and the coldness with which we eventually stare at other such pictures.

The desensitization I have described leads to a rational fear: Is our capacity for sympathy finite and soon exhausted?[2] If so, it might indeed be important to retain first impressions, even the painful and shocking ones. They become talismanic: fixed ideas of our once-and-future power to feel, to experience *something*. It is in pursuit of such defining memories that we abandon the issue of representational limits and seek to "cut" ourselves, like psychotics who ascertain in this way that they exist. As if only a personal or historical trauma (I bleed, therefore I am) would bond us to life.[3]

Ideally, impressions should always be first impressions; yet more significant is the possibility of breaking through the numbness, one's own or another's, with the help of a story. The fantasy so often harbored by Holocaust survivors during their ordeal, that they would find someone after liberation who would listen to their experiences, really sympathize with them, is partly motivated by a wish to recapture their own power of response,

disabled or depressed in the camps.[4] Those who hoped for their story to
have this effect were disappointed.

Yet describing the role of the listener in Yale's oral testimony project,
Dori Laub makes the impossible wish play a structural role:

> The listener . . . is a party to the creation of knowledge de novo. The testi-
> mony to the trauma thus includes its hearer, who is, so to speak, the blank
> screen on which the event comes to be inscribed for the first time.[5]

Does the story create the listener or does the listener enable the story? To
ask this question is to understand that testimony's *prise de parole*, its conditions of production, involve an active audience. However many times the
interviewer may have heard similar accounts, they are received as though
for the first time.[6] This is possible because, while the facts are known, while
historians have labored—are still laboring—to establish every detail, each
of these histories is animated by something in addition to historical knowledge: there is a quest to recover or reconstruct a recipient, an "affective
community."[7]

Yet the testimonies have surprises even at the level of fact: the kind of
fact historians rarely listen to, from the everyday life of the camps or hiding
places. Too often, as the novelist Georges Perec writes, the big stylized incidents of *histoire événementielle* usurp all others: "L'Histoire avec sa grande
Hache avait répondu à ma place: la guerre, les camps" ("History with a
capital H [or, its great axe] had replied in my place: the war, the camps").[8]
In the testimonies no one talks in place of the survivor. Stories converge,
but voices remain individualized, haunted by the present as well as the past,
by ricochet thoughts about life now (many years later) rather than then,
and often distinguished by what I can only call raw poetry[9] as well as a
directness that turns the testimonies collectively into wisdom literature.

In Dori Laub's comment many things come together: the midwife role
of the interviewer-listener; the hope that the elicited words will inscribe
themselves on the mind of the auditor; and the renewal of compassionate
feelings.[10] The interview, conceived in this way, is a social act, however
temporary and precarious; it returns to survivors some trust in communicability, both with themselves through their memories and with a world that
remains a treacherous place. The witness's identity in the face of a continuing traumatism is reinforced.[11]

But one feature I want to stress above the rest. The testimony-encounter
avoids the danger of "secondary trauma," previously described. The narrative that emerges through the alliance of witness and interviewer does not

present, however grim its contents, either a series of fixed images that assault the eyes or an impersonal historical digest. The narrative resembles that most natural and flexible of human communications, a story[12]—a story, moreover, that, even if it describes a universe of death, is communicated by a living person who answers, recalls, thinks, cries, carries on. The hope is, then, that secondary trauma, insofar as it is linked to violent yet routinized images, will not injure either the witnesses recalling the events, or young adults and other long-distance viewers to whom extracts of the testimonies are shown.

I am hardly the first to worry about the increasing prevalence of psychic numbing accompanied by fascination, and which is usually the consequence of *primary* trauma. It would be ironic and sad if all that education could achieve were to transmit a trauma to later generations in a secondary form. In this fifth decade after the collapse of the National Socialist regime, the disaster still has not run its course.[13] No closure is in sight: the contradictory imperatives of remembering and forgetting are no less strong than before.

Indeed, they may have reached an impasse at the institutional as well as the personal level. The public explosion of memories in testimonies, monuments, books, films, and museums sends a danger signal. "Anyone who underwent the Holocaust," Aharon Appelfeld warns us, "will be as wary of memory as of fire. It was impossible to live after the Holocaust except by silencing memory."[14] What of the present, then, of our time, in which the mute is removed from that memory?

In a surprising number of survivors the silenced memory did not fade; it became what Charlotte Delbo names "deep memory," but which is retained side by side with ordinary consciousness. "So you are living with Auschwitz?—No, I live next to it."[15] Our experience in the Yale project has been that survivors remember with astonishing clarity. At the same time, they often feel as if they had never left the place where so many perished. They too seem to have died during those terrible years, and now are self-haunted ghosts. "I am not among the living, I died in Auschwitz and no one notices it," Charlotte Delbo wrote.[16]

This sense of unreality points to a continuing death-in-life, and witnessing does not always lift the curse. "[Testimonies] are actually repressions," Appelfeld says surprisingly, "neither introspection nor anything resembling introspection, but rather the careful weaving together of external facts in

Holocaust Testimony, Art, and Trauma

order to veil the inner truth." By "inner truth" Appelfeld does not mean the fire of memory itself but a darkness it lights up: the survivors' sensation of non-identity, of a ghostly self damaged by "years of suffering [that] slowly erased the image of humanity within. . . . "[17]

Since each witness conducts his own struggle with memory, it is likely that some will avoid introspection and flee from a real reckoning toward the recital of externals. Yet many witness-accounts in the Yale Archive are powerful precisely because a repression *is* overcome and memory returns. Not everything is told, but the struggle, clearly visible, is part of the testimony. It is only a person who knows memory as the enemy, and recognizes the necessity of oblivion, who has the right to talk like Appelfeld. Indeed, Appelfeld acknowledges that he too fled from memory—into art. A turn from historical memory to art was crucial to his inner life after the Holocaust. "We must transmit," he instructs us, "the dreadful experience from the category of history into that of art."[18]

Transmission—the passage from personal to cultural memory—is crucial; yet I believe that Appelfeld's understanding of the genre of testimony is too narrow. He has not differentiated its function adequately from that of historical information. To "transmit the dreadful experience" we need *all* our memory-institutions: history-writing as well as testimony, testimony as well as art. Testimony, in fact, considered not just as a product but also as a humanizing and transactive process, does exactly what Appelfeld wishes art to do: it works on the past to rescue the "individual, with his own face and proper name"[19] from the place of terror where that face and name were taken away. Moreover, especially in the form of video, testimony also touches the present: a present characterized by secondary trauma. It provides an alternate form of transmitting the dreadful event, a non-traumatizing mode of representation, neither as hypnotic as art, nor as apparently impersonal as history-writing,[20] nor as contagious yet cold as the routine videocast.

What I have said so far is that the videotestimonies retrieve "deep memory" as well as specific, informative details of the terror and the suffering. Traumatic incidents are described, often in unforgettable fashion; their remembering is recall and reflection rather than compulsive flashback. Though speech may stumble, get ahead of itself, temporarily lose its way, it is *voice* as well as *memory* that is recovered from moments of silence and powerlessness.

An image too is reclaimed: that of the survivor's humanity. The video-visual medium does not exist for the sake of the narrative but to re-embody the survivor and replace demeaning and sometimes injurious Nazi photos which, till recently, were a staple of Holocaust museums. We cannot allow only images made by the perpetrators to inhabit memory.[21]

It would be false, however, to claim the witness-accounts as an art form: they resist the paradigm of artistic mastery, as well as other types of psychic integration. They are intrinsically repetitive and accumulative—we have to attend to them one by one by one. They do not yield easily to generalization, although they may be influenced by social and literary conventions[22] which buffer, and so transmit, extreme experiences.

What has not been fully appreciated is that the witness accounts are linked to social reality twice over: through their explicit content, of course, a picture of social reality in extremis, but more subtly through the time and place (the memory-milieu) in which they are recorded.[23] We learn about the survivors' resettlement and present circumstances.

The concept, moreover, that the testimonies are public acts of witness helps to build ad hoc communities of interviewers and organizers. Just as the literary work is said to have an implied reader with whom the author enters into a relation, even a sort of contract, so testimonies evoke a trans-generational recipient through the survivor's willingness to record and the ad hoc community's readiness to listen.[24] The testimony project is based on the hope of finding a witness for the witness. In actuality, of course, the tension that surrounds this communicative effort is never completely removed: many survivors question whether an experience like theirs can constitute a "legacy"—can find its audience or be absorbed into our system of education.[25]

I consider the testimonies, with their balance of realism and reticence, to be a less problematic form than docudramas that seek to overwhelm with naked imagery, or, at the opposite end of the spectrum, symbolic modes that aspire to mystery or generality. Yet I feel it necessary to examine both of these alternate modes. My plan is to turn first to the issue of visual realism or simulation, and then to Paul Celan as an intriguing and extreme example of reticence.

The major argument for not limiting realism is simply from reality itself. Given the rise of our exposure to violence in the streets or the media, contemporary artists tend not only to magnify a brutal realism but to adopt a style that emphasizes incidents rather than character, and graphic horror rather than indirect disclosure.[26] It can be argued, moreover, that there is no way to avoid secondary trauma except by avoiding reality itself. Returning to highly stylized and sophisticated genres has a disadvantage which the founder of pastoralism admits. Vergil's spokesman says in the ninth Eclogue, "poems such as ours, Lycidas, have no more force in time of war than doves when an eagle comes." To deal honestly with extremity may require extreme representational means, and an acceptance of a degree of desensitization that is the by-product of realistic media.[27]

But even should we support the value of extreme representations, and say that life makes a degree of sensory numbing necessary, one consequence of secondary trauma is indefensible. A massive realism which has no regard for representational restraint, and in which depth of illusion is not balanced by depth of reflection, not only desensitizes but produces the opposite of what is intended: an *unreality effect* that fatally undermines realism's claim to depict reality. Yet precisely an effect like that is usually blamed on the aesthetic element in art, which is mistakenly targeted for not being close enough to realities. The aesthetic, an alternate and deliberate mode of distancing, is denounced for its supposed coldness to social and historical concerns, or else for exploiting them, for allowing the spectator to take pleasure in watching the suffering of others.

After the Holocaust there is a spiritual hunt to de-aestheticize everything—politics and culture as well as art. As Adorno phrased it in his harshest and most famous statement, it is a sign of the barbaric (that is, of lack of culture) to write poetry after Auschwitz. He refused the arts a role even in mourning the destruction, because they might stylize it too much, or "make an unthinkable fate appear to have some meaning."[28] Yet art creates an unreality effect in a way that is *not* alienating or desensitizing. At best, it also provides something of a safe-house for emotion and empathy. The tears we shed, like those of Aeneas when he sees the destruction of Troy depicted on the walls of Carthage, are an acknowledgment and not an exploitation of the past.[29]

A last argument for realistic purism is that art is simply less faithful than history in holding the line against a feared *recession* of reality. Most historians are intensely suspicious of any discursive or creative mode that deviates from realism or clear, referential touchstones. They see positivistic accuracy as the last remaining safeguard against relativism and revisionism. Others who are not historians focus on a fictionality secreted by the media, on images repeated by them which become metonyms for reality. It is feared that mechanical reproduction, glossily efficient, will corrode over time the distinction between history and fiction.[30]

There must be historical veracity, but we cannot neglect the paradox that cinematic realism produces its own unreality effect. Spielberg's version of *Schindler's List*, a film that follows the documented facts, and takes pains to reconstruct the Kracow ghetto with some faithfulness, can be faulted on two counts. One is that it is not realistic enough. It still compromises with Hollywood's stylishness in the way it structures everything by large salvational or murderous acts. But the second is that the very cruelty and sensationalism of the event, reconstructed through a spectacular medium, exerts a magnetic spell that alone seems able to convey the magnitude of the evil. Spielberg has created a fact on the screen, and the moral challenge passes to the viewers.

Modern realistic media, then, even in the hands of as brilliant a movie maker as Spielberg, remain shadowed by an unreality effect more subversive than aestheticism. We are spellbound, yet something in us keeps saying "This is (only) a film."[31] The artist must now outwit not only art but also technique, or what Adorno diagnosed as the fetishizing of technique.[32] By contrast, the impact of the testimonies is extraordinarily intimate. For without either aesthetic distance or simulated realism there is no unreality effect. Ghostliness is here confined to the witness as *revenant*, who delivers what Delbo in a charged phrase calls "mortal truth."

> There is a pain—so utter—
> It swallows substance up—
> Then covers the Abyss with—Trance
> So Memory can step
> Around—across—upon it—
>
> —Emily Dickinson[33]

The crucial question becomes, in fact, not whether a realistic art is possible (it is), but whether experience is possible, or under what conditions. This Kantian turn is already suggested by Adorno's remark on "the extremity that eludes the concept."[34] Trauma theory raises the same issue.

Walter Benjamin, in "The Story Teller," noted an inverse relation between the battlefield ordeals of World War I veterans and their ability to represent them. Freud also, after that war, demonstrated that trauma was the result of living through extreme experience without experiencing it— without being able to integrate it emotionally or mentally. The disturbances associated with trauma are, according to Freud, an attempt of the system to prepare retroactively for a shock that had already taken place, to catch up with and master it. Memory, and especially the memory that goes into storytelling, is not simply an afterbirth of experience, a secondary formation: it *enables* experiencing, it allows what we call the real to enter consciousness and word-presentation, to be something more than trauma followed by a hygienic, and ultimately illusory, mental erasure.[35]

Memory, then, limits and enables at the same time. When we talk of trauma we mean events or states of feeling that threaten this limit: extreme physical or mental pain, for instance, and also extreme pleasure. They puncture lived time and exist only as phantasms. But memory is evidence of continuity: that the future will have a past. Travel advertisements that tell us how much pleasure we would have remembering a spot not yet visited merely exaggerate a truth. "To exist historically," Arthur Danto has written, "is to perceive the events one lives through as part of a story later to be told."[36]

This future-oriented aspect of memory, jeopardized by traumatic conditions that reduced victims to what camp jargon called "muslims," is precisely what is reclaimed in the narrative testimony of survivors and perhaps in storytelling generally.[37] What was a degrading passivity shows itself as a capacity for listening and observing that now breaks out of dormancy. *Yet it does not break out—wake up—entirely*, for the story's hypnotic charm, or our reluctance to destroy illusion, points to the transmission of something like a trance state as well as an experience. Those familiar with Colcridge's "The Ancient Mariner" will recognize the effect: how the Mariner's glittering eye and tale cast their spell on the reluctant auditor. It is as if art generated that trance in order to circumvent trauma, preparing both author and auditor for a terrible or sublime experience always about to happen, or which has already happened.[38]

Storytelling, then, seems at once to anticipate and to postpone a fulfillment. The desire for experience, *for being a contemporary witness of one's own life, fully present to it*, points to an expectation satisfied only at an imagined horizon that merges sublimity and death. (Emily Dickinson gives a powerful if ironic image of that epiphanic horizon in "I heard a fly buzz—when I died.") Alternatively, that horizon as an origin, as a developmental event lodged deep in the past, compels a virtually endless effort to recover an originary trauma that must be brought into the space of conscious experience. Life, viewed this way, turns into a quest, centered on that defining but unconsciously experienced event. (Alain Resnais's and Robbe-Grillet's *Last Year at Marienbad*, with its doublings and repetitions, romances that quest.) The quest terminates only when the event is fully visible: that is, exposed as an identity mark.[39]

Ideally, this recovery of experience, its passage to conscious and articulate status by means of testimony, art, or therapy, will not reproduce trauma by contagion. Wordsworth understood this fact. In his memory-poem *The Prelude*, he discerns a pattern—some will call it a myth—of development. He depicts the poet's mind as able to overcome psychic shock until it is "From all internal injury exempt."[40] Such invulnerability, however, may border on indifference or insensibility: without shock, how can there be sympathetic identification? Perhaps that is why Coleridge, contra Wordsworth, keeps storytelling *within* the compulsion to repeat, and describes it, in "The Ancient Mariner," as a purgatorial seizure that gives only temporary relief:

> Forthwith this frame of mine was wrenched
> With a woful agony,
> Which forced me to begin my tale;
> And then it left me free.

> Since then, at an uncertain hour,
> That agony returns;
> And till my ghastly tale is told,
> This heart within me burns.[41]

The sense of being a survivor, of having outlived a malignant or sublime or uncanny intensity, often enters into art by partly unconscious mimesis. To clarify the role of the unconsciously mimetic, I turn to Freud's understanding of repetition-compulsion.

In *Beyond the Pleasure Principle*, Freud alludes to Tasso's Tancred, who twice, each time unintentionally, inflicts a grievous wound on his beloved. Is Tancred's "malignant fate," Freud wonders, unconsciously willed, that is, driven by "early infantile influences"? In recognizing the pattern Freud shows himself an excellent literary analyst: meaning is made possible by this movement from unmarked to marked. But does Tasso, in creating the repetition, present a symptom or a symbol? The sequence which could resolve that difference between compulsive symptom and veiled or integrated symbol spans the individual work in its entirety. Hence there is often, especially in art with a strong storyline, what Benjamin calls a "chaste compactness which precludes psychological analysis"[42]—precludes, that is, a psychological reduction or decoding. Such art demands of us considerable "reticence."[43] The episode from Tasso's *Jerusalem Liberated* allows uncanny resonances to emerge but does not demystify the Christian-Romantic theme of an erotic wound's necessary if ambivalent relation to holiness.

Let me recall, moreover, another doubling of a wound, this time unmarked. Alypius opened his eyes when he heard the shout of the crowd in the Roman Circus and "drinks in" the blood. This is an unmarked repetition because Alypius can be considered as Augustine's double. For even if the meditation on Christ's wounds was not as ardent in Augustine's day as in later Catholicism, it is impossible not to recognize here the transumption of the Roman blood-sport by a Christian fatality.[44] What remains difficult to describe is the mechanism whereby a repetition that moves its subject from the unconscious into the domain of word-presentation, or from an unmarked to an elliptical form of marking, participates in the process of closure and healing.[45]

Reading or listening, as part of the therapeutic process, respects words by respecting the wound in words, the "wundgelesenes" (Paul Celan). Yet reading the wound, I have argued, is not just reading for the wound. It does not mean locating the trauma reductively, or literalizing figures and fantasies in the name of realism. It asks how art "symbolize[s] the wound that will not be shown."[46] I would like to conclude with one of Celan's rare prose compositions, "Conversation in the Mountains," and then one of his poems, because a respect for reticence, for representational limits, is, in this author, not a formula but an obsessive scruple. We cannot read Celan's life from his work: how then is that work related to the Holocaust? Can so reticent an art, with a style that marks an absence, be a form of testimony?

The facts we have are meager: Celan was born in 1920 in Czernowitz; his parents were murdered in the Shoah; he himself endured hard labor and perhaps a detention camp. He was troubled by mental illness and committed suicide in 1970. Even his name, Ancel, is changed to become a cypher: while Ancel/Amsel hints at blackbird, Celan is an obscure anagram. He is the greatest poet of the postwar years writing in German; the interpretation industry has him well in hand, yet no consensus exists about the meaning of his words. One thing is quite obvious, however: there is trouble whenever in his writing the intimate pronoun "du" surfaces, or tries to surface. Many poems, till the end of the war, are addressed directly, through that "du," to the poet's mother. After that the act of addressing another or a lost other or the other within turns problematic.[47]

"Conversation in the Mountains" (1959) presents a Jew who wordily invokes an equally wordy other: "do you hear me, do hear me, you do, it's me, me, me whom you hear, whom you think you hear, me and the other. . . . " The repetitious prose is antithetical to the increasing sparseness of Celan's poems at that time,[48] yet here as there the *you* or *semblable* is a ghostly figure. Through the "do you hear me," through such insistent calling, a theme is parodied that will also appear in "The Meridian": "The poem wants to go toward another, it needs that other, it needs an opposite. It searches for, it speaks itself toward him."

A loneliness in the very place of encounter which the poem moves toward, is too general a theme to be historicized. Those with losses less severe than Holocaust survivors also feel that loneliness and a need for community. But I find relevant what Maurice Blanchot says, when he looks back at his pre-Holocaust stories and asks himself if they are dated. Could they be written today in the same style, or must our mode of representation change? He answers that as art, and not something else, they cannot change. "No matter when it is written, every story from now on [from after Auschwitz] will be from before Auschwitz." Whatever its content or time of genesis, storytelling always displays "the glory of a 'narrative voice' that speaks clearly, without ever being obscured by the opacity or the enigma or the terrible nature of what it communicates."[49]

Yet after such a catastrophe, narrative fiction, Blanchot also remarks, may have "lost the foundation on which another language could be raised—through the extinction of the happiness of speaking. . . . " Speech is threatened at its source—not because of its technical inability to represent what happened, but because something has gone out of our voice, an innocence ("the happiness of speaking") maintained in prior times despite everything. The very *will to speak* is at risk.[50]

It is that "happiness of speaking" which has abandoned Celan's "Conversation." The compulsion to talk remains, but the hope for a genuine encounter, a genuine conversation, seems desperate. The shock given to speech cannot be repaired by art or a natural balm. In Celan's strange performance, voice is betrayed into an inconsolable monologue.

How does one make poetry out of the unhappiness of speaking? The dilemma is heightened because poetic speech in Celan's mother tongue, in German poetry with its immense riches, now mocks him.[51] The persistence of a luminous and aesthetic element, a "happiness of speaking" that exists, according to Blanchot, "before all distinctions between form and content," defeats the expectation that, after the Shoah, our perception of art, and of the complicit culture, would alter.[52] Celan confesses: "Only one thing remained reachable, close and secure amid all losses: language. Yes, language. In spite of everything, it remained secure against loss. But it had to go through its own lack of answers, through terrifying silence, through the thousand darknesses of murderous speech. . . . In this language I tried, during those years and the years after, to write poems: in order to speak, to orient myself, to find out where I was, where I was going, to chart my reality."[53]

Deliciously, sadly, with equal measures of pathos and irony, Celan stages his "conversation" as a distinctively Yiddish back-and-forth.[54] A once communal, now spectral form of speech haunts Celan's German. Moreover, in a caricature of the Jewish effort to fight idolatry through renouncing images, the words stumble on, blind to nature, and are said to profane the silence of the hills. Yet they do this without conveying a call or a sense of being addressed as Abraham was (*Hörstdu Hörstdu*, "do-you-hear"),[55] or of having been struck and purified by a divine force. What Celan himself names a "missed encounter"[56] ends with a curiously exalted yet self-subverting *hineni*: "me here, me, who can tell you all this, could have and don't and didn't tell you. . . . " There is no revelation, no logos event.

In fact, words put out eyes: an original deprivation is evoked, a Jewish form of askesis that leads to unnatural verbalism. There is a trauma within the trauma and it is associated with language. The wound is also a word-wound, tied to a collective identity or cultural fate. Celan extends the biblical command concerning images and turns it against the images in words. Though not everything in his strange story is negative (the garrulous words take on a life of their own and *orient* themselves as in the force field of an invisible magnet),[57] we cannot hide the uncomfortable fact that they approach self-hate at times. "[T]hose cousins have no eyes, alas. Or, more exactly: they have, even they have eyes, but with a veil hanging in front of them, no, not in front, behind them, a moveable veil. No sooner does an image enter than it gets caught in the web, and a thread starts spinning, spinning itself around the image, a veil-thread. . . . " The unhappy consciousness of speech has been there all along, a Jewish fate even before the Holocaust.

Let me close with a single poem, a mock aubade. Its sparse, elliptical style, so different from the prose of "Conversation," adds a verbal to a visual asceticism:

> After refusal of light:
> the day, bright, echoing
> wake of the messenger.
>
> The euphoric message,
> shrill and more shrill,
> find to the bleeding ear.[58]

"Light-refusal" evokes a visual sacrifice. But it may also rehearse the Christian charge that the Jews blinded themselves to the new revelation, or were put into a position of imperfect witness by God ("Conversation" refers to "the veil in the eyes"). The transition from eye to ear is not a healing one: the light, the happy news, becomes more shrill as it finds its way to a bleeding ear. The movement is from "Lichtverzicht" to "Lichtzwang," from a refusal of light to being forced by, or into, the light.

The Longest Shadow

The question raised, then, and I believe it emerges from Celan's poetry as a whole, concerns the possibility of witness—in particular, of Jewish witness. The light that shines in the darkness, whether we identify it with Christian or with Enlightenment hopes, is part of the trauma rather than the solution.[59] Celan starts beyond light, beyond heliotropic witnessing: in his world the sun is set, dawn yields black milk, a candle is loved only as it burns down, the word remains in the dark.[60] He demands of himself an act of testimony[61] equal to a blind and perhaps endless journey of recovery, one that gives itself to "snailshorn perception" (Keats) or the barely visible breath, the "Atemwende" of utterance.[62]

No wonder Celan renounces "the glory of a 'narrative voice' " or any luminosity that would fill the emptiness. He imposes on himself the command to silence all "Augenstimmen," "eye-voices." Increasingly laconic, he adopts a Mallarmean and totally nonconfessional language of witness, "without I and without You, purely He, purely It, . . . purely They, nothing but that."[63] Even grammar, the stubborn basement of language-identity, is affected. His poetry displays a type of ellipsis that omits the verb or leaves it uncertain who speaks or is addressed. The first stanza of the "Refusal of Light" poem has no verb; the second, if we construe "find" as an imperative, renders the subject of the verb impersonal.[64] Do we not glimpse a ghostliness here that so often haunts survivors, "I died . . . and no one seems to notice it"?

Only speech survives this death, or writing as orphaned speech. Celan's poetry tends toward an absolute construction and becomes a splintered epitaph. Whatever the origin of his loss, a word-wound scars the entire range of his work. In his last poem Celan seems both to challenge and mock us to read that wound. Perhaps he is also challenging and mocking himself. "You read," he demands, and continues: "the Invisible / pressures the wind / into limits" (*Zeitgehöft*). The Invisible may be Celan himself, who aspires to the most reticent self-presence.[65] Trauma is given a form and disappears into the stammer we call poetry, into a fissure between speech on the page, seemingly so absolute, and an invisible writing that may not be retrievable. This is, in truth, a disaster notation.

Notes

1. The evidence for this fact, though anecdotal, is overwhelming. Frank Rich, of the *New York Times*, reporting that sixty-nine students from a mainly black and Latino high school in California "laughed and joked during a scene [from Spielberg's *Schindler's*

List] in which a Nazi shoots a Jewish woman in the head," quotes a local Rabbi concluding that the incident had nothing to do with antisemitism. "He and other Jewish leaders took the students at their word when they blamed the disruption at *Schindler's List* on their ignorance of history, their immaturity, and their desensitization to violence. 'We see violence in our community all the time,' explained Mirabel Corral, 16, one of the students ejected from the movie. Next to the real thing, the black-and-white bloodshed of *Schindler's List* looked laughably fake." *New York Times*, February 6, 1994, sec. 4: 17. Even the Rodney King tapes, played over and over again by the media, could not continue to shock.

2. "When, kneeling beside the baskets, we had to unroll the bandages covering those human trunks to check on the scarring process, then wrap them up in fresh bandages, each of us wondered whether she could do it forty times a day. One of my aides said: 'I'm going to use up here the whole supply of pity God gave me for a lifetime.' " Charlotte Delbo, *Days and Memory*, trans. Rosette Lamont (Marlboro, Vt.: Marlboro Press, 1990), 48.

3. Our development, Wordsworth writes more sanely, goes from strength to strength, "if but once we have been strong."

4. This state came about as a combination of physical and psychological stress. "You was too tired to exist. . . . You was indifferent to everything. You was like a vegetable." Fortunoff Video Archive for Holocaust Testimonies (HVT-35), Yale University. Testimony of Zoltan G., quoted in Lawrence Langer, *Holocaust Testimonies: The Ruins of Memory* (New Haven: Yale University Press, 1991), 47.

5. "Bearing Witness," in Shoshana Felman and Dori Laub, *Testimony: Crises of Witnessing in Literature, Psychoanalysis, and History* (New York: Routledge, 1991), 57.

6. Not naively, however, for a listener patently ignorant of Holocaust events would seem motivated by mere curiosity and jeopardize the trust between the parties.

7. See also the section on "Les récits" in Michael Pollak's *L'Expérience concentrationnaire*, which deals with this "volonté d'écoute" and other conditions and motivations of testimony-giving. The idea that memory is not even possible without an "affective community" goes back to Maurice Halbwachs. The issue of the addressee, sensitively discussed, and accompanied by the close reading of a Yale testimony, is found in Irene Kacandes's " 'You who live safe in your warm houses': Your Role in the Production of Holocaust Testimony," in *Insiders and Outsiders: Jewish and Gentile Culture in Germany and Austria*, ed. D. C. G. Lorenz and G. Weinberger (Detroit: Wayne State University Press, 1994), 189–213.

8. From *W, ou, le souvenir d'enfance* (Paris: Donoel, 1975). Perec's situation is that of the second generation in its acutest form: where the Holocaust survivor, through the lived quality of his reportage, fills in a neglected dimension, a history within History. Perec, whose mother disappeared into Auschwitz when he was a very young child, is pointing to the very absence of that detail which his deprived imagination always seeks, and which is usurped—filled in too grossly—by schoolbook history.

9. On natural literature, and how recorded speech shows that character "lives in the linguistic road as well as the destination," see Anna Deveare Smith's introduction to her *Fires in the Mirror: Crown Heights, Brooklyn, and Other Identities* (New York: Anchor Doubleday, 1993).

10. I am wary, however, of Laub's positive view of what I have called secondary trauma. "By extension, the listener to trauma comes to be a participant and co-owner of the traumatic event. . . . " *Testimony*, 57.

11. In photojournalism, visualizing the witness is reinforced by reduplication (e.g.,

showing citizens of Weimar looking at the horrors of Buchenwald), but in videotestimony the witness is, so to say, enabled to reinforce him/herself. For photojournalism, see Barbie Zelizer, "The Image, the Word, and the Holocaust" (unpublished).

12. Though having the appeal of stories, they can be clearly and formally distinguished from fictional narratives. See below, note 25.

13. My presentation takes up what I have called "secondary trauma" but not directly the question of the transmission of trauma from the survivor generation to the generations after. I am not qualified to evaluate the significant research that has been done on intergenerational issues by Martin Bergmann, Milton Jucovy, Judith Kestenberg, Anna Ornstein, Dori Laub, and others. Nor the suggestive thesis about a "transgenerational haunting" put forward (in a general rather than Holocaust-related context) by Nicolas Abraham, "Notes on the Phantom," in *The Trials of Psychoanalysis*, ed. Françoise Meltzer (Chicago: University of Chicago Press, 1988), 75–80. But I recognize that there is an intersection not only of family issues and the public domain but specifically of representational issues and pedagogy: of transmission at a time when education takes over from direct experience, since the survivor generation is passing from the scene.

14. *Beyond Despair: Three Lectures and a Conversation with Philip Roth* (New York: Fromm International, 1994), ix. All my Appelfeld quotes are from this book.

15. See Charlotte Delbo, *Days and Memory*, and Lawrence Langer, *Holocaust Testimonies: The Ruins of Memory*. In general, then, unless we deal with very young survivors, Holocaust memories are not "recovered memories."

16. "Je ne suis pas vivante. Je suis morte à Auschwitz et personne ne le voit." *Le convoi du 24 janvier* (Paris: Éditions de Minuit, 1965), 66. Another way of understanding the death-feeling is that the camp experience disclosed an insidious fact about the world generally. Robert Lifton, opening his *The Nazi Doctors: Medical Killing and the Psychology of Genocide* (New York: Basic Books, 1986), quotes a Holocaust survivor's comment which is deeply if unconsciously gnostic: "This world is not this world."

17. Jorge Semprun puts it even more harshly in *What a Beautiful Sunday!*, trans. Alan Sheridan (San Diego: Harcourt Brace Jovanovich, 1982). Memory, he says, can paradoxically become the "best recourse against the pain of remembering, against the dereliction, against the unspoken, familiar madness. The criminal madness of living the life of a dead man." It is Langer's significant contribution to distinguish the various types of survivor memory in *Holocaust Testimonies*.

18. *Beyond Despair*, introduction, xiv.

19. *Beyond Despair*, 22.

20. But for historians, as Saul Friedlander and Dominick LaCapra have pointed out, emotion does intervene through "transference." See, e.g., Friedlander, "Trauma, Memory, and Transference," in *Holocaust Remembrance: The Shapes of Memory*.

21. These "Holocaust icons" include the found images of photojournalists when the camps were liberated.

22. See the well known studies by David Roskies and Alan Mintz. Cf. also Annette Wieviorka's analysis of early *récits de déportation* in "On Testimony," *Holocaust Remembrance: The Shapes of Memory*. Langer's work on *oral* testimony modifies this emphasis on the persistence of convention. The written memoir is shown to be more susceptible to literary mediation.

23. Pierre Nora claims that *lieux de mémoire* come into being when the *milieu de mémoire* is lost; but in oral testimonies there is a sort of recovery of the latter. Not of the original milieu; rather a new one, however second best, comes into view. Though testimonies are

fragmentary and anti-monumental, they share with monuments the varying imprint of the time in which they are received.

24. Cf. Nanette C. Auerhahn and Dori Laub, "Holocaust Testimony," in *Holocaust and Genocide Studies* 5 (1990): 447–62. Peter Brooks in *Reading for the Plot: Design and Intention in Narrative* (Cambridge: Harvard University Press, 1992), talks of a "contract that calls the narrative into existence."

25. It is even problematic to claim that the testimonies are instructive. That we seek to derive moral lessons from them argues our own need and suggests that the contract of which we have spoken, as well as the intelligibility of the survivor's experience in the world outside the concentration camp universe, are conditions of transmission that fall more heavily on the listener than in narratives of art. While a few testimonies are comparable to folktales in which the survivor overcomes impossible obstacles (in narratives of art, Brooks claims, "the specifically human faculty of ingenuity and trickery, the capacity to use the mind to devise schemes to overcome superior force, becomes a basic dynamic of plot," *Reading for the Plot*, 38), almost all show that the concentration camp universe made such plotting impossible. The shock given to what Brooks treats under the heading of "narrative desire" is what I will look at more closely in the concluding section on Paul Celan. The narrative impulse is totally subsumed by the need to bear witness, which keeps the witness alive involuntarily. This is made clear by Jankiel Wiernik's *The Death Camp Treblinka: A Documentary*, ed. Alexander Donat (New York: Holocaust Library, 1979), which begins, "Dear Reader: It is for your sake I continue to hang on to my miserable existence," and in which the author describes himself as an Ahasuerus: "I am a nomad. . . . Do I look like a human being? No, definitely not. Disheveled, untidy, destroyed. It seems as if I were carrying the load of a hundred centuries. The load is wearisome, very wearisome, but for the time being I must bear it. . . . I, who witnessed the doom of three generations, must keep on living for the sake of the future."

26. Whether we like it or not, there is a competition to test rather than strengthen the limits of each medium. Today we are ages away from reflections like those of Lessing in the eighteenth century, who postulated a canon of beauty that would restrain the depiction of pain and suffering in statuary and painting. The future is more with Spielberg's *Schindler's List* than with Louis Malle's *Au revoir les enfants* or Truffaut's *The Last Metro*. The issue of the limits of realism in Holocaust representations is raised strongly by Lawrence Langer, *The Holocaust and the Literary Imagination* (New Haven: Yale University Press, 1975), as well as by Sidra Ezrahi, *By Words Alone* (Chicago: University of Chicago Press, 1980), and Ilan Avisar, *Screening the Holocaust* (Bloomington: Indiana University Press, 1988), esp. chapter 1.

27. The comic realism of writers like Cynthia Ozick is based on the indigestible mess of realia mocking our powers of perception, our counter-creativity. The result is a de facto restoring of the link between realism and comedy, as in the *genera dicendi* system.

28. Adorno, "Commitment" (1962), in *The Essential Frankfurt School Reader*, ed. A. Arato and E. Gebhardt (New York: Continuum, 1982). Also "After Auschwitz," in *Negative Dialectics*, trans. E. B. Ashton (New York: Continuum, 1983).

29. This fact does not preclude, of course, hypocrisy or the perversion of sympathy: it is always necessary to keep Tolstoy's story in mind, in which a countess weeps in the theater while her coachman freezes to death outside.

30. The concern for realism is not lessened by the fact that in a media age "realism" is undermined by another feature. When history returns as film, says Nancy Wood, referring to Anton Kaes's work, we judge "the interpretive cogency of images . . . not in

relation to a historical referent but in relation to the preceding images from which they have drawn." See Wood on the "representational fallacy" in "The Holocaust: Historical Memories and Contemporary Identities," *Media, Culture and Society*, 13 (1991): 368–72.

31. Cf. Estelle Gilson on *Schindler's List*: "Masterful and moving as *Schindler's List* is, there were moments, however, I had trouble believing in it . . . during a killing scene set in a camp, I confused reality and the perception of reality once more. I told myself I wish this were a fiction. . . . " *Congress Monthly*, 61 (March, 1994): 12.

32. In "Education after Auschwitz" (1966), Adorno suggests that this development, which played its part in the mentality and the apparatus leading to mass extermination, is linked to a type of person who is incapable of love. I should add that the bitter attack on art launched by Adorno after the Holocaust was also aimed at culture before the Holocaust: he found that German society had been corrupt long before the Nazis made that truth brutally clear. His insight, supported by a Marxist perspective still widespread today, is given additional weight by the atmosphere of insouciant bourgeois pastoralism so subversively portrayed in Appelfeld's *Badenheim* and *Age of Wonders*. Yet Adorno did not demand a purge of all nonrealistic devices. He knew that "aesthetic incompatability," as Marcuse names it, perhaps updating Brecht, is an inherent and effective element by which art resists rather than conspires with a too literal and dominant mode of representation.

33. *The Complete Poems of Emily Dickinson*, ed. Thomas H. Johnson (Boston: Little, Brown, n.d.), 294, no. 599.

34. Cf. Hans Jonas, quoted by Emil Fackenheim: "At Auschwitz 'more was real than is possible,' " in "Holocaust," A. A. Cohen and P. Mendes-Flohr, eds., *Contemporary Jewish Religious Thought* (New York, 1988), 402. See also Blanchot on "the impossible real" as "That which . . . cannot be forgotten because it has always already fallen outside memory": *The Writing of Disaster*, trans. Ann Smock (Lincoln: University of Nebraska Press, 1986), 29. Epistemological conditions of possibility are, in the case of survivor testimonies, less relevant than social ones, but they help to pose the issue of "experience" more universally. The best sociology-inspired pages on the testimonies are by Michael Pollak, "La formation d'une mémoire collective," *L'Expérience concentrationnaire*, 244–47. On trauma and experience, see also Cathy Caruth, introduction to the special issue of *American Imago*, 48 (1991): 1–13.

35. The conventions, social or literary, which art shares with what is often called the collective memory, also display this formal power to make experience intelligible and to transmit even sublime or dreadful events. Epistemologically it remains uncertain whether they are artificial forms or derivatives of permanent mental structures whose origin in biology or history cannot be recovered. Conventions or not, structures or not, they must seem to renew themselves through the transmitted experience. Otherwise Kafka's "frozen sea" cannot be broken through, and *experience* is not communicated but deadened once more by the very forms that make it possible.

36. Danto, *Narration and Knowledge: Including the Integral Text of Analytical Philosophy of History* (New York: Columbia University Press, 1985), 342–43.

37. See also chapter 8, "The Book of the Destruction."

38. A simple remark in Benjamin's "Story Teller" suggests the same bypass: "The more self-forgetful the listener is, the more deeply is what he listens to impressed upon his memory." Such receptivity repeats or simulates, in a nontraumatic way, traumatic stress as it eludes what Freud calls the psychic shield.

39. *Dating* the event, or a secondary obsession with dates generally, may, at one and the same time, reflect trauma and seek to limit it. Jacques Derrida has a remarkable essay

Holocaust Testimony, Art, and Trauma

focusing on such dating in Paul Celan. See "Shibboleth," first translated in G. H. Hartman and S. Budick, eds., *Midrash and Literature* (New Haven: Yale University Press, 1986).

40. That description is actually applied to poetry itself, rather than the mind producing it; but it is clear Wordsworth views them as homologous.

41. The contagion of trauma, or the transmission of secondary trauma, forms the basis, in Coleridge, for a deeper sense of community. Yet while more realistic in his understanding of this fact, Coleridge is also more symbolic than Wordsworth in depicting it. His isolation seems ultimately greater than Wordsworth's, who remains wary of unintegrated memories but acknowledges them within a daily-life setting that suggests the mutual responsiveness of man and nature and no need for a violent breakthrough of imagination or correspondingly sensational modes of representation. Such differences at the level of individual psychology, however important, are less significant than Kai Erikson's distinction in "Notes on Trauma and Community" between individual and collective trauma. It is collective trauma that the Holocaust survivor faces, "a blow to the basic tissues of social life that damages the bonds attaching people together and impairs the prevailing sense of community." See *American Imago*, 48 (1991): 455–72.

42. My observations here have been greatly helped by Carol Bernstein's "Ethical Ellipsis in Narrative," in *Dialectic and Narrative*, ed. T. R. Flynn and D. Judovitz (Albany: State University of New York Press, 1993), 225–32.

43. The act of interpretation, in other words, is itself among the sequelae of an "unconscious" experience and subject to the same defenses. Concerning this interpretive reticence, abetted by the hypnotic charm of art, much more needs to be said. We avoid tearing the veil away; we hover "between enlightenment and fantasy," like children "who know something they did not know before, but who make no use of the new knowledge that has been presented to them." See Freud, "Analysis Terminable and Interminable" (1937), *Standard Edition*, 23; and Nadine Fresco, "Remembering the Unknown," *International Review of Psycho-Analysis*, 11 (1984): 419.

44. That one type of blood heals and the other corrupts only foregrounds the idea of a homeopathic remedy. Compare the spear of Achilles, which alone can cure the wound it inflicts, or "telephism," as Jean Starobinski names it in *Le remède dans le mal* (Paris: Gallimard, 1989), 191ff.

45. On this, cf. "Words and Wounds" in Geoffrey H. Hartman, *Saving the Text* (Baltimore: Johns Hopkins University Press, 1981). The healing process, in any case, may not be possible without Maurice Halbwachs's "affective community."

46. Avital Ronell, in *differences: A Journal of Feminist Cultural Studies*, 4 (1992): 2, 13. Yet for many the realistic mode, or at least something as explicit as testimony, will be necessary. This is the case of the children of survivors, and perhaps the generation after as a whole. Its condition is described by Nadine Fresco: "[The survivors] transmitted only the wound to their children, to whom the memory had been refused and who grew up in the compact void of the unspeakable." "Remembering the Unknown," 419. See also Elaine Marks, "Cendres juives," in *Auschwitz and After: Race, Culture, and "the Jewish Question" in France*, ed. Lawrence D. Kritzman (New York: Routledge, 1994). The moral as well as generic problem of maintaining a "historical ideal in imaginative writing" is discussed, with special reference to Celan, by Berel Lang in *Act and Idea in the Nazi Genocide* (Chicago: University of Chicago Press, 1990), 138–39.

47. See also Laub and Auerhahn, "Holocaust Testimony," 454–57, on "The Anti-Dialogic Structure of Survivor's Speech," and John Felstiner, "Translating Celan's Last Poem," in *American Poetry Review* (July–August 1982). The *position* of the witness, the person who could address, or be addressed by, the extreme event, but either is no longer

The Longest Shadow

"there" because of that event, or has disappeared into it, is at the center of Dori Laub's observations in *Testimony*. Without turning the Holocaust survivor into a clinical category, it is important to see that, as in autism, automatism of address has been disrupted, and a new referential system must be built up. This concern is equally apparent in art, and especially in poetry with its tension between grammar and rhetoric (figures of speech), or its shifting boundaries between person and thing, or its making *things* more personal (less impersonal) than *persons*. See, e.g., the moving account of Donna Williams, *Somebody Somewhere: Breaking Free from the World of Autism* (New York: Times/Books, Random House, 1994).

48. After his first two collections, *Sand aus den Urnen* (1948), and *Mohn und Gedächt-niss* (1952), Celan cultivates a precocious *Spätstil*, so condensed that it is barely intelligible at first reading. The "Conversation" dates from 1959, when his style is still in transition.

49. See Blanchot's "postface" to *Vicious Circles: Two Fictions & "After the Fact"* (Barry-town, N.Y.: Station Hill Press, 1985), 68. Blanchot may have recalled Adorno's modification in the 1960s of his absolute stricture against art. "It is now virtually in art alone that suffering can still find its own voice, its consolation, without being immediately betrayed by it." The modern *locus classicus* for the imperturbability of the aesthetic medium is Mallarmé's "Governments change: but prosody always remains intact," from "The Crisis of Verse," which brings the "surprising" news that even (French) prosody is changing: "[T]hey have done violence to verse."

50. Blanchot's own narrative art after the war evolves from the plotless fluency of his *récits*, punctured by luminous phrases and incidents, to the fluid stutter of fragments assembled as *L'Ecriture du désastre*, (Paris: Gallimard, 1980). What is involved in this cae-sura between past and present words—in this writing of disaster—is even more forcefully illustrated by oral testimonies. There, a discontinuity often opens up between words then and words now. This is a major point in Langer's *Holocaust Testimonies*.

51. No wonder he announces in "The Meridian" that "The poem is the place where all tropes and metaphors want to be led *ad absurdum*." This "reductio" changes its means but not its end from the time of "Death Fugue" to the extremely elliptical Celan. For quotations from Celan I use Paul Celan, *Collected Prose*, trans. Rosmarie Waldrop (Man-chester: Carcanet, 1986), and *Paul Celan: Gesammelte Werke 3* (Taschenbuch, Frankfurt a/M: Suhrkamp, 1983). It is interesting to compare the American poet Jerome Rothen-berg, for whom the destroyed culture of Yiddish is a *dibbuk* among the *dibbuks*, an un-satisfied dead spirit that robs a powerful poetry of its reason for being. See his *Khurban* (1993).

52. Blanchot opens *The Writing of the Disaster* with: "Disaster ruins everything by let-ting everything be as it was." Wordsworth, in the second book of *The Prelude*, describes how after the death of his mother, the external world, though bonded to him through her, did not collapse: "and yet the building stood as if sustained / By its own spirit!" In Vasily Grossman's *Forever Flowing*, a survivor returning after thirty years from the Stalin gulag (Kolyma) visits the Hermitage art museum and has a "Dorian Gray" experience: "It was unbearable to think that those paintings had remained as beautiful as ever during the years in camp which had transformed him into a prematurely old man. Why hadn't the faces of the madonnas grown old too, and why hadn't their eyes been blinded with tears? Was not their immortality their failure rather than their strength? Did not their changelessness reveal a betrayal by art of the humanity which had created it?" (trans. Thomas P. Whitney).

53. "Speech on the Occasion of Receiving the Literature Prize of the Free Hanseatic City of Bremen." When Celan says he was "enriched" by it all ("It gave me no word for

what was happening, but went through it. Went through it and could resurface, 'enriched' by it all") it is easy to cite his early "Death Fugue" and the charge against it of euphony and aesthetic stylization. His critics did not see the subversive aspect of his lyricism: they felt too much its happiness rather than the "thousand darknesses" of speech. The *ad absurdum* method is fully developed in "Conversation in the Mountains."

54. Celan evokes a Jew who "does golus" like Abraham, but whose words go nowhere. (I wish to acknowledge here stimulating thoughts in the same direction by my colleagues Claudine Kahan and Benjamin Harshav.) For the Yiddish form of this conversation, cf. Ruth Wisse, "Two Jews Talking: A View of Modern Yiddish Literature," *Prooftexts* 4 (1984): 35–48.

55. Both Laub/Auerhahn and Felstiner suggest that such moments constitute an anti-Shema or parody of the central prayer of Judaism: "Hear, O Israel. . . . "

56. "[A] year ago, I commemorated a missed encounter in the Engadine valley by putting a little story on paper where I had a man 'like Lenz' walk through the mountains." "The Meridian," *Collected Prose*, 53. The allusion is to Georg Büchner's Lenz (the name is also a poetic name for the spring season). The "encounter" experienced by Büchner's Lenz seems to repeat Hölderlin's in a different setting: Hölderlin had traveled toward the south until "Apollo" struck him.

57. We understand better, reading this prose, Celan's statement in "The Meridian" that "art is the distance poetry must cover, no less and no more," the distance to "the strangeness, the place where the person was able to set himself free as an—estranged— I." "The Meridian," 45, 46.

58. "Nach dem Lichtverzicht: / der vom Botengang helle, / hallende Tag. // Die blühselige Botschaft, / schriller und schriller, / findet zum blutenden Ohr." *Eingedunkelt*, in *Paul Celan, Gesammelte Werke*, 3 (Frankfurt a/M: Suhrkamp, 1983), 142. The editors date this unpublished series 1969. A volume entitled *Lichtzwang* (Light-Compulsion) was published in 1970, the year of his death.

59. Central to all the questions we have raised is whether a model of non-integration can be developed that would have therapeutic value in psychoanalysis and emancipatory and expressive value in art. In philosophy and religion too the model would scandalize by its resistance to transparency or totalization. I am not saying that all traumatic experience can be aligned, even on this differential axis, but that a general theory, in continuing to rethink its terms, and what is equally important, to speak them, should keep Levinas's axiom in mind: "The interval of space given by light is instantaneously absorbed by light."

60. Cf. his characterization of Christ as "Augenkind" in the poem "Eis, Eden," of those eyes as "helle Erden," and generally his parody of the Christian hymn and its motifs of redemptive light and warmth. On this subject, see Winfried Menninghaus, "Zum Problem des Zitats bei Celan und in der Celan-Philologie," in *Paul Celan*, ed. W. Hamacher and W. Menninghaus (Frankfurt a/M: Suhrkamp, 1988), 188–89 (note 9). Sometimes Celan's oeuvre as a whole, at least in its cryptic dimension, appears as an antistrophe to Hölderlin's praise of inspirational Greek art, "Wo, wo leuchten si denn, die fernhintreffenden Sprüche," from "Brot und Wein"—in other words, his opposition to a metaphorics of light, of illumination, may run deeper than any particular ideological source.

61. Compare Shoshana Felman on Celan, in Felman and Laub, *Testimony*, 25–40.

62. Cf. "The Meridian": "Enlarge art? On the contrary, take art with you into your innermost narrowness."

63. "Conversation in the Mountains," my translation from p. 171 of the German (Suhrkamp) edition. I agree with Françoise Meltzer that Gadamer's dialogic view of

Celan, which presupposes the possibility of conversation, of "an a priori thou and 'I'," misses his dilemma. See her "Paul Celan and the Death of the Book," in *Hot Property: The Stakes and Claims of Literary Originality* (Chicago: University of Chicago Press, 1994).

64. Though "Findet" may be a predicate (the message "finds its way" to the bleeding ear), the positive image of light would still be undermined by line 5. Cf. the "Trübung durch Helles" in Celan's poem for Nelly Sachs, "Zürich, zum Storchen" (*Die Niemandsrose*).

65. At first one is tempted to think of the "Invisible" as God or the source of inspiration. But has Celan, by a daring ambiguity, applied to himself his bitter formula in *Atemwende* (1967): "Niemand / Zeugt für den / Zeugen" (Nobody / bears witness / for the witness)? If "Niemand," in this stanza from "Aschenglorie," has the force of a proper name, a self-effacing Celan could be saying: "I am Nobody, yet must validate the idea of witness by my poems."

Index

Geoffrey H. Hartman, Sterling Professor of English and Comparative Literature at Yale University, is a cofounder of the Fortunoff Video Archive for Holocaust Testimonies at Yale and its Project Director. One of his generation's leading literary scholars, he has explored the nature of interpretation in such books as *Minor Prophecies: The Literary Essay in the Culture Wars, The Fate of Reading, Criticism in the Wilderness, The Unmediated Vision, Easy Pieces,* and *Beyond Formalism.* In more recent years he has also devoted significant attention to examining aspects of the classical literary tradition of Judaism, as reflected in his editing of *Midrash and Literature.* His work on the cultural and political implications of the Holocaust is represented by *Holocaust Remembrance: The Shapes of Memory* and *Bitburg in Moral and Political Perspective.*